9/02

D1224330

Castles and Fortified Cities
of Medieval Europe

Castles and Fortified Cities of Medieval Europe

An Illustrated History

JEAN-DENIS G.G. LEPAGE

McFarland & Company, Inc., Publishers

Jefferson, North Carolina, and London

Library of Congress Cataloguing-in-Publication Data

Lepage, Jean-Denis.
Castles and fortified cities of medieval Europe :
an illustrated history / by Jean-Denis G.G. Lepage.
p.   cm.
Includes bibliographical references and index.
ISBN 0-7864-1092-2 (illustrated case binding : 50# alkaline paper) ∞
1. Fortification—Europe.   2. Fortification—Middle East.
3. Castles—Europe.   4. Castles—Middle East.   5. Military history, Medieval.
6. Military art and science—Europe—History—Medieval, 500–1500.
I. Title.
UG428.L47   2002   623'.194'0902—dc21   2002001351

British Library cataloguing data are available

Manufactured in the United States of America

*McFarland & Company, Inc., Publishers
Box 611, Jefferson, North Carolina 28640
www.mcfarlandpub.com*

CONTENTS

v

ACKNOWLEDGMENTS

I would like to thank Eltjo de Lang and Ben Marcato,
Simone and Bernard Lepage, Bébert le Breton, Anne Chauvel,
the abbot Jacques Jouy, Marta Vieira dos Santos,
Jeannette à Stuling and Jean-Pierre Rorive.

PREFACE

Witnesses to centuries past, castles are still to be seen everywhere in Europe today. Whether standing in ruins, forgotten in dark forests, or well preserved and transformed into hotels, museums, concert halls or offices, they are places of mystery and greatness, the legacy of a civilization that lasted for a thousand years. They are treasures handed down to us from the Middle Ages, the period conventionally dated from 476, when the Ancient Roman empire collapsed, to 1453, when the capital of the Eastern Latin Empire, Constantinople, was taken by the Turks. Roughly speaking, then, the Middle Ages cover the period between 500 and 1500.

In the popular imagination, the medieval era has long been considered a bleak and barbarian period. In fact, however, the European Middle Ages were not a millennium of unceasing violence and permanent disorder. It is true that in the early Middle Ages, between the 5th and the 9th century, civilization, knowledge and art were in relative decay because of invasions and disorder. But after the 10th century, three major influences (Ancient Roman culture, Germanic customs and Christianity) were working in combination to effect significant change on medieval society. That combination reached its apogee in the 13th century.

The brilliant and original medieval civilization was marked in the 14th century by a series of catastrophes: wars, epidemics, social and moral crises. In the 15th century, the European world recovered and underwent technical, social and cultural transformations. The following period, called the Renaissance, was in many ways a continuation of the Middle Ages but also an important breakthrough that opened the planet Earth to exploration and discovery.

Those ten medieval centuries mark a long and difficult transition between the ancient Roman era and the modern one. When the Middle Ages came to an end, tribal and local organizations had vanished, and most European nations had their own identity, their own language, their own particularities. Nature had been brought under man's dominion. The repartition of towns, villages, communication axes, administrative limits and landscapes established by the end of the medieval period would, on the whole, remained the same until the Industrial Revolution in the second half of the 19th century.

During the medieval millennium, the castle was a common feature of the European landscape. The word castle (coming from the Latin word *castellum*) conjures up a whole range of images, from the sugary Walt Disney picture of a pinnacled fairytale palace to the dark and sinister lair of Count Dracula. Legends abound of treachery, hidden treasures, loyal heroes defeating evil dragons and wicked barons, gallant knights rescuing damsels in distress, and besieging forces doused with cascades of boiling oil. Although some legends are based on historical events, in most such stories the portrayal of castles is largely fiction. The historical reality of castles is somewhat more prosaic.

Originally a castle was an independent, fortified dwelling place, probably exhaling a strong smell of farm. Its original purpose was to shelter a lord, his family and his men as well as to defend a territory. In time of war, the peasants of the neighborhood could find refuge behind its walls. The construction of a castle depended on private initiative directly connected to feudalism; the fortified buildings illustrate the decaying political and military authority and reflect a social order based on lust for power. In this sense a private "castle," designed for daily life and occupied by both civilians and warriors, is quite different from a "fort" (a stronghold built by the state to defend a strategic point and manned only by a military garrison) and from a "citadel" (an urban fort).

Some castles played a major role in medieval history. They were besieged, burnt, retaken, rebuilt, enlarged, and sometimes abandoned. Many others were insignificant, never mentioned, left alone for ages. As methods of warfare improved, castles grew in size, height and strength to meet the increased threats from assault, but as the times became more peaceful and central authority was restored, many of them were transformed into beautiful and airy palaces. Many castles have disappeared, but thousands are still standing today, having withstood the violence of war and the attrition of time. Adapted, reconstructed, modernized, or in ruins, they constitute today an important heritage and a rich historical legacy.

It was not only castles that required solid defenses to keep enemies at bay. The prosperity of some ecclesiastical properties made them tempting targets for invaders, and as a result, they built fortifications to protect their inhabitants and property. Towns were collective dwelling places and economic centers that played an important role after the 12th century; they too were fortified by methods borrowed from castle architecture.

Today's surviving castles, vestiges of religious fortifications and urban remains represent a permanent record of our past. They attract many visitors, affording them a direct and dramatic rendezvous with history. Medieval architecture deserves our admiration, especially when we consider the size and sturdiness of the works in light of the lack of means of construction, the weakness of technological methods, the shortage of manpower and the low budgets. Castles and towns were living structures that evolved over time, according to political circumstances, economic conditions and military situations. That is part of the charm of medieval castles and towns: All are different, depending on the natural site, the period, the material used, and the intentions, rank and fortune of those who built them. All castles, however, have certain features in common: living accommodations, supply stores, a place of worship, observation and communication means, and passive and active artificial defense works reinforcing a carefully chosen natural site.

The castles, fortresses, palaces and towns described in this book are intentionally not always the best known. Other books have discussed the well-known works, and the subjective choice that I have made represents a heterogeneous grouping, showing the development and diversity of western European military medieval architecture, including fortifications in France, Britain, Germany, Austria, the Netherlands and Belgium, Spain, Portugal and Italy as well as Palestine (connected to western Europe by the Crusades).

Over the centuries, fortification has evolved a language of its own. Instead of an inconvenient glossary placed at the end of the book, I have chosen—for the reader's comfort—to explain the large number of specialized terms within the main text by means of drawings, cross-sections, reconstructions and impressions. These illustrations are based on my own photographs, sketches drawn on the spot, and other sources. Attention is focused on the essential points, and I have eliminated annoying present-day elements such as late additions, wandering tourists, road signs, parked cars, vegetation and other things disrupting the general view. City drawings are based on ancient ground-plans. Unfortunately, town representations before the 16th century are few, and those that exist are often unreliable, so reconstruction of medieval and Roman walls is a process of deduction from vestiges visible on old maps. In this process, imagination, guesswork and experience are needed to spot walls, ditches, foundations of towers, and other traces of fortifications.

Dimensions in this book are given in metric form as this is now the standard measurement of archaeology. The reader is reminded that 2.54 centimeters = one inch; 30 centimeters = one foot; 0.91 meters = one yard; and 1.609 meters = one mile.

The complete history of castles and towns in medieval Europe will never be written. The subject is so complicated and enormous that it would take a lifetime of dedicated work, and much of it would be details of interest only to a minority of knowledgeable readers. This book reflects my own opinions and predilections. I have selected, neglected and omitted items of equal importance. While acknowledging the infinite diversity of the castles and towns I have illustrated, I have attempted to point out some of the general features medieval fortifications have in common. Another writer would doubtless have produced a completely different story within the same framework. This book's aim is clear, simple and humble: to show the general reader—the reader with an interest but little specific knowledge in this subject—the importance of castles and towns in the Middle Ages, the way of life that developed in and around them, and the historical and technical evolution of European medieval military architecture.

I would like to close this preface with a reminder about military architecture as a whole. Fortifications have an undeniable beauty; through the ingeniousness and balance of their conception, the quality of their execution, the solidity of their mass, the sobriety of their shape and the majesty of their proportions, they arouse real aesthetic emotion. They radiate an impression of quiet strength by the strictness of their geometry and by their functionality, yet their rigorous efficiency is tempered by high shapes that harmonize with decorations and ornaments. Let us not be blinded, however, by romanticism.

Ruined walls overgrown in vegetation, majestic citadels, peaceful towers reflected in the calm waters of moats or isolated castles standing watch over jagged mountains have cost fortunes at a time when most of the population suffered misery and poverty. Let us not forget that fortifications were built by the hard work of generations of humble and exploited people. Let us keep in mind that these places of prestige and feudal glory have also been, in their time, places of suffering, fear, violence, war and death.

Jean-Denis Gilbert Georges Lepage
Groningen
January 2002

1

THE DECLINE OF FORTIFICATIONS
FROM THE 5TH TO THE 9TH CENTURIES

ROMAN FORTIFICATIONS

After six hundred years of struggle for expansion under the Republic and the early Empire, the Romans undertook a huge program of border fortifications, called limites (singular: limes), to defend their possessions. The first limes was established in Germany, along the rivers Rhine and Danube, under the reign of the emperor Domitian (81–96). The program was continued by Trajan (97–117), Hadrian (117–138) and subsequent emperors.

The limes was a line of defense composed of fortified towns, forts (castra), camps (castella) and watch towers (burgi), linked together with ditches and earth walls (vallum) crowned with wooden stockades. Border towns, forts and camps communicated with each other by means of military roads.

Inherited from the civilizations of Greece and the ancient Near East, permanent Roman fortification already displayed all the main characteristics of future medieval fortification. The Roman town was enclosed by a wall, called a curtain. The wall was constructed of masonry about 2 to 6 m thick and was usually about 10 m high. The upper part of the wall was arranged as a wall-walk and protected by a breastwork as high as a man; the breastwork was pierced with openings (crenels), which allowed defending forces to hurl their missiles at the enemy without, and solid standing parts (merlons or pinnae), which provided shelter. Curtains were reinforced by towers, either round or semicylindrical, higher than the curtains and jutting out. Their roofs were either covered by timber and tiles or left as open terraces where artillery machines could be placed. The various stories of the tower were arranged as storerooms or dwelling-places. Windows in the tower let the light come in and the spears or missiles out.

Town-gates were not numerous. In a city with a regular ground plan, gates were placed in the lengthening of the cardo (main north-south street) and the decumanus (main east-west street). The gatehouse was a compromise between a military stronghold and a triumphal arch, with decoration, windows, galleries, and statues. It included two defensive towers, passageways for carts, and smaller doors for pedestrians; the passages could be closed by heavy doors and a portcullis (a strong wooden barrier which could be raised and lowered by machinery).

THE BARBARIAN INVASIONS

In 394 under Emperor Theodosius's reign, paganism was abolished and Christianity became the official Roman religion. The triumph of Christianity was a major turning point for the history of Europe, marking a complete change in mentality and a major break between ancient time and pre-feudal times.

The decay of the Roman empire began in the third century AD. For many reasons—notably imperial despotism, the rise of Christianity, the shift of forces to the East, and the difficulty of maintaining an empire of such huge dimensions—Rome and Italy gradually lost control. The Romans learned that the frontier limes, though often cunningly placed along rivers and mountains, were not impassable.

Urban Roman gatehouse

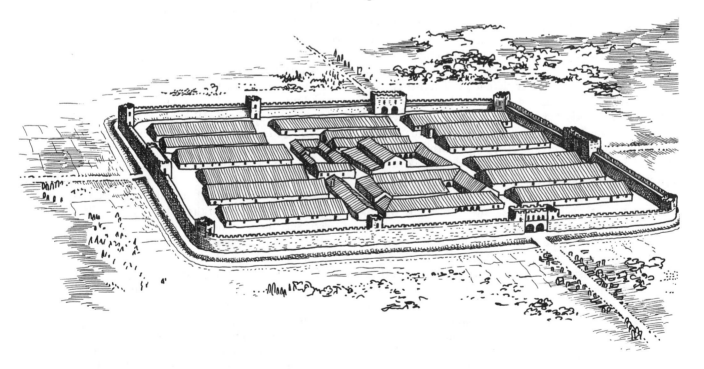

Roman castrum—The castrum (also called castellum stativa)
is a permanent fort intended to control, pacify and romanize a region.

Left: *Roman watchtower (burgus).*

The fragile balance between Romans and barbarian Germanic tribes was broken in the beginning of the 5th century. Taking advantage of internal Roman anarchy and military weakness, Germanic raiders launched audacious attacks; facing little resistance, they settled and founded their own kingdoms. After years of confusion made worse by the expeditions launched by the Asiatic hordes of brutal Huns in 450 and 451, the western Roman empire collapsed and was divided into numerous and chaotic barbarian realms.

In the course of these endless conflicts, the Western empire politically ceased to exist. The final blow happened in 476 when the Heruli tribe seized the eternal city of Rome. Their warlord, Odoaker, overthrew the last Roman emperor, Romulus Augustus, and proclaimed himself king of Italy. This date conventionally marks the end of the empire and the beginning of the Middle Ages.

Over the course of about one hundred years, from the middle of the 5th to the middle of the 6th century, Europe had been profoundly upset, with the Roman administrative centralization replaced by diversity and political partition. The barbarian invasions, it is generally recognized, resulted in violence, destruction, insecurity, large scale banditry, and the ruin of trade and economic life, as well as depopulation brought on by epidemics. However, the so-called barbaric Germanic tribes also brought with them a new and dynamic civilization.

In terms of fortification, the 4th, 5th and 6th centuries were characterized by a significant decrease of urban life and a revival of defense works to face violence and invasions. The typical town was reduced to a small nucleus that could be better defended. The urban surface, called the castrum, was diminished to 6 to 30 hectares. New walls were hastily raised using stones and construction materials from buildings of the abandoned neighborhoods. In certain cities of southern Europe (Arles, Nîmes or Rome, for example), the huge oval amphitheater intended for circus entertainment was transformed into a fortress called the castrum arenarum.

The barbarians had defeated the Romans by war of movement, but having become settlers themselves, they rapidly rediscovered the need for fortification. Upon the Gallic-Roman heritage they built new strongholds. The Visigoths, established in southern Europe, fortified their capital of Toledo as well as Alarcón, Siguenza, and Daroca in Spain; they built numerous castles and city enclosures such as Beja, Evora, Guarda and Lisbon in Portugal, and Carcassonne in southern France.

THE MEROVINGIAN DYNASTY

The Merovingian dynasty was founded by a legendary warlord called Merowe, whose successors, Childerik and Clovis, reconstituted a part of the former Western Roman empire. The long Merovingian period, from 457 to 751, is rather obscure because of a lack of reliable written documents, and its history is very complex because of the decay of the Roman heritage and the growing Germanic and Catholic influences. The Frankish warlord Clovis, who ruled from 481 to 511, eliminated all his rivals, imposed himself as improvised king of all Franks, defeated the Alamands and the Visigoths and conquered a large part of Gaul (today France) and Germany.

Clovis was a cunning leader who became a Christian, and his prodigious success was made possible by the support of the Catholic Church, which was the only organized body remaining in the general chaos after the collapse of the Roman empire. Clovis established his capital in Paris and is often, though wrongly, considered the founder of France. Indeed after his death in 511, the Frankish realm was divided among his sons according to Germanic custom. His successors took Burgundy, southern Germany, Saxony and Bavaria. However, Clovis's heritage was rapidly dismantled by severe family quarrels. Progressively, after many bloody civil wars and fratricidal struggles, weakness appeared and the Frankish realm was divided into four major parts: Aquitaine (southwest France), Burgundy (today called Bourgogne, spreading then from Champagne to Provence and including a part of Switzerland), Neustria (nucleus of Clovis's domain in northern France with Paris as capital) and Austrasia (eastern France, a part of western Germany including lands of the Rhine and the Meuse with the capital city of Metz).

Wars were numerous between those realms and by the 7th century, the Merovingian kings had considerably lost their power. The real authority was exercised by the majordomus (mayor of the palace), originally a high domestic servant, who became a kind of prime minister and secured power to himself.

In the military field of the early Middle Ages, the tactical sophistication of the Greeks and Romans was forgotten, and no significant technical improvements were made. The Merovingian army was composed of all Frankish free men, who were required to serve and to finance their own weapons and equipment. The warriors were not trained, and their weaponry, what we know of it, was rudimentary and irregular, though very costly. The men were armed with swords, large battle-axes and long spears; the richest carried a round wooden shield and wore an iron helm and cuirass. Combat took place both on horse and on foot.

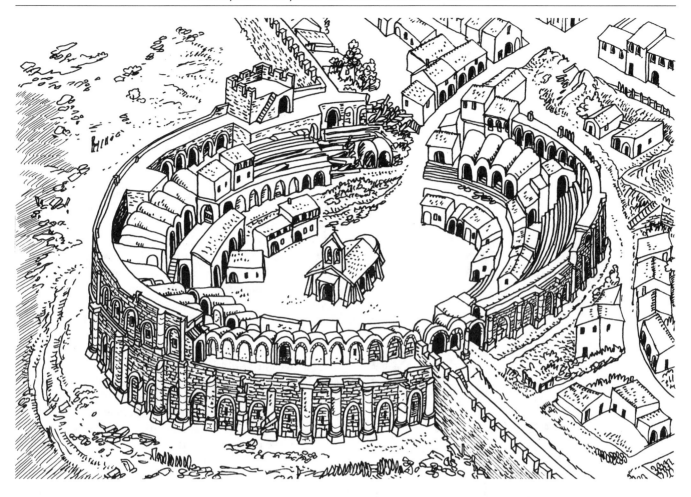

Castrum arenarum

The Merovingian army was fully ruled by Germanic custom and was not so much an army as a gang of ill-organized warriors, certainly not numerous, with no discipline and rather poor efficiency. Though the army was officially under command of the king himself, in the second half of the 7th century command was often entrusted to high officers called graven (counts) and herzogen (dukes). The army was not permanent, but mobilized according to the need of a campaign.

As for fortification, very little is known. Wars were small-scaled and fought by armed groups who practiced offensive tactics in short campaigns; political division, strategic situations and financial predicaments probably did not justify the maintenance or creation of new strongholds. Written documents and archeological evidence are unfortunately lacking. Some ancient Roman villas (large rural farming estates) may have been fortified with earth walls and stockades in the ancient Celtic and Germanic tradition.

As we have just seen, towns were considerably reduced in population and area; most of them had lost all economic and political importance. The most significant cities were the sieges of the local Catholic bishops (in France for example Soissons, Paris, Tours, Orléans, Clermont, Poitiers, Bordeaux, Toulouse, Lyon, Vienne, Arles). In the 8th century, however, some cities in southern France, Italy and Spain increased their defensives capabilities because of a new threat coming from northern Africa: the Arabs, called Saracens, who began to expand in the West. The toponym *"La Guerche"* (derived from *Werki*, meaning fortification in the old Frankish language), which is common in western France, indicates possible strongholds built by the Franks to face aggression and repulse raids launched by the Britons established in Armorica (French Brittany).

THE BYZANTINE EMPIRE

While the Jutes, the Angles and the Saxons (coming from northern Germany and Denmark) invaded the

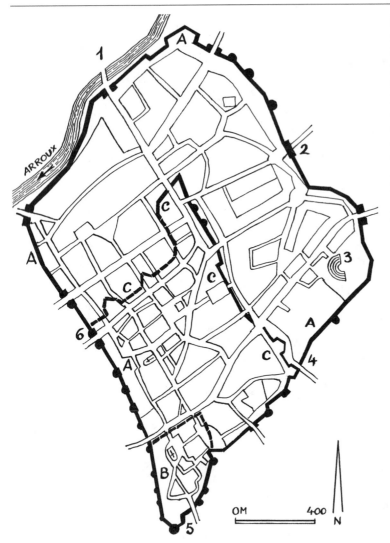

British Islands; while the Franks established themselves in Gaul; while the Visigoths dominated Spain and the Ostrogoths and Lombards occupied Italy, the eastern part of the Roman empire survived and considered itself the one and only Roman heir. From its capital, Constantinople (also called Byzantium, today Istanbul in Turkey), the Oriental Empire dominated the Balkans, Greece, Syria, Egypt and Cyrenaïca (today Libya). The emperor Justinian (527–565) consolidated his power, codified the Roman right, and reformed the administration and the Church. Intending to re-create the whole Roman empire, Justinian took northern Africa, the great Mediterranean islands, southern Italy and southern Spain. But Justinian's conquests were lost by his successors. The Byzantine Empire was weakened and reduced to Greece, Anatolia and a part of the Balkans; nevertheless it retained its prestige and power until 1453, when the city of Constantinople was taken by the Turks.

Byzantine fortifications, notably those of Constantinople, would have a great influence on western military architecture during and after the Crusades. Situated on a promontory, Constantinople was heavily fortified on the land front by the emperor Theodosius II between 408 and 450. The formidable fortifications of Constantinople were composed of three concentric walls, including a ditch 18 m wide and 6.5 m deep, dominated by a crenellated wall 5.5 m high, reinforced by buttresses. About fifteen meters behind this was a second crenellated wall 8 m high and 2 m thick, along with square flanking towers. Behind this, a

Ground plan of Autun (France). Situated in Saône-et-Loire (Burgundy) on the river Arroux, Autun was created in 10 BC by the Roman emperor Augustus (whence its name Augusturum). The prosperous Gallo-Roman town, though playing no significant military role, was fitted with fortifications which enhanced its prestige and wealth. Enclosing a surface of 200 hectares, these fortifications were composed of a crenellated wall 6 km in perimeter, 2.5 m thick and 11 m high including 52 high half-circular towers, four main gates and six secondary posterns. Autun was ravaged by the Vandals, by the Franks in 674, by the Moors in 731, and by the Norsemen in 895. During the invasions, the town was in full decay, abandoned and reduced to a small fortified castrum on the southern hill. In the 12th century it became again a prosperous city which was enlarged and fortified with an enceinte and a circular donjon called the Tour (tower) Saint-Léger (or Tour des Ursulines). The ground plan shows the Roman fortifications (AA) in the 1st century with the Arroux gate (1), the Saint-Andrea gate (2), the theater (3), the Rome gate (4). (B) is the 6th century castrum with the Saint-Lazare cathedral and the episcopal residence. (CC) is the medieval enceinte from the 12th century with the Ursulines dungeon (5) and the Saint-Andoche gate (6). Note that the medieval city, though prosperous and protected by the dukes of Burgundy, was much smaller than the ancient Roman town.

third wall, 12 m high and 4 m thick, was flanked by 96 towers, all 20 m high and arranged to shelter artillery machines.

THE ARABS AND ISLAM

In the 7th century, the prophet Muhammad began preaching in Arabia, and his teachings developed into the Islamic religion. Established in Arabia with Muhammad's emigration from Mecca to Medina in 622, Islam spread into Persia and central Asia.

The Arabs conquered huge parts of the Byzantine Empire, Syria, Egypt (634), the Mediterranean main islands, and northern Africa, and they even vainly besieged Constantinople in 674. The Arabs—Saracens or Moors, as they were called by the western Christians—crossed the strait of Gibraltar in 711, defeated the Visigoths and conquered Spain and Portugal by 718. By 750 the Arab civilization extended from India to the Atlantic and from the borders of Gaul to equatorial Africa.

The Arabian establishment in the Iberian Peninsula resulted in a long and formidable struggle between Christiandom and the Islamic world all through the Middle Ages.

Beja (Portugal). Situated in the province Baixo Alentejo in Portugal, the city Beja was founded by the Romans and called Pax Julia. Beja became a Visigothic town, both a bishopric and a stronghold. The Arabs occupied the city for four centuries, until King Afonso III (1248–1279) reconquered it. The castle was rebuilt about 1310 by King Dinis on Roman, Visigothic and Arab vestiges.

Merovingian soldier

12

Known as the Reconquista, the Christian campaign of reconquest lasted until 1492, when the last Arabian bulwark, Grenada in Andalusia, was retaken by the king of Spain. Yet the refined and brilliant Islamic civilization had a tremendous influence on Spanish society, an influence still perceptible even today.

Arabian fortification greatly influenced military architecture in the Iberian Peninsula even after the Reconquista and in all of Europe during the Crusades. Like many other conquerors, the Arabs made use of existing fortifications as bases for controlling and exploiting the territories they occupied. Where suitable strongholds did not exist, they built their own. Being originally nomadic men of the desert with little experience in masonry, they erected shuttering to take a primitive form of ready-mixed concrete-mortar dried in the sun (called tapia) and reinforced with stones. The resulting structures were rectangular in plan, with square towers at each corner and protecting the gate. Within the walls were constructed living quarters and a mosque. During the long Moorish domination in the Iberian peninsula, the main Arabian elements designed by the alarif (architect) were the al-qasba (alcazaba or fortress), the alcázar (luxurious defended palace for the military governor) and the rhibat (fortified monastery). Important features created by the Moorish architects were the barbican (external work defending the gatehouse), the torre del homenaje (massive square masonry keep) and the atalaya (isolated watchtower); other characteristics were the frayed échauguette (sentry-box), the tower with fringed roof, the typical crenellation outline cut in point, staircase or pyramid-shaped, and very refined and numerous decorations inspired by the art of the Mudejars (Muslims allowed to remain in Spain following the Reconquista, many of whom were highly skilled craftsmen).

THE CATHOLIC CHURCH

The Catholic religion and its administration survived the collapse of the Roman Empire and remained an organized institution within the new barbarian realms. Bishops, who were principally implanted in the towns and often originated from the Roman aristocracy, played a central role in the fusion between the new conquerors and the submitted populations. The bishops and the pope (who originally was merely the bishop of Rome) asserted their spiritual authority as God's representatives by opposing heretic and derivative faiths. They also enjoyed a large temporal power, thanks to the riches and organization of the Church. More or less successfully, the bishops and the clergy spread the Gospel, stimulated the reconstruction of towns (which over the long term meant

the rebirth of commercial activities), tried to oppose violence, helped the poor and sick, and participated in political life by giving their support to the Germanic kings and warlords who became Christians (e.g. Clovis, later Pepin the Short, Charlemagne and Hugh Capet). The barbarian Germanic kings rapidly understood that nothing on an economic, political, social, or spiritual level could be done without the Church's support, and most of them converted to Christianity.

In the troubled post–Roman time, amid the chaos resulting from the invasions, many Christians recoiled from the world and sought the isolation of religious communities, living as monks in monasteries under the authority of abbots. As early as 529, Benedict of Nurcia founded an abbey on Monte Cassino in Italy and created rules for observing vows of chastity, poverty and obedience with prayer and work. Monasteries multiplied and became spiritual and cultural nuclei in a world of disorder and violence.

Irish monks were particularly active in European evangelization in the 7th and 8th centuries, and after 663, Benedictine monks played an important role by giving Europe a united religion. However, theological disputes and political quarrels between the two great Christian poles, Rome and Constantinople, led to a schism in 1054. Christianity was then divided into two parts: the Roman Catholic Church under the authority of the pope in Rome, and the Greek Oriental Orthodox Church headed by the patriarch of Constantinople.

In spite of its severe faults, the Church prevented the disappearance of the Latin civilization and greatly participated in the creation of the medieval world and the rebirth of Europe.

THE CAROLINGIAN EMPIRE

After having conquered Spain, the Arabs continued their aggression in a northern direction. In 720, they took Narbonne in southern France, and for ten years they launched numerous and bloody raids into the Frankish Merovingian territories, notably up to Autun and Bordeaux. The majordomus of Austrasia, Charles Martel (meaning the Hammer), who had taken over most of the powers of the weak Merovingian king Thierry IV, reacted to the Saracen threat by raising an army. He defeated the Moors in Moussais-la-Bataille near Poitiers on 25 October 732.

Charles the Hammer's victory marks an important moment in the history of Christian Europe because the expansion of Islam was stopped. The battle of Poitiers also showed the tactical supremacy of the armored cavalry that would be the mainstay of medieval warfare.

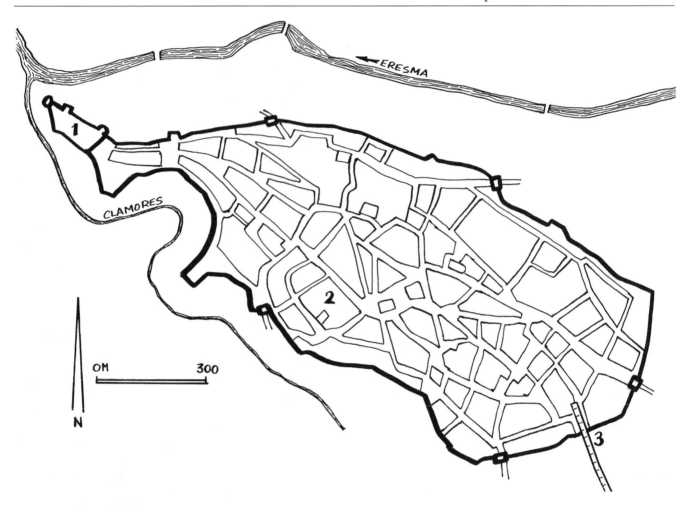

Ground plan of the old city in Segovia (Spain). Segovia was situated in Castilla on a steep ridge 66 m high at the confluence of rivers Eresma and Clamores. The Ciudad Vieja (old city) was created by the Romans and became a Moorish alcázar (stronghold). After the Reconquista, the Moorish fortress was turned into a residence for the kings of Castilla. It was profoundly reshaped in the 15th century by King Juan II in the Mudejar style combining luxurious living accommodations with military elements, a circular dungeon, high walls and towers. Segovia was an important economical, administrative and political center playing a major role in the history of Spain. The ground plan shows the old city with the Moorish alcázar (1), the cathedral (2) and the Roman aqueduct (3).

Exploiting his fame and prestige, Charles Martel brought the rich Aquitaine and the other Frankish kingdoms under his power. His son Pepin the Short (741–768) overthrew the last Merovingian king, Childeric III the Idle, in 751. Cleverly, the cunning Pepin arranged to be crowned king by the pope Zacharias. Thus from an illegal coup he created a legitimate new dynasty, today called Carolingian after his father's name (Charles is in Latin *Carolus*).

Pepin conquered a part of northern Italy from the Lombards in 756. Those territories were yielded to the pope and formed the nucleus of the pontifical state. Pepin continued the struggle against the Saracens, liberated the province of Septimania (today Languedoc in southern France) in 759, and repressed a revolt in Aquitaine from 761 to 768.

When Pepin died in 768, according to unwritten but customary Germanic laws, the reunited Frankish kingdom was divided again between his two sons: Carloman and Charles. Carloman died prematurely, however, and in 771 only Charles remained as king.

A king of enormous prestige, Charles (742–814) is

View of alcázar in Segovia (Spain)

called the Great (in Latin, Carolus Magnus; in French, Charlemagne; in Dutch, Karel de Groote; in German, Karl der Große). He became a legendary sovereign throughout medieval Europe. During his long reign, which lasted for forty-six years, Charlemagne undertook a huge program of expansion, both territorial and religious. With the Church's support, he pursued a policy of aggression and evangelism outside the realm, with unceasing war expeditions establishing the Frankish authority.

In 774, Charlemagne defeated the revolt of the Lombards of northern Italy and proclaimed himself king of both the Franks and the Lombards. He led another victorious campaign against the separatist Aquitaine in 781.

In 787, he launched a successful war against the pagan Avars in the Danube region, but his efforts to drive the Saracens off of Spain were in vain. He conquered Bavaria, Belgium, Netherlands and Luxembourg in 788. Northern Germany and Saxony up to the river Elbe were conquered and Christianized after numerous ruthless wars and atrocious campaigns lasting more than thirty years.

By the end of the 8th century, the period of conquest was complete, and Charlemagne had reconstituted the Ancient western Roman Empire, along with a wide part of northern and central Germany, but without the British Isles and French Brittany.

Champion of the Christian faith, ally of the papacy and the landowning nobility, victor against the Arabs, Charlemagne was henceforth the most powerful sovereign of all western Europe. At Christmas of the year 800, he was crowned emperor by the pope Leon III in Rome.

The new emperor's task was now to defend his possessions from external aggressions. Charlemagne organized the border provinces militarily into so-called marches; this term, originating from the old Frankish word Marka, means frontier. The march of Brittany, created as early as 790, was intended to repulse the boisterous Bretons. In 805, the Avars of the Danube, who could have been a threat to Bavaria, were contained by the eastern march, the Ostmark, which later became Osterreich (Austria). The march of Spain, called marka hispanica (which would become the kingdom of Catalonia), was created in 811 in the south of the Pyrenees; with its capital Barcelona and the fortresses of Vich, Cardona, Girona and Lerida, it was intended to contain the Saracens. At the head of each march Charlemagne delegated a Markgraf (a term that gave us the words margrave and marquis).

The marches formed a strong defensive organization, but unlike the Romans who defended their empire by continuous lines of fortifications and entrenchments with permanent and fixed garrisons, Charlemagne's defenses relied on mobile warriors, mounted on horse, operating an offensive warfare from strategic strong points. Indeed, the emperor had no permanent army; according to the traditional Germanic law, armed forces were raised for every campaign in spring and summer. Charlemagne, as a Frankish warlord, had the right to call up all free men for an expedition. Only the richest of them could be warriors because they were required to pay for their own weapons, military equipment and servants, and they received no pay but were rewarded by booty, land and estates taken from the defeated enemies. Accordingly the Carolingian army could not have been numerous; probably it consisted of a few thousand combatants. As for the huge figures given by the medieval chronicles describing thousands of valiant knights vanquishing hundreds of thousands of wicked enemies, these were written ten centuries afterwards; they do not reflect reality but are intended to impress the reader through rhetorical, allegorical and epic style.

Because of its huge dimensions, its varied pastiche of Germanic laws, its patchwork of populations, and its poor fiscal and administrative structure, the Carolingian empire was a vulnerable construction. Partly, the empire rested on the fighting high nobility and low gentry originating from the Merovingian organization. To this group of aristocrats (who of course were the same privileged cast called up for military service), Charlemagne delegated a part of his power, dividing the empire into counties, provinces, regions and marches commanded by graven (counts or earls), herzogen (dukes) and markgraven (margraves). These powerful officers represented the emperor; they were appointed and dismissed by him and had large juridical, fiscal, administrative, and of course military and police power in their territories. At the regional level they in turn delegated a part of their power to local gentry, barons, viscounts and lords.

Recall, however, that the emperor had a poor fiscal administration and consequently no money; hence he could not regularly pay his officials. On the other hand, land and agriculture were the only wealth in a rural world. The emperor therefore had no choice but to allow nobility and gentry to live on the lands they administrated, drawing their livelihood from them.

The system was complicated by the fact that Charlemagne also appointed the bishops, who became not only spiritual leaders but territorial administrators too. All imperial servants were regularly inspected and controlled by officers called missi dominici (literally meaning sent by the master).

This system, based on loyalty and a personal oath of allegiance between important individuals and the emperor, functioned more or less successfully as long as Charlemagne was alive, and as long as the counts, earls, dukes, margraves, barons, viscounts and other local lords were loyal and willing to accept the fact that they were removable. Actually, however, the system was the great weakness of Charlemagne's empire. The main imperial cohesion was the Church, and naturally the strong and charismatic personality of the emperor, who had the power to impose his will and to control personal relationships between individuals.

Though himself a brutal warrior, Charlemagne sought to bring spirituality, morality and education to his warriors, clergy and populations. His reign was marked by an artistic and intellectual revival, the empire was not invaded, and a semblance of internal peace was maintained, allowing a rebirth of commercial activities, notably in northern Europe. At all levels, however the effects of the Carolingian Renaissance were only moderate.

Wars were fought on the borders of the empire by

horsemen. The tradition, recruitment and structure of the Carolingian army was unsuitable for fixed garrisons in permanent fortifications. Towns, even those few that were relatively prosperous, were not politically and economically significant, and their conquest and possession was not a decisive trump. Therefore military architecture fell into full decay. Existing works and urban fortifications dating from the Roman time were maintained little or not at all. Charlemagne allowed the dismantling of defense works so that stones from fortifications could be used to build churches, notably in Langres, Verdun, Reims, Melun, Frankfurt or Ratisbon, for example. Even Charlemagne's palace in the imperial capital city, Aix-la-Chapelle (today Achen in Germany), was unfortified. Only a few border fortresses and frontier strongholds were erected or maintained in the marches to serve as offensive bases. It is rather difficult to know what they looked like, since documents are lacking and works were later demolished or rebuilt. We may suppose, however, that they were in the Roman-Germanic tradition with stone walls, earth entrenchments, stockades and ditches.

If the land frontiers of Charlemagne's empire were rather well held owing to the marches, the maritime façade (North Sea, Channel and Atlantic Ocean) was poorly defended and vulnerable. As early as 799, Scandinavian pirates began to launch quick and bloody raids. Against them the emperor was powerless because he had no naval force. Charlemagne ordered the installation of fortified surveillance posts on the coasts, near the harbors and by the river-mouths. Those posts, however, were probably not numerous and were not likely strong enough to secure the coast.

Charlemagne's empire did not survive long. Unity was maintained with difficulty by his son Louis the Pious from 814 to 840, but after Louis's death, his three sons and successors quarreled and fought among themselves. The result of these fratricidal struggles was the partition of the huge empire by the treaty of Verdun in 843. Charles the Bald became king of the western part, which would become France; Ludwig the German became king of the eastern part (east of the river Rhine), which would give birth to Germany. Between these two kingdoms, the third brother, Lothar, was yielded a large corridor stretching from the Netherlands up to northern Italy. This absurd and incoherent realm proved impossible to rule, and Charles and Ludwig annexed large parts of it. By 870 Lothar's territories had ceased to exist, but his name can be still found today in the French province Lotharingia or Lorraine.

The division of the Carolingian Empire marked the end of an era, the end of united Europe. The antagonism among the subsequent Carolingian kings, worsened and quickened by new invasions, precipitated the decomposition of Europe into the feudal time.

THE SCANDINAVIAN INVASIONS

The Vikings or Norsemen, Germanic inhabitants of Scandinavia (Denmark, Sweden and Norway), were remarkable ship builders and audacious seamen. During the 7th century, for quite unknown reasons (over-population, lack of land, banishment of nobles, simple lust for pillage?), they began expansion and conquest. Hardy adventurers, they undertook long and perilous sea travels in the Baltic sea, opening commercial routes in the Russian rivers up to the Black sea and even to the Near East. In a western direction they explored and settled in Iceland and Greenland. They probably discovered America five hundred years before Christopher Columbus by exploring the coasts of Labrador and Newfoundland.

In the 9th century they sailed south and conquered the northern part of the British Isles. They came with the intention of trading, but having been badly received, they turned to pillaging and launched bloody raids on the Atlantic coasts. Their long, swift, high-prowed ships could penetrate deep in the hinterland to ascend rivers, from which they launched mobile surprise raids. Before long they seized horses and rode inland, ravaging the countryside.

As early as 809, the prosperous port of Dorestad in the Netherlands was attacked. Chronicles mention Viking aggressions in Rouen in 841 and Nantes in 844. Spain was raided in 844, Bordeaux was besieged in 848, Paris was a target in 845, 856 and 861. The Norsemen passed the Strait of Gibraltar in 859 and spread murder and devastation on the Mediterranean coasts in Spain, southern France and Italy. They sailed the Rhine in 885 and looted Nimegue, Cologne and Bonn. In 886, a huge fleet of Viking ships ransomed Paris and looted the rich provinces of Champagne and Burgundy.

According to chronicles, everywhere they came, the Vikings murdered people and ransomed, looted and burned villages, cities and even churches, monasteries and abbeys—all because they were unscrupulous and devilish pagans who had never known the edifying influences of Roman civilization. But were they really that bad? Were they exclusively responsible for all crimes, thefts, murders and pillages of the time?

Actually, whenever and wherever they were given the opportunity, the Vikings appear to have been rather peaceful merchants, peasants and good administrators. Progressively the Norsemen converted from vagabond looters to sedentary settlers. By the treaty of Saint-Clair-sur-Epte in 911, the Carolingian king of France, Charles the Simple (893–922), yielded the Viking chief, Rollo, a vast territory in the region of Rouen. With astonishing rapidity, the Norsemen (called henceforth Norman) became Christian, learned the French language, mixed with

Carolingian horseman. The Carolingian time saw the beginning of the supremacy of the cavalry on the battlefield. The warrior on horseback benefited from several important technical improvements invented by the Franks. The horseshoe increased the animal's capacity, and speed and mastery over the horse were increased with the use of spurs attached to the rider's feet. A well-designed saddle and stirrups introduced in the 8th century provided more stability, enabling the horseman to use his spear both as a throwing and a shock weapon. Armament consisted of a lance, a long right sword and a battle-ax. Defensive equipment was composed of a long wooden pointed shield reinforced with iron bars, and—for the richest—a metal helmet with nose piece and a coat of mail made of metal rings called a hauberk.

Castle Valkhof in Nimegue (Netherlands). Nimegue (Nijmegen in Dutch) was situated in the province of Gelderland. The city was the capital of the Batave tribe, then a Roman castrum called Noviomagus Batavorum on the Rhine limes. Nimegue was one of Charlemagne's residences, and the emperor had a castle built called Valkhof. The castle and the city were ravaged by the Norsemen in 880. The German emperor Friedrich Barbarossa ordered the reconstruction of the Valkhof in 1155; the castle served as residence for the dukes of Gelderland throughout the Middle Ages. The Valkhof was destroyed by the French in 1796.

the local populations and assimilated manners and customs.

From the region of Caen, the Normans conquered the valley of the Orne River about 933, the Cotentin Peninsula and the British Channel Islands in 1051. The Norman territories became the rich duchy of Normandy. In the 11th century, the Normans settled down in Britain, Sicily and southern Italy.

Norman fortification was characterized by the use of earth entrenchments and wooden palisades. Villages were often circular, in a form called ringfort, but there was also a vast entrenched camp called Hague-Dike, a four kilometer–long earth rampart erected in the 10th century to defend the Hague peninsula in the Cotentin (Normandy). Norman fortifications, notably the motte-and-bailey cas-

tle (see chapter 2), played an important role in early feudal times.

During the 8th and 9th century, the Vikings were not the only invaders to ravage Europe, and other looters contributed to the general insecurity. In the Mediterranean sea, the French and Italian coasts were exposed to Spanish corsairs, Berber pirates, and Muslim raiders whose razzias were, in many respects, similar to those of the Norsemen: sea robbers turning into mounted marauders on land. In eastern Europe, the Magyards, coming from central Asia, brought troubles and insecurity in Germany and even pushed deadly incursions up into Burgundy, Provence, and northern Italy. For a century, the savagery of their raids once again brought Asiatic danger to the European lands. In 955, however, the Mag-

Viking boat. The Norman ship, called drakkar, langskip, karve or knarr according to its size, could sail with its unique mast or be moved by oars.

yards were defeated in Lechfeld by the German emperor Otto I the Great. They established themselves in the plain of the river Danube, converted to Christianity, and created the kingdom of Hungary.

FEUDAL SOCIETY

Over the course of the 10th century, the Carolingian empire was ultimately dismembered. The German part became the Holy Roman empire created by Otto the Great, who was crowned emperor in 962. The French part was divided into seven independent kingdoms characterized by a new social organization that today is called the feudal system or feudalism (from the Latin *feodum*, which means fief, a rural domain or an estate including population and produced goods).

The feudal system—or, more accurately, absence of system—was actually an improvisation resulting from the events previously discussed. The system had many forms, which evolved over time and varied according to region. Roughly speaking, the multiform feudal system was in effect from the decay of the Carolingian era in the 9th century until the end of the 12th century, though some aspects were still alive in the centuries that followed, notably in France until the Revolution of 1789 and in Great Britain even to the present day.

The last Carolingian kings, as weak and as insignificant as the last Merovingian sovereigns, could not stop the disintegration of the empire, as they could no longer guarantee public order, peace, traditional rights or individual security. The end of the first millennium was one of the most tragic times in western European history; insecurity and danger were widespread and established values disappeared along with the last vestiges of the Carolingian Renaissance. From all corners of the continent, invasions by Vikings, Arabs and Hungarians had wrought havoc and destroyed what remained of traditional Frankish civilization. In a climate of state dissolu-

Norse warrior

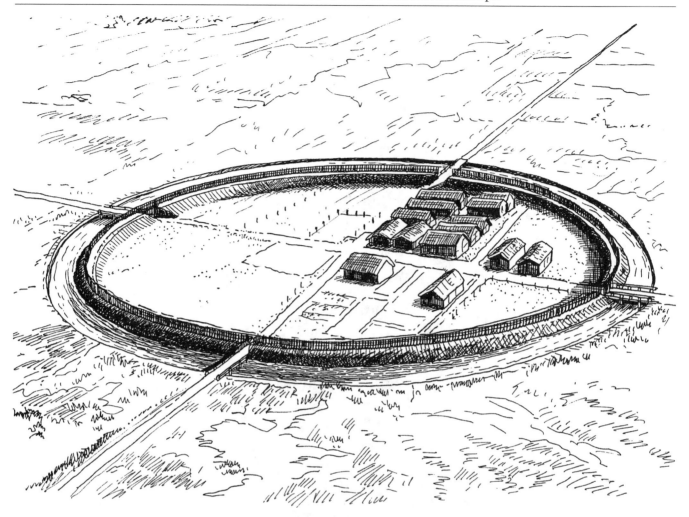

View of a Scandinavian fortified round village. When Scandinavia emerged from its prehistoric period at the end of the 8th century, there were only a few towns—market centers such as Ribe, Birka, Hedeby or Fyrkat. Norse fortifications often followed a standard circular design with ditches, earth walls and palisades. Living accommodations, stores, stables, workshops and other buildings were placed inside the round enclosure.

tion, authority and power were transferred from the royal level to a local scale. The populace, confused and desperate, turned for protection to strong and energetic local lords who could organize measures for self-defense and survival. Authority and power were thus available to whoever could seize and keep them. This being the case, local wars and small conflicts were numerous even after the Scandinavian invasions had ceased.

Feudalism spread from its birthplace in France to other European countries and in particular to Germany, Italy, England and northern Spain. Gradually, Europe was divided in autonomous territories headed by the Carolingian nobility as well as other usurpers who became independent from all centralized power. The cen-

ter of self-defense became the fortified manors and castles ruled by the local lords, which became strongholds where the individual could find relative refuge. Titles and domains became private property, which were transmitted by heritage (in France the right of inheritance became official as early as 877). The new class of powerful landowners had not only territorial holdings but also powers that today belong to the state such as police, finance, justice, public offices, affairs of state and the minting of money.

Feudalism had its origin in the fusion of two institutions: the right of land and vassalage. The right of land represented an individual's lifetime right to use a fief (an estate) granted to him. Vassalage meant the swearing of an allegiance and rendering of service by one man to another in exchange for such an estate as well as for protection. The fief was granted by a mighty lord, called a suzerain, to a subordinate, called a vassal. The bond between the two represented dependence and submission, and it was directly related to the strength of the castle and its lord. Both parties owed one another council and help, which was principally in the form of armed service, called ost.

Out of the semi-anarchy arose social structures and laws based on verbal contract. A pyramidal organization developed, with the king at the top as suzerain to all suzerains; note that the function of king or emperor was never abolished, even though royal power was limited or insignificant. Officially, the chain of authority extended from the king to his vassals (the high noblemen loyal to him), who were suzerains to their vassals (dukes, counts, earls), who in their turn were suzerains to their vassals (marquis and barons), and so on down to the local lords and castellans. Each level of the hierarchy was tied by the bond of homage; each vassal personally swore to be loyal to his suzerain, declaring himself that suzerain's man (homme in French, whence *homage*). The system was perpetuated by titles and ceremonies that were observed with utmost rigor.

In practice, however—human nature being what it is—rebellion of suzerain, revolt of vassal, instinct for independence, and greed all led to conflicts, insurrections and local wars, which the king or the high suzerains simply could not stop because they had neither the police power nor the moral authority to do so. The hierarchic chain of loyalty was complicated by the fact that one vassal might swear homage to more than one suzerain. In many cases, low vassals and local lords were almighty within their own fiefs. Any concept of public authority was undermined by the immunity of the dukes, counts, marquis, barons, castellans and lords within their own domains.

The throne at last began to regain power by establishing centralized administration, extending its land holdings by usurpation and by armed force. With the growth of central power, notably in France and England, feudalism began to decline and the power of the lords was checked. These changes, however, developed over three or four centuries. In the mean time, feudalism was officialized by the church: The feudal society was declared the expression of the will of God, who puts each man in his place. At the end of the 10th century, the archbishop of Rheims defined and consecrated three distinct and unequal social classes: *oratores*, *bellatores*, and *laboratores*.

Oratores: Those Who Pray

The first social feudal class was the Catholic Church. By virtue of his position as successor to Saint Peter, and through the prestige of the eternal city, the bishop of Rome became the head of the ecclesiastical structure with the title of pope (also called Holy Father or Pontiff Sovereign), and the Catholic Church was divided into two main branches. The first branch was the regular clergy, composed of abbots and monks living in secluded communities and following a *regula* (rule). The medieval regular clergy had a remarkable capacity for adaptation, constantly transforming and renewing itself according to the evolution of the feudal society. Monasticism, originating from the Near East, spread into Europe in the 3rd century. Though prayer and Godly service were fundamental to the monastic life, faith was not the only reason to enter a religious house. As the European population grew, more and more people found they could not feed their whole families. Placing a son or a daughter in a monastery or a nunnery meant fewer mouths to feed. Certainly, life was better as a monk within the safe walls of a convent than as a poor farmer outside.

Though the monastic orders were all different and observed rules, they also had many common features. From the 7th century onwards, monasticism was directly placed under the pope's authority and thus escaped the subordination of the laic king and the secular bishop. Well-disciplined, committed and sometimes fanatical, present and active throughout Christendom, monks were the best agents of pontifical power. The orders were composed of more or less educated monks who could read, study, translate ancient Hebrew, Greek and Arabic texts, write manuscripts, and pray. This tiny elite was assisted by lay-brothers who were workers, craftsmen, peasants, servants and domestics.

No one can deny that monasticism played a fundamental role as spiritual nucleus in a harsh and illiterate world. As missionaries, monks contributed greatly to the evangelization of Europe. On the intellectual and cultural level, what they brought to civilization was essential. They saved the literary and scientific heritage of the ancient world; they stimulated the progress of science, medicine, literature, technology, art and philosophy; they transmitted knowledge through schools, universities, and handwritten books. Most medieval scientists, thinkers, doctors, historians, theologians, philosophers and other intellectuals were monks.

The second part of the Church was the secular clergy—the spiritual administrator of the profane world. Its structure and hierarchy dated back to the late Roman Empire. The parish, headed by a priest, was the basic unit, usually embracing a village or a district in a town. A number (which varied) of parishes formed a diocese headed by a bishop (the term comes from the Greek *episkopos*, meaning supervisor or guardian). The bishop played a central role in the medieval organization. When the Carolingian empire collapsed, there was no more central authority nor public services; gradually and according to circumstances, the bishop took over and, besides his spiritual mission, fulfilled a social and economical role. It was he who directed the organization of daily life by helping the poor, by opening markets and hospitals, and by building bridges, dikes, roads, fortifications, churches and, later, cathedrals.

Both branches of the Church were feudal landowners, and as such disposed of the same rights as the laic ruling hierarchy. However, ecclesiastical wealth was not personal but collective; church property could not be transmitted by inheritance because monks, abbots, priests, bishops and all other clergymen were supposed to observe chastity and thus, officially at least, did not have children.

The Church was also a good business. Neither branch paid taxes. Clerical resources came from the dime, a tax corresponding to one tenth of the goods produced by the population. Wealth also flowed in from members of the nobility who, hoping to gain salvation, gave the Church money, land or feudal rights over estates. Another source of income for the Church was the sacraments, benedictions and offices that had to be paid. The Church also reaped big profits from shrines, sanctuaries and pilgrimages: Saint-Martin in Tours, Mont-Saint-Michel and Rocamadour in France, Saint Peter's sepulture in Rome, Santiago de Compostella in Spain and, the most prestigious of them all, the holy city of Jerusalem in Palestine.

Bellatores: Those Who Fight

The second privileged social class of the feudal system was the nobility, composed of warriors organized in a pyramidal vasselage. Originally the task of this class was the physical defense and protection of their subjects, but gradually the bellatores' power became paramount.

The lord was a fief-holder and manifested his authority from a stronghold. His drew his resources from the work and production of the population attached to his domain. He collected various taxes, and banalities (obligations) were imposed on the subjects, such as required use of the lord's mill, market, bakehouse, bridge, press-house and brewery. The community was also subjected to various labors such as maintenance of the fortress and roads.

The noble class of feudal society was a complex body, at first made up of men from a great variety of conditions. It was not a closed group, at least originally; anyone smart, cunning, strong and powerful enough could join and declare himself a ruler. But gradually, it became a hereditary and hermetically closed aristocracy, sharing

a peculiar vision of the world, a special mentality, with its own values and a common way of life. Whatever their position, power and wealth, noblemen distinguished themselves from the common folk by their privileges. They did not pay taxes because, in theory at least, they shed their blood for the community's defense. In a world dominated by scarcity, precariousness and poverty, their way of life was marked by an abundance of food, clothing, and possessions, and they lived in more or less comfortable fortified residences (castles, strong-houses, donjons and so on).

Laboratores: Those Who Work

The third feudal social class was that of the common people, composed of all those who were not noble and who did not belong to the Church. The laboratores were the most numerous—about 90 percent of the population—and it was they who fed the two privileged classes. All were country-dwellers, living from and in direct contact with nature; their existence directly depended on conditions of ground, climate and geography.

The manorial system was not the same all over Europe, nor did it stay the same in any one region through the whole of the Middle Ages. There were always differences in the way the system worked between one estate and another, one region and another and one period and another. Local customs and both local and national economic pressures affected the way things worked. Accordingly it is impossible to give an accurate description of this class that would cover all the various European regions over a period of about a thousand years. Nevertheless, it can be said that the most characteristic features of the laboratores were a modest life, strong family and community ties strictly dominated by the lord and controlled by the Church, hard labor in meadows and fields, and poor or miserable resources due to economic dependence on the local ruling lord. The peasantry was composed of people with various juridical status. Many were serfs (a term from the Latin word for slave), i.e., peasants attached to a domain; others were villeins (in ancient times, workers attached to a Roman villa), who owned a small piece of land; and a few were free laborers.

Life is the countryside was hard. People worked from dawn to dusk every day of the year until they were unable to work any longer. The basis of the manorial system was the exchange of land for labor. The local landlord was expected to protect his subjects, and he in turn expected the villagers to work a fixed number of days on his own estate; the rest of the time they worked on their own land. The villagers were also obliged to use the lord's mill, bridge and facilities and to help build and maintain castles, roads and bridges.

Most of the population lived in simple houses. The

View of Mont-Saint-Michel (France). This remarkable Benedictine abbey is situated on a small island in the mouth of river Couësnon near Avranches in the department of Manche. At the same time an abbey, a village and a fortress, the origin of the place is attributed to the angel Saint Michael, who ordered the bishop of Avranches to build an oratory on the rocky Mont-Tombe, as it then was called. Work began in 1023, and in 1080 the monastery housed a hundred monks. The king of France, Philippe Auguste, decided to enlarge the abbey; the building called "la Merveille" and the cloister were built between 1221 and 1228. The abbey of Mont-Saint-Michel was continually embellished in the following centuries, but during the French Revolution and the days of the empire (1789—1815) it was turned into a prison and damaged. Since 1874, the Mont-Saint-Michel has been restored, and today it is the most prestigious and the most visited French historical monument.

walls were made of wooden beams and sticks covered with mud. The roofs were thickly thatched with reeds or cornstalks so that the rain ran off easily. People ate cereals and vegetables most of the time, with chicken or pork for special occasions. Resources came from agriculture, gardening, fishing and poaching (hunting was strictly forbidden to the commoners and jealously reserved to the nobles). Agriculture had seen progress since Roman times: Plowing was deeper and brought air into the soil, animal traction was improved by the invention of the horse-collar, and crops were rotated on the land, giving better harvests. The energy of wind and water was exploited by means of

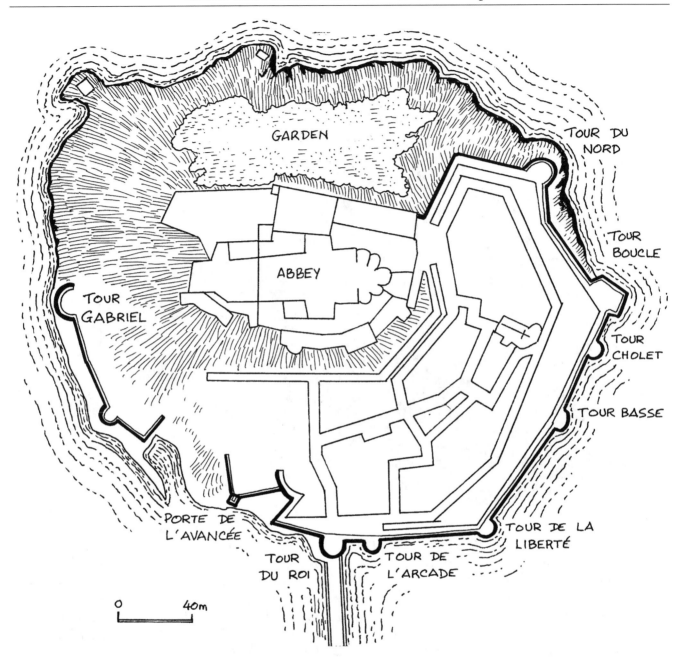

GARDEN

TOUR DU NORD

TOUR BOUCLE

ABBEY

TOUR GABRIEL

TOUR CHOLET

TOUR BASSE

TOUR DE LA LIBERTÉ

PORTE DE L'AVANCÉE

TOUR DU ROI

TOUR DE L'ARCADE

0   40m

Ground-plan, Mont-Saint-Michel (France). An abbey and a place of pilgrimage, the Mont-Saint-Michel was also a stronghold that was fortified during the Hundred Years' War in the 14th and 15th centuries. Symbolizing the struggle against the English, the Mont was defended by walls, ten towers and a gatehouse. The fortifications were adapted to firearms about 1440. The Mont-Saint-Michel, well protected by its wall and its situation off shore, has never been taken by force.

mills as early as the 10th century. Leather, wool, hemp and flax provided materials for the textile craftsmen.

Until the 10th century, the medieval landscape was dominated by huge forests, with domains, cities, villages and abbeys mere isolated outposts. The forest was economically very important for medieval society, providing villagers with wild plants, herbs, honey, mushrooms and wood for construction and fuel. In the 11th and 12th centuries, however, vast pieces of forest were cleared, new lands were brought under cultivation on a large scale, marshlands were drained, and rivers were dammed up, allowing new settlements, population growth and relative prosperity. Rural communities were installed near abbeys and castles. Some villages grew and became cities.

2

The Revival of Military Architecture from the 10th to the 12th Centuries

EARLY MEDIEVAL FORTIFICATIONS

The collapse of the Roman Empire, the establishment of Germanic realms and dreadful invasions marked the beginning of a new era. The decline of institutions, the lack of military means and the complete decrease of central power brought far-reaching changes, while insecurity gave rise to the first medieval castles. During the 9th and 10th centuries, which were dominated by violence and troubles, there was a general revival of fortification. Fortifications reflected the local power of the numerous lords; they reassured the frightened common folk and allowed the protection of people and property. Organized defenses, even rudimentary ones, offered the possibility for a small garrison to resist mounted attackers. Two types of fortification gradually appeared: urban and rural.

Urban fortification was often due to the initiative of the local bishop, who sometimes organized the people for survival and self-defense. Not before the 12th century, however, would cities regain the importance they had had in the Roman empire, as we shall see in chapter 5. Much more significant was rural fortification, which evolved following the Celtic, Roman and Germanic tradition. Farms, villages and hamlets were isolated, more or less at the mercy of nature and vulnerable to outlaws, raiders and invaders. Fortified, they constituted a type of primitive refuge, which went by various names: for example, borough in Britain, Burg in Germany, burcht in the Nether-

lands, ferté, plessis and bourg in France. Those terms survive today in the names of numerous villages and towns.

Rural fortifications were characterized by the use of wood and earth. A common feature was the stockade or palisade, widely used since ancient times. It was a barrier, fence, breastwork or a defensive wall made of pointed tree-trunks, set vertically in the ground. The cohesion and solidity of the poles were reinforced by ropes, transverse beams and stones forming foundations in the ground. The stockade was very often placed on an earth wall, created by digging a ditch and heaping up the soil on the inner side of the excavation. This was the easiest and earliest permanent method of marking a boundary or creating a fortified perimeter. Sharp sticks, dead bushes or thorny hedges were sometimes placed in the ditch to provide further protection (prefiguring barbed wire). The top of the earth wall behind the stockade was flattened to create a wall-walk (also called allure), permitting circulation and defense.

The combination of ditch and earth wall formed a passive obstacle, while the stockaded parapet sheltered the inhabitants within from enemy missiles and provided for the active emplacement of combat. This primitive form of fortification constituted a considerable defense, but it needed constant maintenance. Another drawback was that if the palisade was relatively cheap and rapidly raised, it was vulnerable to battering ram and fire.

The inhabitants could also find protection in the church, which was very often the only stone building in

Cross-section of wooden and earth defense. The cross-section shows the ditch (which was sometimes double) and the earth wall crowned by a palisade and a wall-walk. The gate-house was possibly a wooden tower with a primitive drawbridge.

the village. Constructed in great numbers before the erection of the stone castles, fortified churches were a common feature not only on the pirate-infested coasts or in the regions exposed to Saracen raiders, but all over Europe. The village church could easily be converted into a defensive structure with just a few adaptations. By narrowing the windows in loopholes, crenellating the top of the walls, reinforcing the doors and using the bell-tower as an observatory and a donjon, churches and cathedrals were turned into fortresses. Furthermore, medieval country churches were usually surrounded by the village cemetery; if the cemetery wall was well maintained and adapted to defense, it could be used as an external line of combat. So, with determination, a good deal of luck and many prayers, the frightened villagers were in some cases capable of resisting a gang of bandits, a party of looters or a group of raiders.

Examples of fortified religious buildings are numerous throughout Europe: Sé Vilha (old cathedral) in Coïmbra and Lisbon in Portugal, the church of Signy-le-Petit and Liart in the French Thiérache, the church of Saintes-Maries-de-la-Mer in Camargue, the cathedral Saint-Etienne in Agde and the cathedral of Albi in France or the Sankt-Michaelis Kirche in Hildesheim in Germany, just to mention a few.

THE MOTTE-AND-BAILEY CASTLE

With the progressive institution of feudalism everywhere in Europe, a rudimentary form of castle appeared. The term castle, coming from the latin *castrum* and its diminutive *castellum*, designates a fortified building, a dwelling place for the local lord, a political and economic center which provided shelter to the population of the fief in case of danger.

Originating from the French regions between the Loire and Rhine rivers, the so-called motte-and-bailey castle was a transition between the post–Roman refuge and the medieval stone castle. Continuing Germanic tradition, the motte-and-bailey castle was characterized by the digging and heaping up of a huge mass of earth, and the use of wood, material which was everywhere available and easily used by non-specialists.

Rather little is known about motte-and-bailey castles, but the Bayeux tapestry illustrates those at Dol, Rennes, Dinan and Bayeux in France and Hastings in England; the tapestry and a little archeological evidence give some indication of their structure.

The motte proper was a conical mound which might vary considerably in size (between 6 and 15 m). The

29

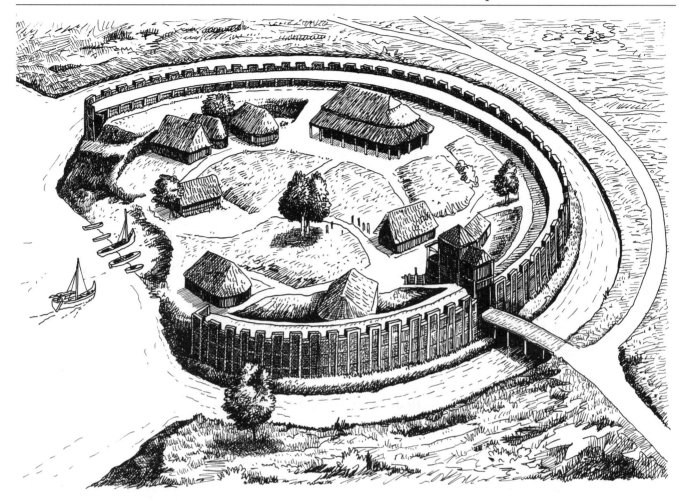

Hunneschans. The small fortified village of Hunneschans was situated near Uddel in the Netherlands. Probably built in the 7th century by the earl of Veluwe Diderik, the village was oval-shaped and leaned on a lake. It was fortified by a ditch, which could be filled with water from the lake, and an earth wall crowned by a stockade. Hunneschans was in some ways similar to the Scandinavian and British ringforts. It was used as a refuge for the local peasantry until the 13th century.

motte could be completely man-made—an important or even enormous undertaking—but if there was a suitable hill in the area it would be adapted by scarping, that is, cutting vertically down the sides and digging away the lower slopes. In certain cases, to avoid the shifting of materials and to provide greater stability to the motte, alternating layers of stone, peat, clay, chalk, rubble, gravel, brushwood or sand were inserted between rammed or beaten down layers of earth. Finally the whole mound was revetted with a thick coat of clay to keep out water. With this technique the builders could create a dry place in a possible swampy area, or keep the castle out of reach of the river in low lands. The base of the motte was surrounded by a ditch, which may have been filled with water. Some of the material for the motte was derived from the ditch, but in some cases additional materials

Opposite: Saintes-Maries-de-la-Mer. This fortified church, situated in the Camargue in southern France, was built and fortified against the Moors in 1144. It included a bell-tower arranged as a keep, thick walls with few openings, a high chapel and a wall-walk fitted with machicolation in the 14th century.

31

The fortified bell-tower of the church of the abbey of Moissac (France)

were required to bring the mound up to any appreciable height.

Artificial or man-made, the top of the motte was flattened in order to constitute a platform, which was defended by a stockade and an earth rampart. In the middle of the platform stood a timber tower, which served as either an observatory or, more frequently, a fortified wooden house where lived the dominus (lord), his family, his few warriors and some servants. This building was called the tower or great-tower, though other words were used, including donjon, dungeon, keep, odel, dunio, domus, domicilium or castellum.

The great-tower was frequently quadrangular or, less commonly, round. Often it rested on foundation pits to take heavy and strong timber posts. The tower usually included one to three stories in which one living room, sleeping accommodations, missile-supply, food and water stores were arranged. The top of the pitched or sloping roof was frequently designed as a small lookout post, a kind of watchtower allowing a wide view of the countryside around it. The entrance to the tower was above ground level and could be reached only by a removable timber bridge or a ladder. Anything else about the appearance of the tower is a matter for speculation, but it was very unlikely that there was not some attempt at decoration in the form of painting, carving or sculpture, since not only preservation but also beauty, pride, ostentation and prestige were always involved in fortification.

As the name suggests

Cathedral of Lisbon (Portugal). The cathedral of Lisbon was built in the 12th century, probably by the French master masons Bernard and Robert, by order of king Afonso Henriques. Like the cathedrals of Porto, Coimbra and Evora, it was also a fortress.

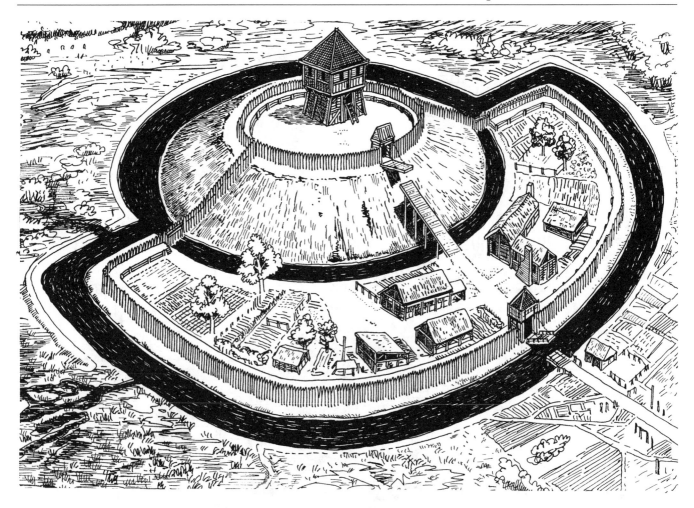

View of a 10th century motte-and-bailey castle

most mottes were accompanied by a bailey. Situated at the foot of the mound, the bailey (a term coming from the French word *baille*, also called basse-cour or bascourt, meaning low yard) was an enclosed area usually in the form of a half-moon, D- or U-shaped. Typically a bailey was constructed with a few auxiliary buildings (for example an oven, a well and cistern, storehouses, a granary, a bakery, stables) and a few huts intended for servants and craftsmen (baker, smith and so on). There was also a small yard where the warriors could train, a garden for herbs and vegetables, some fruit-trees, and a small meadow for a few horses, cows, sheep and pigs. The bailey formed a kind of small village permitting the castle community to live and survive in quasi-autarky.

The bailey was enclosed by a ditch, an earth wall and a stockade. Its entrance was defended by a small gatetower and a primitive drawbridge over the ditch. Communication between the keep on top of the mound and the bailey down below was by means of a flight of steps up the slope to a gateway in the palisade and a small and

narrow bridge which could be easily destroyed by the castle inhabitants to prevent entry by the enemy. The hierarchical separation of the motte-and-bailey castle in two parts was obvious. The upper part reflected the lord's authority; it was a nobleman's residence and a place of command. The lower part was for the servants, whose task was to make their master's life as comfortable as early medieval life allowed.

The dimensions of the motte-and-bailey castle were generally calculated according to the range of a bow. This very ancient weapon was revived in the time of Charlemagne, and its employ was the dominating influence in medieval warfare and fortifications.

The simple structure of motte-and-bailey castles allowed for much variation in design, shape, dimensions, and arrangement. Each was a unique system specifically intended to meet the requirements of that particular geographical and political situation. Though baileys were often elliptical, they could also be square, rectangular or round. The motte might be erected in the middle or on

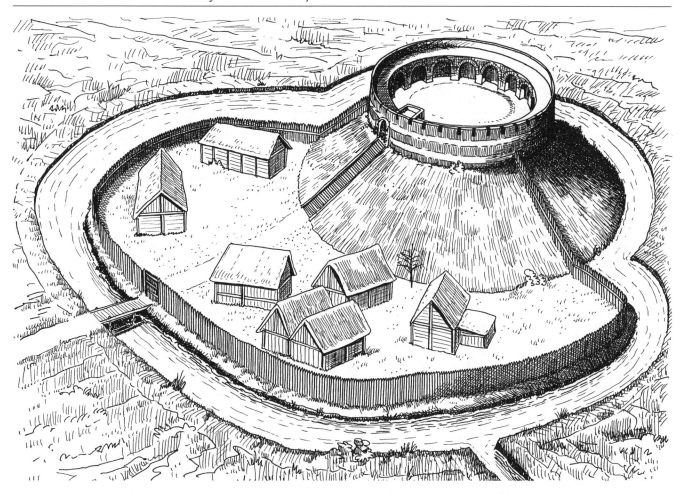

View of a shell-keep (see page 37)

one side of the bailey. Certain motte-and-bailey castles were built by an association of families, resulting in two or more mounds with residential towers and several baileys.

Simple to conceive without the science of an architect, rapidly and rather inexpensively erected by non-qualified villeins and serfs, and easily rebuilt after a siege, the motte-and-bailey castle had many advantages. It was, however, vulnerable to battering ram and fire. In addition, the site had to be regularly maintained and refurbished because time, rain and wind fill in ditches and erode mounds and earth entrenchments, while wooden parts become rotten.

The motte-and-bailey castle was a residence in peacetime and a refuge for tenants of the neighborhood with their cattle and goods in time of war. It was a safe where taxes were collected and tolls levied; it was a small economical, juridical and administrative center; it was the siege of a small-scale political authority dominating a territory (fief) including villages and inhabitants. Its main

purpose, however, was to be a center from which the lord's rule and order were maintained, a stronghold to deter or repulse aggression from external foes as well as a solid military base for mobile warfare when the lord launched raids and attacks on his enemies.

Made of perishable materials, motte-and-bailey castles were direct ancestors to medieval stone donjons and castles. They were characteristic of the chaotic early Middle Ages, the troubled 9th and 10th centuries when local wars were numerous because of the weakness of the royal authority. Thousands must have been built, some permanent, others erected as temporary expedients only to be abandoned and destroyed when royal and ducal order was reestablished. Though particularly common in northern France, motte-and-bailey castles were built throughout Europe, from Italy to Denmark and from Brittany to Poland. After the invasion of England by William the Conqueror in 1066, motte-and-bailey castles were constructed on a large scale by the French Normans to subjugate the Anglo-Saxons. Norman motte-and-bailey cas-

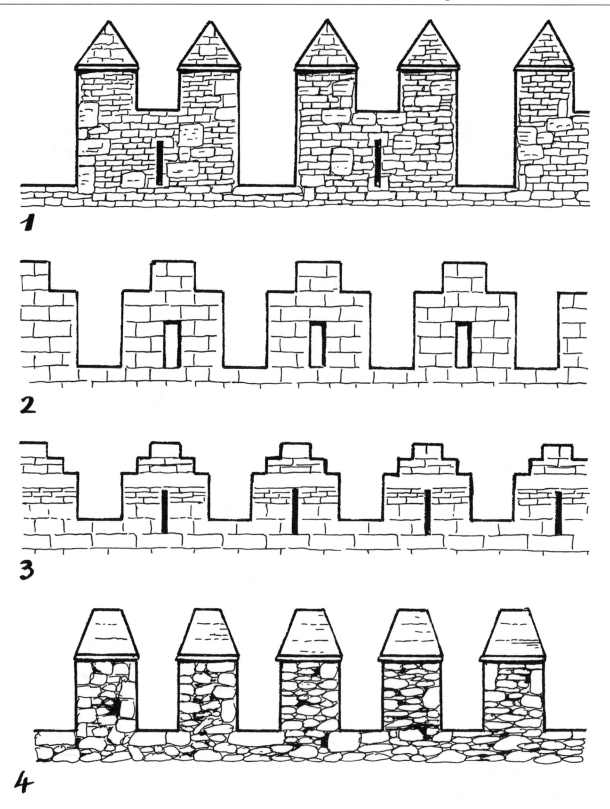

Various forms of Spanish merlons: (1) castle of Maqueda, (2) castle of Manzaneque, (3) castle Belmonte, (4) castle Guadamur.

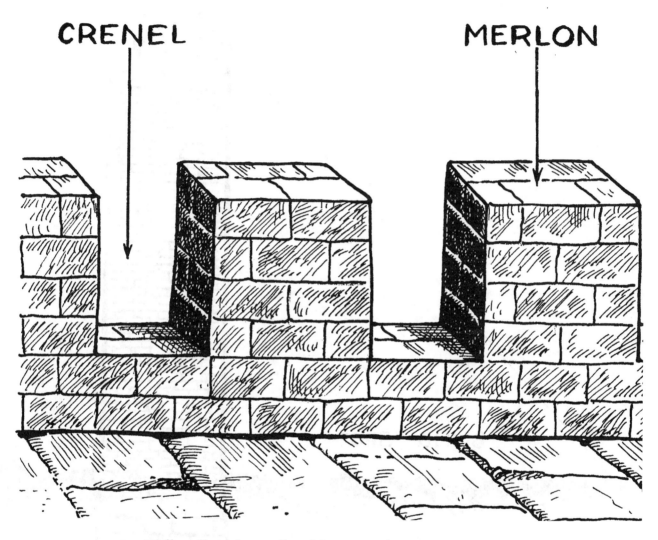

Wall-walk and crenellated breastwork (see page 48)

tles featured a variant called a shell-keep that included a circular stone wall on top of the mound.

Because they were made of perishable construction materials, most motte-and-bailey castles have disappeared. The earthworks have completely vanished, the excavations have been filled in, and timber works have left no trace on the surface. Only those castles that were later rebuilt in stone have survived (Gisors in France and Berkhamsted, Launceston and Restormel in Britain, for example). In France, however, some survive in the toponymy: La Mothe-Fénélon (Lot), La Mothe-Achard (Vendée), La Mothe-Fouquet (Orne), La Motte-Josserand (Nièvre) or La Motte-Tilly (Aube).

Interested readers planning a vacation in western France may want to visit the clever and historically reliable reconstruction of the Haie Jaulain motte-and-bailey castle in the village Saint-Sylvain-d'Anjou situated east of Angers (Maine-et-Loire).

THE FIRST MASONRY DONJONS

Wooden palisades were relatively easy to burn, dismantle, or pass through. Ditches could be crossed. Fire was a hazard to the wooden motte-and-bailey castle tower, from internal domestic sources at all times, and

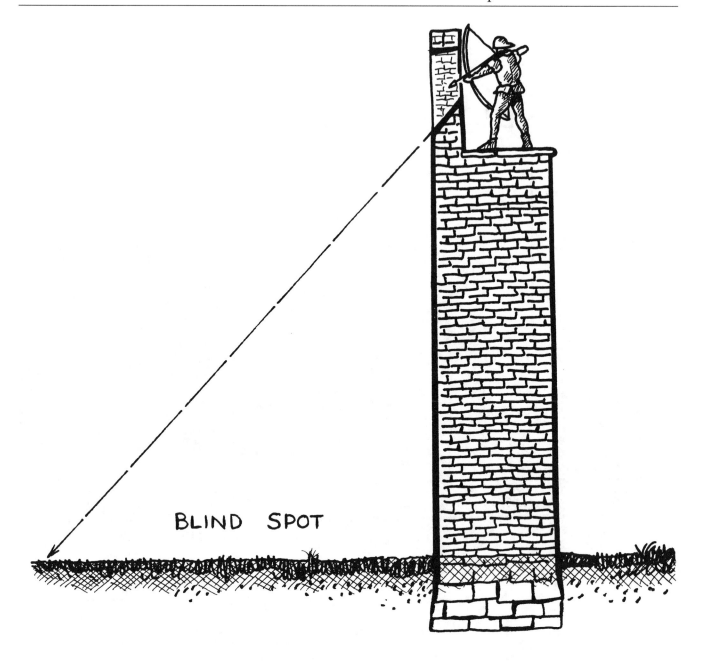

BLIND SPOT

Cross-section of a medieval wall showing the blind spot. Blind spots (see page 49) or dead angles were areas around a fortress where the defenders could not see and their weapons could not reach their enemies.

from external, hostile action in time of war. Subsequently, from the 11th century on, the wooden residential tower—the central element of the motte-and-bailey castle—was gradually replaced by a more durable tower of stone. The transition took place gradually, in a loose fashion. The choice between a timber castle and one of stone depended on the particular time and conditions, including natural elements. In mountainous rocky sites, it was difficult if not impossible to dig a ditch or to plant a stockade, and the only solution was masonry buildings, constructed with stones coming from the vicinity. Simultaneously, Romanesque religious architecture was making tremendous progress, significantly stimulating the development of craftsmanship in the building trades. Architects, quarrymen, master-builders, masons, and stone-hewers were some of the increasingly available craftsmen whose

Cross-section of a wall fitted with hoarding (see page 49)

Hoarding (see page 49)

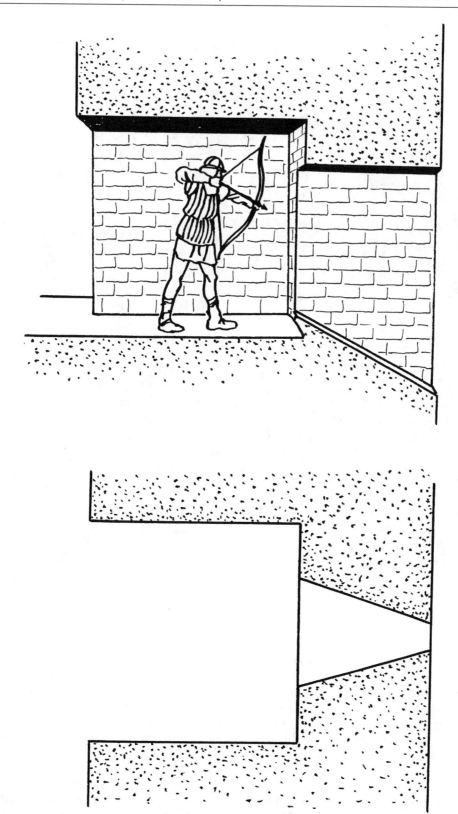

Cross-section and ground plan of a loophole with combat niche (see page 52)

Inside view of a shooting niche (see page 52)

knowledge and experience were valuable to military architecture.

Stone keeps varied considerably in size from very large examples to very small ones. It goes without saying that building a great-tower of masonry takes time and costs a lot of money to pay the designing architect, the planning master-builder and the working skilled specialists. Only the richest and most powerful lords could afford such a luxury.

The first significant masonry great-tower was that of Langeais, credited to the count of Anjou, Foulque Nerra (Fulk the Black), who ruled over the lush and fertile valley of the Loire, southwest of Paris. Fulk had developed

a strategy of establishing wooden motte-and-bailey castles to exploit each newly won patch of Angevin territory, and to serve as springboards for further conquest. Realizing the advantages of a masonry building combining military purposes and his own proud strength, he founded the castle of Langeais, situated west of Tours in the Indre-et-Loire (France), in about 994.

Langeais marks an important evolution in medieval fortification, being the oldest stone keep in France and a model for masonry great-towers of the early Romanesque period. Built on a motte, it was a simple rectangular tower 7 m × 16 m in plan. The donjon, demolished in 1841, probably had smallish, roughly hewn walls about

Atienza (Spain). The village of Atienza was situated about thirty kilometers northwest of Sigüenza in Castilla La Mancha. The castle was built by the Moors and reconquered by the king Alfonso VI in 1085. Today only the square donjon is preserved.

43

Luneburg. The donjon Luneburg was situated near Neerlangbroek in the province Utrecht (Netherlands).

Nogent-le-Rotrou. The château Nogent-le-Rotrou, situated in Eure-et-Loir (France), was founded by the count of Perche, Geoffrey III, probably between 1005 and 1028. It was composed of a massive rectangular donjon 17 m wide, 24 m long and 35 m high; the walls, reinforced with buttresses, were 3.5 m thick at the base and 1.5 m at the summit. The donjon was enclosed with a wide bailey and a gatehouse built in the 13th century furnished with machicolation in the 15th century. Though it suffered a fire in 1428 the castle is well preserved today.

12 m high, 1.5 m thick at the base and 0.70 m thick at the top. The walls were reinforced by buttresses and the tower had wooden floors. Entrance was by means of a small projected tower placed some 3 m above ground level. The Langeais donjon does not seem to have included active defense organs such as crenels and loopholes; probably it was merely a passive carapace. Between 1465 and 1467, a new fortress was constructed in the vicinity of the old keep by Jean Bourré (minister to the French king Louis XI).

Over the long term, stone towers helped to create, reinforce and maintain a hierarchy within the nobility. Because of their wealth and its usual accompaniment of military power, some kings, counts, earls and dukes were able to subjugate many vassals, barons and marquis, who in turn dominated poor noblemen and landowners as well as impecunious knights and squires. Heavy masonry fortification was a significant step in the evolution of the power that permitted kings and dukes to impose their will on their vassals. The time was coming when only the wealthiest would be able to build, confiscate or dismantle castles according to their own interest and strategy.

Motte-and-bailey castles did not disappear overnight. Just because something new was invented does not mean that everything of earlier design was immediately aban-

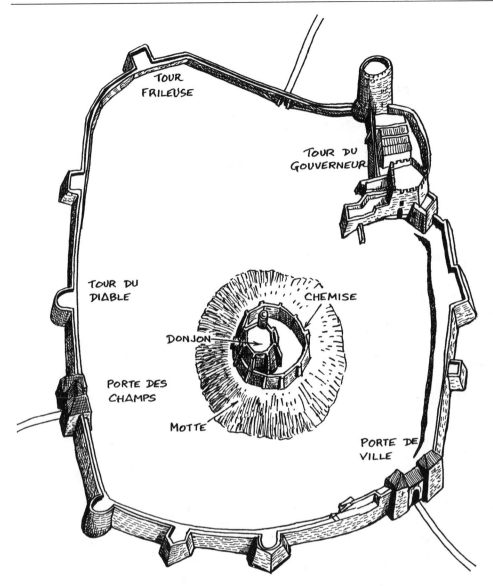

doned. Until the middle of the 13th century, many local landlords of relatively modest means could not afford, or were not allowed by their suzerains, to build masonry castles. Though many illegal or unauthorized stone castles were built, many low vassals had to be satisfied with rudimentary strong houses, simple towers, fortified farms and poorly defended manors.

Masonry donjons, keeps and great-towers fulfilled the same function as motte-and-bailey castles. They were very often the residence of a lord, his family, his warriors and his servants. They reflected power and authority, but the impressive towers were foremost self-supporting military strongholds. The great-tower was high, massive and vertical, and its foundations were strong and resistant in order to help to distribute the huge weight of the building. Walls were always very thick in order to resist the battering ram; they were often reinforced with powerful masonry buttresses. The tower's ground-plan was usually square or rectangular, allowing a convenient internal layout. It was composed of a various number of stories including

Gisors ground-plan. Gisors, situated near Les Andelys in the department of Eure in Normandy (France), displays an imposing Norman fortified site. The château was built between 1097 and 1106 by the master-builder Robert de Bellême, on order of the English king William II to defend the valley of the river Epte forming a border with France. The castle was composed of an artificial motte (20 m high, 70 m in diameter at the base, and 24 m at the top level) on the summit of which an octagonal stone keep was built; this was enclosed by a chemise (shirt) with crenellated walls 10 m high reinforced by buttresses. The motte, donjon and chemise were enclosed by a wide bailey wall erected about 1123 by Henry I. The external wall included towers, two main gates and a secondary postern. In 1193, Gisors was yielded to the king of France, Philippe II Auguste, who ordered the construction of the powerful Prisoner's Tower (28 m high) and the Governor's Tower in the northeast corner. Gisors castle was further refurbished during the Hundred Years' War between 1375 and 1379. The château was abandoned in the time of Henry IV at the end of the 16th century, and today its majestic ruins stand above the river Epte.

Gisors: the donjon and the shirt

a blind vaulted ground level used as a store-room. The entrance to the great-tower was placed on the first floor above which other rooms were vertically arranged. The aula or hall was a kind of multi-purpose living room, and the camera was a sort of sleeping room. A special space was arranged as a chapel. The top level of the tower offered accommodation for a few guards. Finally, the summit of the building was fitted with a roof and a crenellated allure (wall-walk), allowing guards to watch over the surrounding countryside and providing a place for active defense.

As previously mentioned, the wall-walk and crenellated parapet (breastwork) were already known and used by the ancients and the Romans. The wall-walk was a communication allowing the garrison to move rapidly from one place to another, and the crenel was a hollow space between two solid man-high merlons. Though the shape of the merlons and the width of the crenels varied enormously, the purposes were the same: The crenel allowed defenders to shoot arrows and throw down missiles, while the merlon offered shelter while reloading a bow or crossbow. To crenellate a wall was also a question of prestige and social status; the construction of merlons and crenels was allowed by suzerains to vassals only by means of a special license. Crenellation was paramount all through the Middle Ages and was popular even beyond that time as a civilian architectural decoration, since it shows up well against the sky.

Active defense consisted of repulsing assault ladders and was effected vertically from the upper position, by throwing down missiles (mainly stones) or shooting arrows

White Tower in London. London, originating from a Celt oppidum (pre–Roman fortress) contructed on a ford at Westminster, was colonized in 43 AD and fortified by the Romans. Londinium, as it was then named, became the capital of Great-Brittany in the 2nd century AD. After the victory of Hastings in 1066, the duke of Normandy, William the Conqueror, became king of England and ordered the construction of the White Tower near the Thames. Erected between 1078 and 1097 by the bishop of Rochester Gandulf and master-builder Guillaume Le Roux, the White Tower was a rectangle 35.9 m long by 32.6 m wide with four corner turrets. The walls were 31 m high, 4.6 m thick at the base and 3.3 m at the summit. In the Middle Ages, the fortress was the royal residence, a citadel enclosing the inhabitants, an arsenal, a prison and the center of administrative life.

Rochester (Britain). Rochester, situated east of London in Kent, was founded by the Romans. Called Durobrivae, the fortified city was intended to defend the mouth of the river Medway and the road from Dover to London. Rochester castle was originally a motte-and-bailey castle built by the Normans. About 1087 the bishop Gandulf ordered the erection of a stone donjon similar to that of London. Rochester castle was a massive square 21 m by 21 m, 36 m high, divided in four stories with corner turrets. Between 1127 and 1142, the castle was enlarged and reshaped by archbishop of Canterbury Guillaume de Corbeil.

downwards. This way of shooting, called plunging fire or vertical flanking, left many blind spots (also called dead angles)—see illustration, page 38) at the foot of the tower. Indeed, unless the defenders leaned dangerously far out of the crenels, they could not see and their weapons could not reach their enemies. Accordingly a special disposition, called a hoarding, was invented to avoid this dangerous drawback.

A hoarding, also called hourd, brattice or propugnacula, formed a wooden balcony made of removable scaffolding, a kind of roofed timber gallery jutting out from the external surface of a wall. (See illustrations, pages 39 and 40.) Hoardings were placed on top of the wall of the donjon at parapet level, later on walls and towers. They were composed of planks attached to strong overarching timbers and short poles (called putlogs) fixed in corbelled stones in the masonry and in holes. The putlog holes, sometimes in two rows, ran all along the top of walls, towers and donjons. Sometimes hoardings were permanent fixtures; in other cases they were erected in an emergency in time of war, the timberwork being kept in store. In the hoarding floor were openings through which the defenders could watch their enemies and throw missiles down on them when they reached the very foot of

Richmond castle. The castle of Richmond, situated in the valley of the Swaledale river (North Yorkshire in Great Britain), was an imposing masonry donjon built in 1071 by the Norman baron Alain le Rouge (Allan the Red). Securely installed on top of a cliff dominating the river, Richmond keep was 30 m high and presented many similarities with Rochester castle and the White Tower of London.

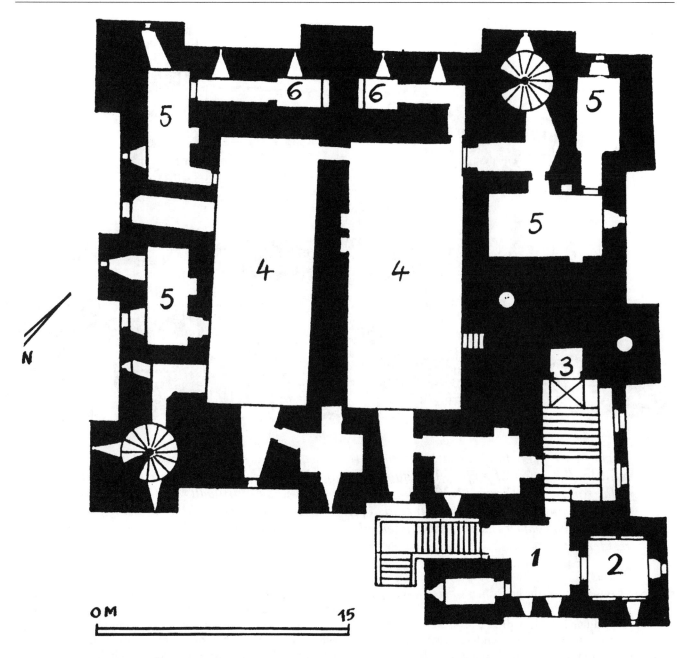

Ground-plan of Dover castle. Strategically situated in the Strait of Dover and considered key access to England, Dover (called then Dubris) was founded by the Romans in 43 AD. The castle was constructed by master-builder Maurice l'Ingénieur between 1181 and 1188 by order of Henry II (1154–1189). Its core was composed of a keep similar to that of the White Tower in London: It was a square tower 30 m x 30 m and 28 m high with corner turrets. The walls were extremely thick for a Norman design, reaching 6 m. The keep was divided in three stories; the ground-plan here shows the second floor with (1) the entrance, (2) the chapel, (3) the drawbridge, (4) two vast halls, (5) chambers and living quarters and (6) latrines. The donjon was surrounded by a bailey and two concentric enceintes with towers dating from the time of King John (1199–1216) and his successor, Henry III (1216–1272).

51

Loches castle. Loches was situated near Tours in Indre-et-Loire (France). The donjon, built by the count of Anjou, Foulque Nerra, in the 11th century, was a massive rectangular tower 37 m high, 23.30 m long and 15.40 m wide with walls 2.80 m thick reinforced by buttresses. The tower included four stories and a side-building housing the entrance and a chapel. Loches castle, later enlarged, became one of the French kings' favorite residences.

the wall. Consequently, the hoardings offered a very good vertical flanking.

Yet hoardings had their drawbacks. Made of wood, they were very vulnerable to incendiary missiles. Besides, they concealed crenellation and made it useless, and accordingly they had to be fitted with their own loopholes. Because of these drawbacks they were replaced by the end of the 13th century by permanent masonry machicolation.

The internal rooms of the stone donjon were furnished with various domestic facilities such as latrines, aumbries (wall cupboards), food-stores, a cistern for drinking water, and fireplaces. Floors were made of heavy planks held by strong beams resting on corbelled stones, and access between the various levels was by means of ladders or narrow staircases. Openings were rather few and placed rather high, if possible out of range of enemy projectiles. Those narrow vertical windows—called loop-

holes, murder-holes or arrow-splits—were intended to let fresh air and light come in, but in the event of a siege, their main function was as combat emplacements from which the defenders could shoot down arrows. Loopholes usually widened out to form a small fighting niche with side benches. They also had a great deterrent function because enemies never knew if they were occupied by defenders armed with lethal bows and arrows.

The entrance to the donjon was the weakest spot. For this reason there was only one entrance, placed at the first level. The door was accessible only by a removable ladder or a spiral staircase (built in a small masonry turret called a forebuilding) and a narrow drawbridge. The spiral stairs were adapted to defense, turning counter-clockwise so that an aggressor was forced to present his vulnerable right side (the shield was always worn on the left arm). The door was usually intended to let only one

Altpernstein castle (Austria). The castle Altpernstein was situated on a steep dominating promontory in the province Niederösterreich. The castle was built between 1007 and 1055, and enlarged in the 12th century by the lord Pilling von Pernstein.

person at a time. Made of strong oak planks reinforced with heavy nails and metal plates, it was closed and blocked from inside by means of strong transverse beams. Because large loads could not be transported through the narrow entrance, they were hoisted by a crane and a winch placed on top of the building.

The turret containing the spiral stairs sometimes continued up to the top of the donjon to lead to all floors. In some cases, it rose above the building to become a small round watchtower. A guard could be placed inside the watchtower to sound an alarm with a bell or a horn in case of danger. The watchtower was fitted with a mast to which the lord's flag or banner was attached to wave in the wind.

For obvious tactical and strategic reasons, keeps were always constructed in places with a difficult access such as a ridge with sloping sides, between the meandering streams of a river, or on a cliff or hill. If it was built in a plain, the keep often included a ditch or a motte, or

else its base was "emmotted," which means that huge masses of earth were heaped up around its substructures to resist battering rams and to make tunneling impossible or at least very difficult.

The vicinity of the donjon was defended by a comprehensive range of fortification dictated by each particular case: thorny hedges, earth entrenchments with palisaded walls, and ditches. If the nobleman who ordered the building of the castle had some money left, those rudimentary defenses might be replaced by a lower stone enclosure called a chemise, shirt or mantle. The shirt was a simple wall with a variable height and thickness, sometimes fitted with towers. It protected the base of the keep, and if fitted with a walkway and a parapet, it provided a place for an external line of combat. The shirt also isolated the building and enhanced its prestige.

Characterized by its height and its massive thick walls, the keep was intended to create a strength ratio fa-

Reconstruction of castle Oostvoorne (Netherlands). The ruins of castle Oostvoorne are to be found near Rotterdam in province South-Holland. The castle was built at the end of the 12th century by the lord of Oostvoorne. The castle presents some similarities with an English shell-keep, being placed on a motte 60 m in diameter and 10 m high. There was a central 13 m high square tower built about 1160, and an oval shirt made of bricks; the enceinte was later reinforced with four towers and a gatehouse. Oostvoorne, like many Dutch castles, was a waterburcht—a castle surrounded by a wide, wet ditch. Abandoned since the 16th century, castle Oostvoorne is today completely in ruins.

vorable to the defenders. Its height increased the dominance of the defenders and worsened the inferior position of the attackers. The imposing mass of the great-tower was a deterrent to attackers and ostentatiously reflected the presence, the power and the authority of the lord.

From the 11th till the first half of the 12th century, keeps offered a reasonably good solution to security problems because of the simplicity and inadequacy of siege methods. The defense afforded by these masonry mastodons was more passive than active, but it allowed a handful of defenders to resist a fairly large besieging force. Such massive great-towers could be taken only by treason, attrition or surprise.

DAILY LIFE IN EARLY CASTLES

During the 10th and 11th centuries, living conditions in the motte-and-bailey castles and masonry keeps were rather harsh and dull. Daily life was spent in the aula. Light was feeble, coming from a few loopholes or narrow windows which also let cold drafts penetrate; at night they were shielded by cloth or closed by wooden shutters, and the only light was provided by smoky torches, lanterns and guttering candles. In spite of wood burning in the fireplace, the hall was swept by stench, cold and drafts. Humidity dampened the walls, and the

Reconstruction of castle Montfoort (Netherlands). Montfoort was situated on the Yssel River west of Utrecht; like Oostvoorne, it was a waterburcht. The castle was constructed by the bishop of Utrecht to resist the boisterous and expansion-minded neighbors, the counts of Holland. Looted and badly ravaged by Louis XIV's troops in 1672, the castle is now in ruins.

chilly air was disturbed by bad smells and smoke. The smoke, after eddying round the hall, escaped through a louver, an opening in the roof above the central hearth. Sanitation was primitive, and cleanliness was little regarded in many homes. Because the floor was often cold, it was sometimes covered with planks, furs and carpets.

Domestic utensils and furniture were rudimentary. The table was a plank supported by two trestles, not always covered by a tablecloth. Ordinary folk sat at the table upon wooden benches, forms, stools and bushes of straw; chairs were the perquisite of the higher ranks. A few bins, chests and boxes serve as wardrobes and cupboards. Beds were merely straw mattresses in which several people slept without privacy. The fireplace was used for both heating and cooking. Food was generally roasted meat and boiled vegetables; drink was strong beer and some bad wine served in drinking horns and bowls. Meals were collectively taken in poor terra-cotta plates and pewter dishes; knives were used, but forks were as yet unknown, and guests ate with their fingers.

The castle was functioning in autarky, the community living retired within itself. With no means of mass communication, any news that arrived at the castle was often weeks or months old.

The lord was frequently a brutal and illiterate person who was bored when he could not go out, riding his horse, inspecting his fief and administrating his domain with the assistance of his provost. His chaplain was very frequently the only literate man of the household and served not only as a religious servant but often too as a secretary, maintaining correspondence and written records.

Chaves (Portugal). Situated on the river Tâmega in the northern province Tras-os-Montes, Chaves was an ancient Celtic oppidum, then a Roman town called Aquæ Flaviæ founded about 78 AD. Occupied by the Moors, Chaves was reconquered by the Christians in 1160. The 12th century square medieval donjon (Torre de Menagem) was reconstructed by order of King Dinis (1279–1325) and used as a residence for the dukes of Bragança in the 14th century.

Steen castle, Antwerp (Belgium). Antwerp, situated on the river Scheldt, was the second important town in Belgium after Brussels. The Steen castle was a part of the first urban fortifications constructed in order of the German Ottonian emperors about 980. The castle and the Saint-Walburg church were the core of the old city (called Burcht), which was defended by a wet moat, an earth wall and a palisade. The Steen castle as it appears today is the result of considerable enlargements in the 14th century.

The greatest adventures in a lord's life were feasts, tournaments, jousts, and travels such as going to war or off on a pilgrimage, or sailing away to the Holy Land for the Crusade. His main day-to-day pleasures were physical and military training, but usually his favorite entertainment was hunting. Hunting gave the lord an opportunity to show off his strength and skill, but it also provided the community with furs and brought additional food. Hunting was also a means of getting rid of wild animals regarded as noxious or dangerous (bears, wolves, foxes, weasels). Game such as deer and wild boars were hunted on horseback with spears and a pack of hounds. Birds and rabbits were hunted with a tamed falcon. Falconry was an art and a science demanding

hard work, care and patience to train a wild bird to attack and catch smaller birds and to bring them back to the falconer. Hunting was jealously reserved for the nobility, and poaching was strictly forbidden and repressed with brutality.

In periods of war, when a conflict was expected, or when a gang of bandits was known to be in the area, life in the castle became tense. Brattices were installed, security measures were rigorously increased, the entrance was carefully guarded, and sentries were doubled. At night security was reinforced by ferocious hounds. The drawbridge was lowered only when all arriving persons had been identified and checked out. Secret passwords were used before entering the fortress. Nobody was allowed to

Castle Peñaran (Spain). The castle Peñaran was situated in southern Castille. Just like castles Peñafiel, Soria, Berlanga and Gormaz, it belonged to a chain of fortresses constructed along the river Douro in the 11th century to defend the region against the Moors. Peñaran included a massive square tower and a crenellated enceinte reinforced by towers following the outline of the hill.

depart the keep without a strong armed escort. The peasants of the neighborhood were allowed to find refuge within the keep's shirt with cattle, food and goods. Even the harvest and vintage seasons were a time for extra security, during which the lord and his mounted men patrolled around fields and vineyards to protect harvesters against hungry looters and wicked marauders.

The lord had married his wife for her dowry, to increase his territorial power, to put an end to a war or a family vendetta, or to consolidate an alliance. Wife and daughters were under the lord's tutelage and directed the domestic life and the servants. If the lord died or could not rule anymore because of illness or captivity, the wife led the domain until the rightful heir was old enough to rule, according to a legal settlement of regency in her favor.

The castle routine followed the rhythm of seasons: Life, closely related to and dependent on nature, was punctuated by petty pleasures, daily worries, harvests and vintages, religious feasts, births, marriages and mourning. The slightest incident took on the proportions of an event; when the community was visited by a group of pilgrims, a traveling friend or a relative, wandering merchants, a religious dignitary, a party of begging monks, or the suzerain, it gave residents the opportunity to organize a reception or banquet and to obtain news and gossip from the outside world. When a group of tumblers, jugglers, singers, troubadours, minstrels or trouvères stopped in the castle it was a time for fun and rejoicing. Southern France and Italy had, however, a more refined cultural life because many rich noblemen lived in town in luxurious urban palaces where they maintained idle and mannered courts with sophisticated and affected entertainments. Sponsored and encouraged by rich sovereigns and high noblemen, an abundant literature of courtesy was created and developed, in which women,

Guimarães castle (Portugal). Guimarães is situated southwest of Braga in the province Minho. The 28 m high donjon, placed north of the city, was founded about 960 by the countess of Mumadona in order to protect the town and its monastery. Guimarães was the cradle of Portugal. The French knight Henri de Bourgogne, count of Portucale (originally the region of Porto), installed his residence in Guimarães and enlarged the castle with a triangular enceinte. His son, Afonso Henriques, born in 1110, became the first king of Portugal in 1139. Guimarães has kept the donjon, the enceinte and the Paço dos Duques, the palace of the dukes of Bragança, built near the castle in the 15th century.

chivalry and idealized love replaced coarse military vainglory. In the course of the 12th century, a new breed of nobility appeared, characterized by a strong elitist spirit, exclusive manners and distinctive rites influenced by the ideal of chivalry.

THE EVOLUTION OF CASTLES IN THE 12TH CENTURY

During the 11th and 12th centuries, the number of imposing masonry keeps apparently did not increase significantly, probably because of the huge cost. The model remained very much as previously described: a rectangular donjon of a height between 20 and 30 m, the entrance placed on the first level, three or four stories, few openings, a shirt, and so on. But toward the end of the 12th century, important changes took place in the castle plans, giving rise to a process of evolution and development. These changes were due largely to the experience gained in the Crusades by western military engineers, who for the first time had made a close acquaintance with Middle East culture and the mighty fortifications of the Byzantine empire. The most significant of these changes was the general discarding of the rectangular masonry keep in favor of a circular outline. The progress of Romanesque religious architecture had brought about the domination of cylindrical volume and round form in churches (in the apse, the apsidal chapel, and the chancel). These technical improvements influenced military construction, and many works built in this period present

10m

0

Cross-section and ground-plan of the Tour Blanche in Issoudun. Built on a 16 m high motte between 1187 and 1195, the Issoudun donjon (Indre, France) gives a good example of 12th century rounded form.

The donjon of Provins. Situated on the river Durteint, Provins in Seine-et-Marne (France) evolved from a benedictine priory and became in the 12th century the second important town of Champagne (after Troyes). The donjon called Caesar's Tower was built by count Henri I from 1152 to 1183 on an artificial motte; the square donjon was 17 m x 17m, 25 m high (45 m including the motte), with walls 4 m thick. The general construction was similar to that of a Romanesque church bell-tower.

61

Conisborough. The donjon of Conisborough was situated between Sheàeld and Doncaster in southern Yorkshire (Great Britain). It was built between 1166 and 1172 by Hamelin Plantagenet, half brother of Henry II. The tower was cylindrical with five stories. The walls were 4.5 m thick, their base strengthened by a sloping apron and reinforced by six huge buttresses. The donjon and its walled bailey were placed on a motte surrounded by a ditch.

Bruck in Tyrol (Austria). The castle Bruck was situated in the Isel valley near Lienz in the province Carinthia. It was built by Graf von Görz in the end of the 13th century. The castle includes a high square donjon (Berchfrit), a residential house (Palas), a crenellated enceinte, a shield-wall (Schildmauer) and an outer enclosure. Today the castle Bruck houses a Tyrolian museum.

round, oval or polygonal forms. The donjon of Provins (France) had many similarities with a church bell-tower. Even more sophisticated ground-plans were used. The plan of the Tour Blanche in Issoudun (France) was almond-shaped. The quatrefoil plan, consisting of four interpenetrating round towers, was used for the King's Tower in York (Britain) and the Etampes donjon (France).

The cylindrical ground-plan became more and more common because of its several advantages. Space for space, it allowed significant economy in the materials used. Blind spots around the tower were reduced because the view and the field of fire were better from the top of a circular building. Round walls were more resistant than sharp corners to tunneling and to thrusts of the battering ram because stones in curved walls shoulder each other by pushing thrust laterally. A round tower lends itself readily to dome-vaulting on all or at least on the principal floors, and thus can be made virtually fireproof.

There were also disadvantages to the cylindrical plan. Circular rooms were less practical for daily life than rectangular ones. What's more, a round building was much less stable over time than a rectangular one. Consequently, today, many cylindrical donjons lie in ruins, while square and rectangular great-towers are on the whole better preserved.

Cylindrical towers were far from the rule, however. Many castles—in Portugal, Spain and Italy, just for example—remained massive rectangular buildings. German and Austrian castles in the 12th and 13th centuries were characterized by a special type of great-tower called a bergfried in Germany and a berchfrit in Austria. This was a large tower generally not used as dwelling place but as a military building. Varying in shape, often square but also rectangular, pentagonal or (infrequently) circular, some bergfrieden were reinforced on their most vulnerable face by a Schildmauer, a high and thick wall screen-

Échauguette on buttress

Échauguette on cul-de-lampe

Brattice

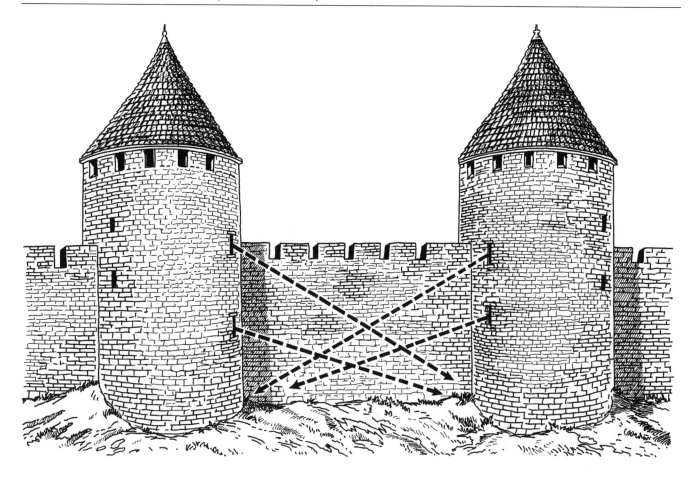

Schematic view of horizontal flanking

ing the inhabited parts. Examples can be seen in the castles Wassenburg, Bruck, Kinzheim and Andlau.

In the 12th century, active defense of castles and keeps was increased by new architectural elements. One such element was the échauguette (sentry-box), which served as both an observation post and a combat emplacement. Intended for one guard, it was a small round or polygonal masonry tower fixed on corbels, a buttress or a cul-de-lampe, and overhanging the angle formed by two walls on top of a tower, a donjon or a belfry. It was fitted with loopholes, and its summit was either covered by a roof or open and fitted with crenellation. The échauguette also offered a nice decoration with its detached silhouette and its elegant curves.

Protection of the entrance was increased by the installation of a brattice. This element was a small projecting balcony of either masonry or timber, resting on corbels. Its floor was fitted with an opening permitting defenders to throw missiles down upon assailants. Its summit was either roofed or open and furnished with one or two crenels. The brattice originates from the Middle East.

Throughout the 12th century, the donjon remained the most important defensive work, but its vicinity became more and more fortified by various elements influenced by the Middle East. At the same time that the castle builders were experimenting with round, multiangular and four-lobed donjons, they were devoting more and more attention to the walls around the fortress. The previously discussed shirt and the bailey enclosure became in certain cases an external wall. The purpose of the external wall was to protect hall, chapel, and ancillary huts and stores, and to provide a first line of defense. The external enclosure was composed of a masonry wall (called a curtain) fitted with a wall-walk, a crenellated breastwork, échauguettes and projecting towers, allowing the rebirth of the principle of flanking.

Flanking was one of the essential principles of fortification. It was the disposition of two parts of a defense work in such a way that enemies attacking one part were exposed to fire coming from the second. There were two main forms of flanking: vertical (as previously discussed, i.e., from an upper position

Niort Castle (France). The castle of Niort (Deux-Sèvres in France) was constructed by the duke of Aquitaine and the king of England, Henry II, about 1170. It was composed of a huge donjon enclosed by an enceinte with sixteen towers. Niort became French in 1436 by the end of the Hundred Years' War. The castle was dismantled in the beginning of the 17th century by order of cardinal Richelieu, minister of King Louis XIII. Only the keep has been preserved, one of the best examples of the 12th century Romanesque great-tower.

View of donjon of Falaise (France). Falaise, in the Calvados (Normandy), was one of the medieval residences of the dukes of Normandy. The donjon, built in 1123, was situated on a rocky spur dominating the river Ante. It was a massive rectangular building 23 m wide, 26.60 m long with walls 3.50 m thick. The donjon housed a hall, a cistern, supply rooms and the chapel Saint-Prix. About 1207, the king of France, Philippe Auguste, retook Normandy and had a cylindrical tower built. Called Tour Talbot, it was 35 m high with six stories and walls 4 m thick. The donjon was surrounded by a bailey 600 m in perimeter, flanked by 14 towers, housing a residence, a guard-house, stables, various service buildings, a garden and a well. At the foot of the keep and its bailey, the old town of Falaise was enclosed by walls, towers and gatehouses. In 1418, the château was taken by the English, who occupied it until 1450. By the end of the 15th century the castle was adapted to firearms with embrasures and bulwarks. In 1590, Falaise was besieged and taken by Henry IV. After this time the castle was abandoned. Until 1864 it served as a stone quarry.

downwards) and horizontal. Horizontal flanking was an enfilade fire nearly parallel to the wall and ditch coming from a projecting element perpendicularly placed in relation to the target. This method was very convenient and allowed economical use of personnel: Indeed, it took only a few soldiers armed with bows or crossbows, placed in a projecting tower, to defend a whole length of wall.

The distance between two towers was extremely variable, but as a general rule it was equal to the effective range of bows and crossbows, about 50 m or 100 m. Towers were square, semi-circular or round, fitted with

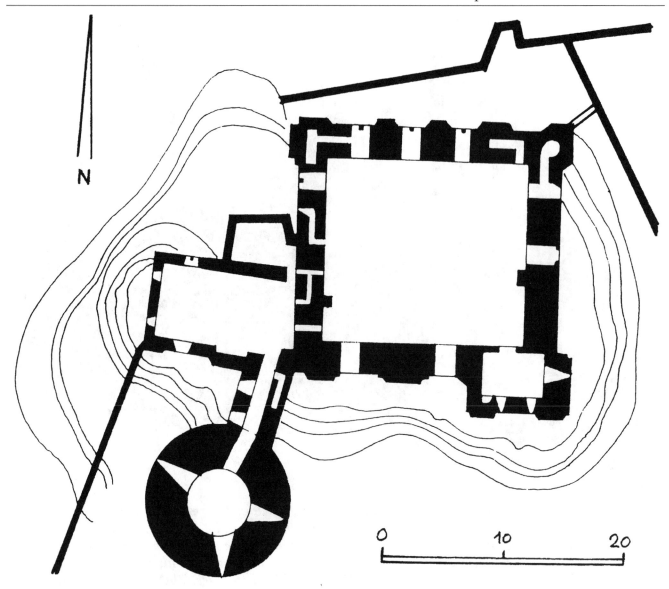

Ground-plan of the castle of Falaise. The square building is the donjon, constructed in 1123; the round tower is the Tour Talbot, erected in 1207. Both towers are linked by a forebuilding containing the entrance with a drawbridge.

loopholes and crenellation, their summit either covered with a roof or arranged as an open platform.

The 11th and 12th century keeps and enclosures bore witness to the efforts, research, and experience of castle builders; they marked a certain improvement, but most keeps were still blind and passive carapaces on their mottes. Not until the Crusades does one see real changes influenced by Arabian architecture.

THE CRUSADES

As long as the Arabs held the Holy Land, access to Jerusalem stayed open to the Western pilgrims, but the situation changed in 1073. In that year, Palestine was conquered by the Turkish Seljuks, and from that time Christians were no longer welcome in Jerusalem.

In 1095 Pope Urban II called for a crusade to free the Holy Sepulcher. Thus began two centuries (from the seizure of Antioch in 1098 to the fall of Acre in 1291) of western European involvement in a dramatic adventure called the Crusades. Though initially motivated by religious passions, the Crusades came to be characterized by greed; by a passion for conquest, combat and prowess; and by racial hatred and racism. They also proved a con-

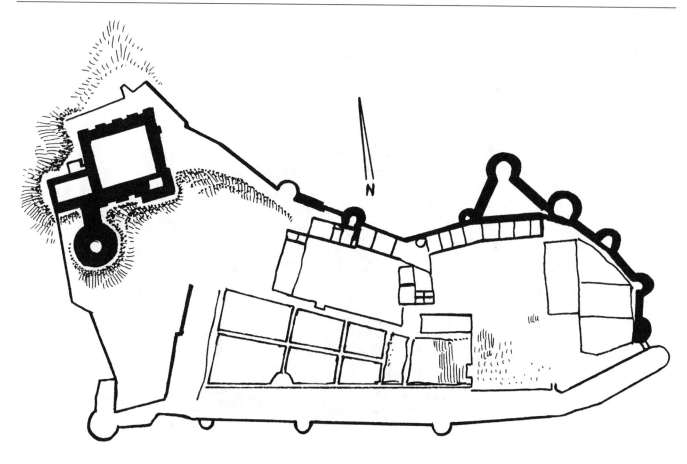

Ground-plan of Falaise castle and bailey

venient outlet to divert the energy, greed and aggressiveness of adventurers, feudal lords and boisterous knights— a channel into which violence could be diverted and sanctioned.

Effectively the Crusades represented the backlash of Christendom against Islamic conquest. The Byzantine emperor was also politically motivated, since he wanted Western assistance in expanding his territory and stabilizing his frontier. Meanwhile the pope and the German emperor saw the expeditions as bringing some measure of unity to Christendom.

As early as 1096 the first Crusade departed for the East. This spontaneously assembled crowd of ill-prepared pilgrims was slaughtered and decimated on the way to Jerusalem. A year later a second expedition, militarily organized and well structured by feudal barons, departed, and in 1099 they managed, after a long journey and much suffering, to retake the holy city. Under the authority of Godfrey of Bouillon and his brother Baldwin, the Crusaders organized the conquered territory according to the European feudal system. The Frankish kingdoms of Outremer (Beyond the Sea) were created including the kingdom of Jerusalem, the principality of Antioch, and the counties of Edesse, Jaffa, Tripoli and Outer-Jordan.

After about a century of relative peace interrupted by periods of war, the Christian rulers were defeated in 1187 by Sultan Saladin. Jerusalem was lost, and the Crusaders from then on dominated only a limited coastal stripe in Lebanon. Other expeditions were organized to reclaim the territory for Christians. Some of these were led by great feudal lords, and even kings of France and England as well as emperors of Germany participated. Finally, however, all attempts failed because of political quarrels and economic rivalry within the Christian camp.

In 1270, the death of the French Crusader king, Louis IX the Saint, marked the last crusade. The dream of a permanently Catholic Palestine came to an end when the last Christian bulwark, Acre, was taken by the Muslims in 1291.

The Crusades mark an important moment of European history. Manifesting the rebirth of European vitality, a spiritual and material renaissance, they had significant influence on the evolution of medieval society.

71

Count Castle in Ghent (Belgium). The château des Comtes (in Flemish Gravensteen) was erected about 1180 by the count of Flanders, Philippe of Alsace, on the emplacement of an 11th century stronghold. The Gravensteen includes a massive rectangular donjon, an elegant residence and various buildings for the commons enclosed in an oval curtain flanked with échauguettes resting on buttresses. The castle was defended by a strong gatehouse and a wet ditch with water supplied by the river Lys. The castle was the count's residence but also intended as a citadel to control the rich and boisterous citizens. From the 14th to the 18th century, the castle was used as municipal tribunal and prison. The Gravensteen, restored between 1889 and 1913, today is one of the charms of the medieval city Ghent.

They gave rise to renewed commercial activity, the profits of which flowed mainly to the Italian ports of Venice, Genoa and Pisa. Luxuries from the orient, including many plants and fruits as well as various goods previously unknown in Europe, were imported. Socially, the Crusades helped to weaken the position of the feudal lords, hastening the reestablishment of the royal authority (particularly in France) and the development of free cities.

In matters of fortification, the Crusades were also very important, for they introduced to the Western world efficient methods of siege warfare and sophisticated defensive techniques. In the early years of the Crusades, the Christians, backed by good armies, had the initiative, but their strategy was poor and the frontier of their long kingdom was weak; eight hundred kilometers of sandy desert formed a springboard for Muslim raids and counter-offensives. After the initial western enthusiasm there was a continuous shortage of armed forces, and fortifications were the only way to defend the vulnerable realm of Outremer.

The castles erected by the crusaders in Palestine were profoundly original buildings. In the 11th century, castles were still influenced by western tradition. For almost half a century the crusaders lived a life of comparative peace in increasing comfort, either in captured fortresses of an-

Bragança castle (Portugal). Bragança is situated in the province Tras-os-Montes, close to the northern border with Spain. The city, installed at an altitude of 660 m in the Serra de Nogueira, has preserved its 43 m high square donjon built in 1187 as well as its urban walls from the 12th century. The region was founded as a duchy in 1442, and the dukes of Bragança played a significant role; they reigned over Portugal from 1640 until 1910 and in Brazil from 1822 to 1889.

cient foundation or in newly built castles similar to those of their homelands. They were indeed strongholds for the governance of conquered lands, controlling farming areas, oasis and desert crossroads. But from 1144 onwards, a succession of new Muslim leaders restored Arabian pride and rekindled the missionary zeal of Islam by organizing djihad (holy war) against the infidel foe. Though marked by long truces, periods of relative peaceful coexistence and mutual understanding, the Crusade wars were cruel, radical and fanatically led because both sides were equally assured of eternal life if they fall in battle.

Progressively, the crusader fortifications evolved into gigantic fortresses, killing-grounds with weapons systems designed to enable a few defenders to hold out as long as possible, or in the worst event, to sell their lives as dearly as possible. Usually located on some inaccessible mountain-top, intended for both active and passive defense, castles usually included a huge square keep forming a highly protected core and concentric rings of walls flanked by towers providing efficient external defensive positions. Walls were thick and fitted with solid parapets and arrow-splits.

In peacetime, fortresses were economic centers administering farms and estates. In wartime, they formed collective chains of interdependent strongholds controlling

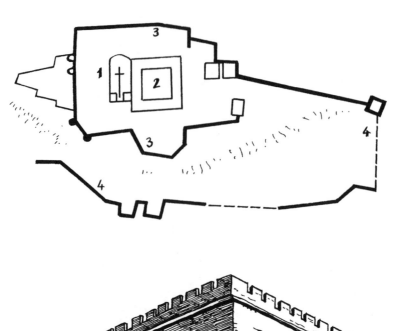

Uclés (Spain). The castle Uclés stands between Cuenca and Aranjuez in Castilla La Mancha. An ancient Roman fort, the castle was built in the beginning of the 11th century as a residence to caliph Mohamed III Al Mostacfi. After the fall of Toledo in 1085, Uclés remained a border place held by the Moors until 1157, when King Alfonso VII retook it. Occupied by the military order of Santiago from 1174 to 1499, the castle became a castle-monastery, combining military demands and the spiritual life of a monastery, justifying the nickname it later assumed, "El Escorial de la Mancha" (an allusion to El Escorial, the huge palace and monastery near Madrid, which was built by King Felipe II between 1563 and 1584). After 1528 the castle-monastery was occupied by the nobleman Francisco de Mora y Gaspar de la Vega and transformed into a residence. The ground-plan shows the situation today: the church (1), the cloister (2), the first enceinte (3) and, down on the steep hill, the external wall (4).

Tarasp (Switzerland). The castle Tarasp is situated near the village Vulpera in the canton of Grisons in Switzerland, close to the border with Austria. The castle was built by the lord of Tarasp in the 11th century as a high square bergfried on a steep hill dominating the river Inn. Owned by various noblemen, it became the property of Duke Sigismond of Austria. Enlarged, transformed and restored over the centuries, the castle today is the residence of Herzog of Hesse-Darmstadt.

Grand-Pressigny. The donjon of Grand-Pressigny was built in the 12th century near Loches in Indre-et-loire (France).

The Krak des Chevaliers. The most famous of all Hospitaler castles, the impressive Krak des Chevaliers was situated on a 650 m high naturally defensible sloping spur overlooking Homs Gap northeast of Tripoli in Lebanon. Founded in 1031 by the emir of Homs, the castle was taken by crusaders in 1110. From 1142 to 1271, the krak (meaning castle in Arabian) was occupied by the Knights of Saint John, who, after the earthquake of 1202, redesigned and transformed it to the most powerful castle ever built in the Middle Ages. The concentric Krak des Chevaliers includes a massive central core with a huge donjon whose walls were 9 m thick, a water reservoir, a deep ditch dug in the rock, and a 600 m external wall with thick flanking towers.

communication, roads, cities, and vital coastal anchorages. The crusader castles were well munitioned with plenty of stones, arrows and combustible missiles, as well as artillery for projecting them. Careful attention was paid to reserves of water and food; many castles had their own mills.

To take care of pilgrims, special monastic orders were created. Confronted, however, with violence, those charitable organizations rapidly became armed militia charged with escorting pilgrims, protecting Christian property and defending the Church. Owing to the fanat-

ical crusade atmosphere, warriors became Christ's fighters; brutal knighthood and pious monasticism became compatible.

The Brotherhood of the Hospital of Saint John-of-Jerusalem (called knights of Saint John, Hospitalers or Johannites) was created in 1070 to assist poor pilgrims in the Holy Land. About 1120, the order was militarized by Raymond du Puy. It became a rich organization and an armed force with international power. The Knights of Saint John played a major role during the difficult Chris-

Belvoir Castle. Situated north of Jerusalem, Belvoir Castle was constructed by the Hospitalers about 1170. The castle had a regular ground-plan organized around a strong core with towers and gatehouse. This central keep was defended by a thick external wall reinforced by square towers and a deep moat. After the defeat of Hattin in 1187 and the seizure of Jerusalem by Saladin, Belvoir was besieged and taken in 1189. The fortress was demolished by Muslims in the 13th century.

tian domination in Palestine. Beside daily care for pilgrims, they participated in all major battles and were remarkable fortress builders.

Driven off the Holy Land after the fall of Acre in 1291, the Knights of Saint John established themselves on the Isle of Rhodes, where they stayed until 1522. In 1530 they were once more attacked by the Turks and driven off Rhodes. They settled next on the island of Malta, where they become known from then on as the Order of Malta. Both on Rhodes and Malta, the order built formidable fortifications.

A group of Hospitalers originating from Germanic lands specialized in taking care of German pilgrims, probably for linguistic and political reasons. Established in the Saint Mary church in Jerusalem, the German Hospitalers were greatly encouraged by the Hohenstaufen emperor during the third Crusade (1189–1192). The Germanic branch of the Hospitalers

became an independent military order called the Brotherhood of the Hospital of Saint Mary of the Teutons, conveniently called Teutonics. Approved by Pope Innocent III in 1199, the Teutonics were organized in a structure similar to that of the Hospitalers from whom they had originated. Together with the newly created German Knights of the Sword (founded in 1204, this order merged with the Teutonics in 1237), they favored German interests, which gave rise to rivalry with the other military monk orders. After the fall of Acre in 1291 and the abandonment of the Holy Land, the Teutonic knights were transferred in 1309 to Marienburg near Danzig (today Gdansk) in Poland. The German knights maintained the spirit of the Crusades by "evangelizing" pagan Slav populations by means of arms, and by conquering vast territories in Poland and in the Baltic region. The Teutonic power reached its apogee in the 14th century, but after the defeat of Tannenberg

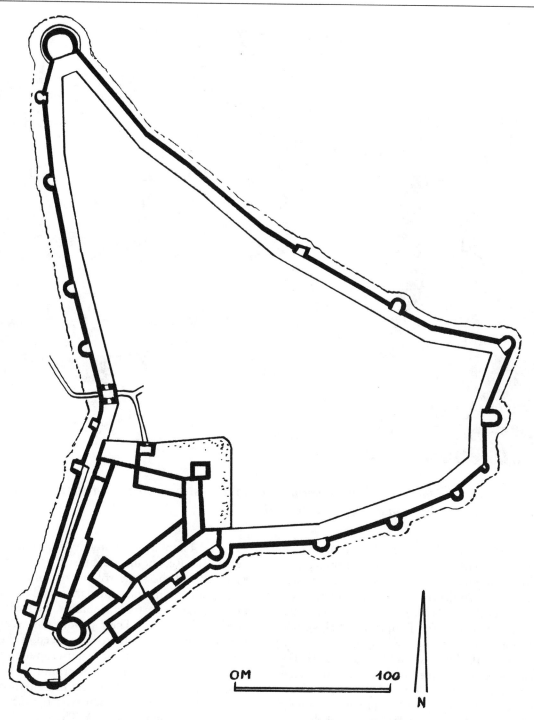

OM   100

N

Ground-plan, castle Margat. The fortress of Margat (Marqab) lies on a vast promontory overlooking the port of Baniyas on the coast of Syria. Constructed by Arabs in 1062, the castle was a point of bitter dispute between Muslims and crusaders between 1116 and 1140. In 1186, the fortress was occupied and rebuilt by the Hospitalers. It was besieged and taken in 1285 by sultan Qala'un. Margat was composed of a double-walled castle lying on the south point and a triangular village or bailey of considerable size defended by walls, towers and moats.

Ruins of castle Margat. The view shows the southeast part of the castle with the main corner Tower of Eperon and the outer wall.

in 1410, the weakened knights were forced to abandon their conquests in Poland and retreat to Prussia.

The Order of Saint Lazare (also called Lazarists or Order of the Saint-Sepulchre) was another branch of the Hospitalers. Founded in 1120, the Lazarists were especially charged with caring for Templars and Hospitalers infected with leprosy, a sickness widely spreading in the Middle Ages in both the West and the East. Until 1187, the Lazarists were also charged with the military defense of part of the walls of Jerusalem.

The Order of the Temple of Jerusalem (commonly called Templar) was founded in 1118 by a French knight named Hugues de Payens. The order took its name from its installation in Solomon's temple (today the El-Aqsâ mosque). The Templars too were transformed into a military force. Their wealth grew considerably, and their power became of international importance. In the 12th century, the order headed an empire embracing some 9,000 commanderies, priories, farms, domains and estates throughout Europe, which produced enormous riches.

The Templars were involved in Spain and Portugal during the Reconquista against the Moors. In Palestine they fulfilled the same role as the order of Saint John. They built, maintained and garrisoned eighteen huge castles and many fortified domains. In Paris they had an enormous fortress. Their prodigious wealth and their banking activities attracted the greed of the French king Philippe IV (1285–1314). The unscrupulous king, short of money, accused them of evil crimes in 1307. Through lies, manipulation, torture and intimidation, Philippe in collusion with the pope achieved the dissolution of the order of the Temple in 1312. The main dignitaries were burnt alive, the members returned to "civilian" life or were transferred to the Order of Saint John, and the order's wealth was confiscated by the French crown. The Templars survived, however, in Spain in the Order of Montesa (created in 1317) and in Portugal in the Order of Christ (1319).

The Order of the Très Sainte Trinité (Very Holy Trinity or Trinitarians) was founded by Jean de Matha

Knight of the Hospital order (Saint John). The Knights of the Saint John order wore a black cape with a white cross later known as the Maltese cross.

Sergeant-brother of the Saint John order

Knight of the Sword and Teutonic knight. The members of the short-lived Order of the Sword wore a white coat with a black sword crowned by a black German cross. The order of the Sword merged with the Teutonics in 1237. The Teutonics wore a white overcoat decorated with a German black cross.

Knight of the Lazarist order

Knight Templar. Knights of the Temple wore a white coat decorated with a red cross. Sergeant-brothers wore a black overcoat with the same cross.

Knight of the Order of Christ. The Order of Christ was formed in Portugal after the dissolution of the Temple order in 1319.

Almourol (Portugal). Situated south of Tomar (district of Santarem), the castle Almourol was built about 1160 on an island in the middle of the river Tage by the sovereign-master of the order of the Temple. Almourol was composed of a massive rectangular keep enclosed by walls flanked by ten half-cylindrical towers.

and approved by the pope in 1098. As the name indicates, the Trinitarian order was founded to worship the Trinity and assist the poor and sick. They were not fighting units; rather it was their job to exchange prisoners and negotiate the liberation of Christians captured by the Muslims during the Crusades. Their important role and their popularity brought them wealth and international reputation with domains and monasteries in Spain, France, England, Germany and Palestine.

Hospitalers, Teutonics and Templars were officially placed under direct papal authority, but in practice they were almost independent. Combining force and faith, the military orders were very popular. They attracted many noblemen, and because of their reputation they accrued much wealth in the form of gifts, donations and domains. Though having different purposes, various ceremonies and different rites, all orders had a similar hierarchy, the same feudal organization and a common structure. All three of them were given the strict Cistercian monk *regula* (established in 1098 by edict of the abbot of Cîteaux, Robert de Molesme), though the rule was somewhat adapted to each order's particular

fighting function and to the severe climate of the Middle East.

The orders were organized following the three feudal social classes in a pyramidal hierarchy. Each order was headed by a grand master, both an abbot and a general, who ruled with a chapter of officers; it was the chapter who secretly elected the master for his lifetime.

All knights, squires and sergeant-brothers came from the nobility. All had to complete an extremely rigorous and physically challenging training program to fight on horse and on foot. They wore a sort of uniform composed of a hauberk (armored coat of mail) and a linen cloth decorated with a distinctive cross. They were issued wooden shields and metal helmets and armed with the typical weapons of the Middle Ages: long right swords, battle axes, war-hammers, morning-stars, spears and lances to which banners were fixed. Horses, weapons and equipment were lent to each knight but remained the order's property because monks were not allowed to own anything.

Knights were divided in squadrons, generally composed of twelve mounted combatants headed by a prior.

View of the citadel of Jerusalem. The ancient city of Jerusalem (in Arabian Al-Quds and in Hebrew Yerushalaïm, meaning city of peace) was built on two hills separated by the river Cedron. The city was founded in the 3rd millennium BC and entered history with the Jewish people by the time of King David (1004–965 BC) and King Solomon, the latter of whom built the temple and the royal palace. The Jewish kingdom was divided in 928 BC and Jerusalem became the capital of the realm of Judah, with fortifications built by Hezekias in 701 BC. Jerusalem was devastated by the Babylonians in 586 BC, and the temple of Solomon was destroyed. After captivity in Babylon, the Jews returned to Jerusalem and rebuilt the temple and fortifications (520–445 BC). After the Greek domination (332–37 BC) and the reign of King Herod, the city was taken by the Romans in 63 BC. Already a holy place in the Jewish faith, Jerusalem as the site of Christ's death attracted Christian pilgrims as early as the 2nd century AD. The Roman occupation lasted until 324 AD. Jerusalem was then occupied by the Arabs in 638 and became an Islamic holy place; the mosque El-Aqsa was erected there in 691. After the first Crusade, Jerusalem became the capital of the Frankish realm Beyond the Sea in 1099, and remained so until 1187 when the city was retaken by sultan Saladin. The fall of Saint-Jean-d'Acre in 1291 marked the end of the Crusades in Palestine.

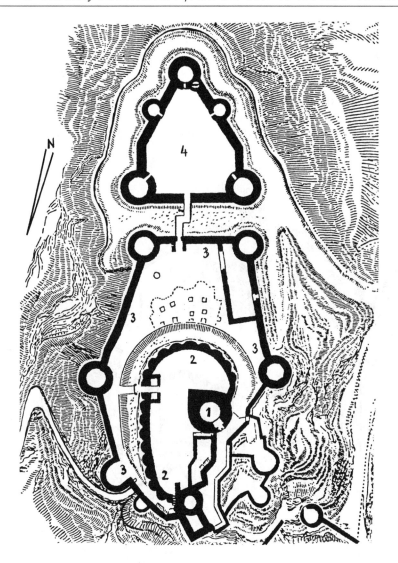

Ground-plan, Château-Gaillard (France). Château-Gaillard (originally called La Roche Gaillarde) was built on a spur dominating the Seine near Rouen (Eure in Normandy). The huge castle was constructed in an astonishingly short time—from 1196 to 1198—by order of the duke of Normandy and the king of England, Richard Lion-Heart. Château-Gaillard, brilliantly testifying to the Plantagenêts' military skill, was one of the first concentric castles influenced by eastern architecture. It was composed of four main parts. There was a huge four-story, almond-shaped donjon (1) with walls 5 m thick, reinforced with buttresses and crowned with crenellation and machicolation. The donjon was hemmed with an elliptical skirt (2) with living accommodations, moat, a gatehouse and a drawbridge. The skirt was enclosed by a low enceinte (3) flanked with towers including various service buildings. Finally, a huge triangular outwork (4) included five towers, a moat and another drawbridge. Though considered impregnable, Château-Gaillard was taken by the French king Philippe Auguste after a long siege in 1204. The seizure of Château-Gaillard resulted in the annexation of Rouen and Normandy. The castle was demolished by Henri IV at the end of the 16th century, but its ruins and vestiges are particularly imposing.

Both warriors and monks—fighting, but also praying and taking care of pilgrims—they represented the paradoxical fusion of religious devotion and destructive violence. The knights were assisted by non-combatant friars, vicars, clerks and chaplains coming from the gentry who provided spiritual and administrative backup.

The lowest members of the orders were non-combatant commoners, subaltern lay-brothers charged with hard labor, craft, service, and logistic and domestic tasks.

All members, exclusively masculine, voluntarily enlisted in the military orders for life. They were carefully selected, and once proven physically fit, morally suitable and spiritually strong, they were initiated and introduced by means of a ceremony. Like normal Cistercian monks, they were required to take a vow to abandon the world, to stay in the order until their death, to be chaste and poor, and to swear an oath of total obedience to the order's rule.

Castello dell'Imperator in Prato (Italy). The town of Prato is situated on the river Bisenzio northwest of Florence in Tuscany. For a long time Prato was a rival of Florence, but it passed under Florentine tutelage after 1351. The Castello dell'Imperator was built by the German emperor Friedrich I Barbarossa von Hohenstaufen (1152–1190), whence its name (Castle of the Emperor). The castello displays many influences of the crusaders' military architecture: regular rectangular plan, square tower, thick and high walls. The crenellation, however, was typically Italian with so-called Gibeline merlons which were dovetail-shaped. The Hohenstaufen dynasty occupied the throne of the Holy Roman Germanic Empire from 1138 to 1254. The German emperors possessed Sicily and built many castles such as Barletta, Catane, Bari, and the most remarkable of them all, the Castle del Monte.

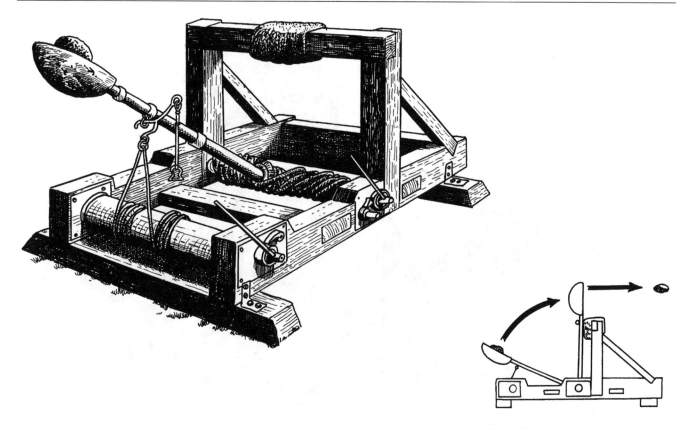

Catapult (see page 96)

Wounded and elderly members of the orders were taken care of in the orders' estates in Europe. They were given such work for the community as their disabilities allowed, and remained in the estates until death.

Hospitalers, Teutonics and Templars provided the crusaders with what they most lacked: a permanent army. Owing to their incomparable gallantry, their spirit of sacrifice, their strict discipline, their implacable rigor, their knowledge of Arabian warfare and their own military experience, they were the backbone of the Christian presence in the Holy Land. However, Hospitalers, Teutonics and Templars did not always behave like the untainted monks and brave knights they were supposed to be. Rather than forming a homogeneous block, they became independent, arrogant, and wealthy temporal powers exclusively favoring their own parties. Hard rivalry between them reflected the conflict-ridden political situation—i.e., the diverging interests of the crusaders which often made their efficiency questionable.

The fortifications built by the military orders were greatly inspired by Byzantine and Muslim styles of military architecture, which were inherited from the colossal realizations of ancient times. The orders constructed, restored, maintained and garrisoned huge fortresses which were at one and the same time monas-teries, fortified barracks and castles. Those fortresses always included a chapel, a room for the chapter, and supply-stores; often they included guest quarters as well. They were intended to house large garrisons composed of members of the military orders but also to accommodate laic knights serving during their time of pilgrimage and mercenaries raised among the local population called Turcopoles.

During the 12th and 13th centuries, the crusader fortifications were greatly improved by new ideas and new elements. The experiences acquired during the crusades were brought back to Europe. The constitution of permanent armed forces and the significant development of siege warfare transformed fortifications in both concept and realization, contributing in no small measure to the full development of medieval military architecture in the 13th century and its brilliant apogee in the 14th.

MEDIEVAL SIEGE WARFARE

Siege warfare is as old as cities, and the evolution of fortifications was directly connected to the challenging improvements of siege warfare. Developed in ancient

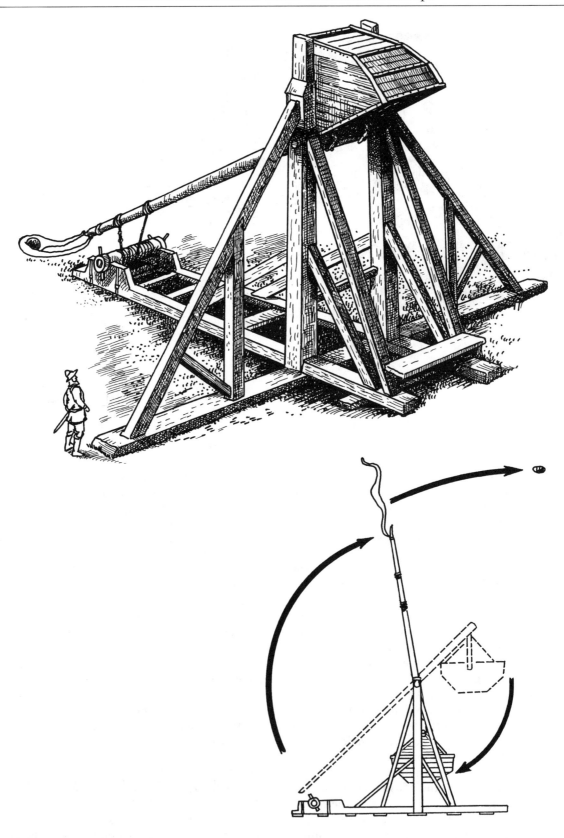

Trebuchet (see page 96)

Belfry (see page 101)

Cross-section of a siege mine with a cat (see pages 102–103)

times, siege warfare was a military science called po-liorcetics by the Ancient Greeks. It has been widely used throughout history because victory frequently depends on the seizure of strongholds, fortresses and towns. This was particularly clear in the Middle Ages when rural castles were the basic political, administrative and economical structure of life.

The purpose of a siege was not necessarily the destruction of the besieged target. The aim might be to bring a rebellious vassal back to submission, or to obtain political and economic compromise. Entrenched behind high walls, defenders were in theory in an advantageous position. History shows, however, that reputedly inexpugnable fortresses, defended by regiments, sometimes fell at the blast of a single trumpet. On the other hand, some modest fortified place, garrisoned by a handful of half-starving men, might for months resist a whole army. High walls were not always sufficient to stop enemies; the outcome of a siege depended a great deal on many factors such as physical courage, individual bravery, logistical preparation, morale, determination and pugnacity.

Besiegers might use several means to achieve the seizure of a fortified place. They could impose capitulation by displaying their force and threatening terrible retaliation (pillage, fire, rape and general massacre). They could launch a surprise attack or a discreet assault at night. They could also infiltrate parties disguised as merchants, pilgrims, traders or travelers in need of assistance. Once inside, the posing party could open the door to armed comrades waiting hidden outside. For this reason all strangers were regarded with suspicion.

Besiegers might also profit from internal quarrels among the defenders and negotiate various advantages with one or the other. What would wars be without traitors? If wars proceeded by mathematical formulae, the side with the best strategists, the bravest soldiers and the most powerful weapons would invariably win. But this is never the case, and treachery is the evil genius of war. Treachery throws a spanner in the works and sweeps plans of genius off the campaigning table. It turns heroism and the art of warfare, the supremacy of weapons and the courage of soldiers in the face of death into a

Cross-section of a battering ram in a cat (see page 103)

farce. How many battles and how many sieges have been decided as the result of iniquitous treachery? Certainly just as many as have been won through bravery.

If intimidation, menace, negotiation, ruse, treachery or surprise failed to bring an operation to a swift conclusion, besiegers were obliged to take the place by force. A military siege was a large-scale undertaking demanding time, comprehensive logistics and considerable organization. Soldiers, engineers and workers, ammunitions, machines, tools, accommodations, water and food supplies, all had to be arranged and accounted for. Weather conditions also played an important role; if it rained, camps and roads became mud pools, bows and hurling machines were useless, and morale collapsed. Even in good conditions, armies of the Middle Ages were slow to move, and they could be mobilized only for short periods; vassals were required to be available for the ost (military service) only forty days of the year. Vassals and peasant-soldiers mobilized by the suzerain became impatient, and many of them wanted to go home when harvest time came.

The first stage of the siege was the establishment of

a tight blockade intended to isolate the place and cut all communication and supply lines. The intended result was a war of attrition; that is, the besiegers intended to wait until the besieged were worn out and exhausted by hunger, isolation, sickness and discouragement. It was consequently important for the encircled garrison to have reliable allies who could come to its rescue and provide sufficient supplies.

In the limited space offered by the castle and its bailey, peasants and non-combatants of the neighborhood found temporarily refuge. In return, they participated in defense or at least tried not to be a hindrance. In some cases, when supplies were gone and the garrison was still refusing to surrender, "useless mouths" (women, children and the elderly) were cast out of the castle.

Sometimes, however, the defenders had left the countryside surrounding the castle empty by "scorched earth" devastation. In such cases the besiegers were, in their turn, short of resources and supplies.

Since the attrition siege was based on logistics and time, the besiegers had to be accommodated in one or more temporary camps. It was of course desirable to protect the

General view of a siege in the Middle Ages.

camps by field fortifications (obstacles, moats, earth entrenchments and palisades) in order to repulse sallies, or counter-attacks, launched by the besieged. A sally was a brisk operation that took advantage of the besiegers' off-guard moments. The besieged would rush out from their fortification, strike, and withdraw within the castle walls before the besiegers could react. Surprise counter-attacks were psychologically quite important for morale, and tactically they might turn the tide of the siege by breaking the blockade, disorganizing and driving the besiegers back.

Pressure on the defenders was increased by archers and crossbowmen deployed behind mantelets and pavis (wooden protective screens) shooting arrows and bolts, some incendiary. More devastating were the bombardments effected by siege machines. These primitive forms of artillery, already employed in ancient times and revived during the Crusades, were called engines. They were designed, built and serviced by specialists called ingeniatores (whence the word engineer).

One such engine, the catapult, was an ancient nevrobalistic weapon that drew its propulsive power from the elasticity of sinews and twisted rope. It was composed of a solid timber framework holding a pivoted arm tightly strained on a rotating roller fitted with twisted rope. The arm was winched down and the missile was loaded in a kind of spoon or a sling. The mobile arm was then unlocked, and, freed from the great tension of the rope, it sprang upward with great strength. The rotating movement of the arm was violently stopped by a transverse beam fitted with a padded cushion, resulting in the projectile being propelled in a high curving trajectory. (See illustration, page 91.)

The trebuchet, probably introduced during the Crusades, was a hurling machine whose propulsive energy was provided by a solid, heavy weight of several tons (a wooden container filled with earth and stones). This counterweight was fixed to the short arm of a huge pivoted beam resting on a solid framework. The missile was loaded in a sling placed on the end of the long arm, which was winched down to the ground and then released.

Archer, 13th century

Under the force of the counterweight, the arm went up, the sling opened by centrifugal force, and the missile was then swung away with a high parabolic trajectory. (See illustration, page 92.)

Projectiles launched by catapults and trebuchets were mainly stones or rocks, which killed men, crushed brattices, scattered merlons, punched through walls, crumbled towers, and destroyed houses and huts. Capatults and trebuchets were also used for psychological and primitive chemical and bacteriological warfare. A besieging force might launch pots of tar, quick-lime and Greek fire, an incendiary substance used by the ancient Greeks and Byzantines. (Greek fire was probably made of tar, oil, sulfur, and other flammable substances, but the precise content is unknown.) These pots would shatter on impact, sending their burning contents flying in all directions, setting ablaze wooden houses and huts in castles, baileys and towns. It was recorded that on at least one occasion, beehives were similarly employed.

Medical experts of those days might not have been fully cognizant of the means by which disease was spread, but they knew it had something to do with dead and rotting flesh; accordingly, the decomposing corpses of men and animals were among the projectiles. Excrement and garbage were also thrown with the intention of humiliating the opponent and poisoning his wells.

More subtly, the defenders' morale could be attacked by parading the captive survivors of a relief party in full view of the garrison, then killing them and hurling their heads into the besieged place. A variation was to speed the living prisoners on their way to their intended destination by catapult.

Crossbow man, 14th century. The earliest crossbows were loaded or spanned by hand. Then as their power was increased, the legs were used to assist the arms in their task, the feet being placed on either side of the bow or in an iron stirrup on the end of the stock. A hooked strap attached to the girdle was often employed, the bow being spanned by straightening the body. When the strong steel crossbow was introduced, various mechanical spanning devices made their appearance. One was the windlass, connected to a metal grapple by a system of cords and pulleys. The grapple was hooked over a cord of the crossbow and was wound up by a large handle until the cord caught behind the nut. Another winder was the rack or cranequin. This was a rack and pinion mechanism with gear wheels contained in a flat round box. The gears were set in motion by the winding handle. The heavy cord loop at one end was passed over the butt of the crossbow, and the grapple at the other end hooked over the string. The toothed bar was then wound back, bringing the string with it. A simpler and quicker device was the gaáe or bender, now usually called the goat's foot lever, which was a lever ending in two curved prongs pivoted with a double hook. The crossbow was a powerful weapon, but it took longer to reload than a normal bow. It was therefore better used in the defense of a castle than on the open battlefield.

Early medieval men-of-arms. The period ca. 600–ca. 1250 was the age of mail. The warrior, fighting on foot or on horse, wore a jaque or hauberk, a knee-length armored shirt of mail, made of riveted or butted-together metal rings. The hauberk had sleeves normally extending to the elbow, but in some cases, the sleeves reached to the wrist and covered the hand forming mittens (muffers or gauntlets). Mail leggings (hosen) and shorter shirts of mail (haubergeon) were also worn as well as leather jackets (gambison). The head was protected by a close-fitting mail hood (coif) attached to the hauberk and a conical-shaped metal helmet often fitted with a bar-like extention (nasal) protecting face and nose. A defensive item was the long almond-shaped Norman shield or a round shield called a buckler.

Hurling machines existed in numerous variants of differing shape, strength and size, with many appellations such as baliste, mangonel, bricole, couillard or perrier, for example. The high curve trajectory of these weapons, hurling over walls, made their use just as effective for defenders as for attackers. When both sides were armed with such weapons, the result was an artillery duel.

The range of these siege engines varied widely, depending on solidity, structure, weight of projectile, length of mobile arm, tension given to twisted rope and so on. Experiments made in the 19th century with reconstructed machines indicate a range up to 450 meters. Loading the devices took some time, so the rate of fire was low, and the aim could be rather haphazard, though some trebuchets were precise owing to the counterweight being slid up and down the short arm to vary the range. Nevertheless, inaccuracy could itself be an advantage, for it could increase fright among the defenders—and if the point of impact was unknown, damage was a certainty in any event. Catapults and trebuchets were deterrent weapons, too; their menacing deployment was sometimes enough to persuade the besieged to surrender.

Catapults and trebuchets had to be very strongly

Armor, 15th century. At the beginning of the 14th century the increasing effectiveness of bow and crossbow meant that arrows could drive through a mail shirt, making some form of plate armor imperative. The result by the 15th century was full armor, turning knights and horses into complete heavy-armored units.

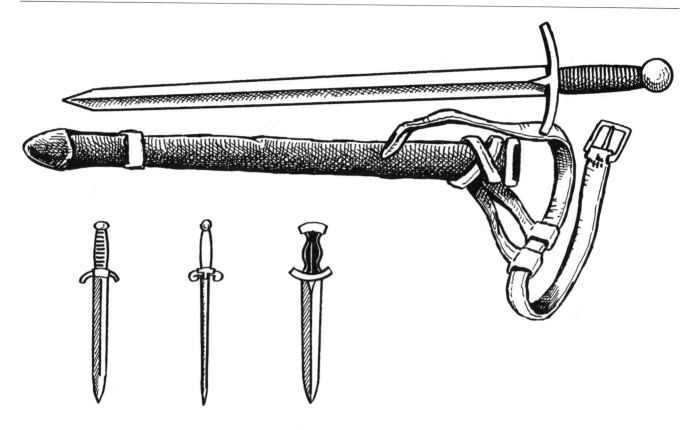

Sword, sheath and daggers

built because they were submitted to heavy mechanical forces. To move them it was necessary to disassemble them, transport them piecemeal and reassemble them on the spot. Hurling machines were gradually superseded and then replaced by heavy firearms (siege guns and mortars) during the second half of the 15th century.

Blockade and bombardment were preparatory actions. They preceded the most important and most dangerous phase of the siege: the assault. The main offensive was always directed towards a weak point of the defense: a low wall, a rampart deprived of ditch, a tower of small dimensions or a hard-to-defend suburb in a town, for example. Once the assailant had disposed of numerous defending troops, the main attack could be completed by diversions on other points that obliged the defenders to scatter their remaining force.

The decisive assault could be done by one of two main ways: either by assaulting the top of the wall or by making a breach. An assault on the top of the wall could be achieved by throwing grab-dredgers fitted with rope or by using scale-ladders. Anyone can imagine the risks this involved—climbing a rope or an unsteady ladder to a height of 10 meters, holding a sword and a shield under a hail of arrows, stones and spears. (Tales of cascades of melted metal or boiling oil cast down by defenders must,

however, be discounted as untrue: These materials were too expensive and too difficult to maneuver in combat conditions from a narrow wall-walk.) If the ladder was not repulsed, the attacker was very vulnerable while ascending and when he reached the top of the parapet.

A much safer method of assaulting the top of the wall was by means of a beffroy or belfry. Used in ancient times, the belfry (called a helepole by the ancient Greeks) was a rolling wooden assault tower as high as the wall to be conquered. Fitted with wheels or large rolls, the tower was designed to be rolled close to the wall and moved by means of capstans, pulleys and ropes maneuvered and winched by a party of men. It was also fitted with ladders, and its summit included a platform where a group of archers could shoot at the defenders. The platform also included a sort of drawbridge that allowed attackers to set foot on the parapet for hand-to-hand combat with the defenders. The belfry was made of timber and consequently vulnerable to fire; it was therefore covered with rawhide or wet turf to resist incendiary projectiles thrown by the besieged. (See illustration, page 93.)

The utilization of this machine was very slow. A belfry had to be built on the spot, along with a steady track for rolling the cumbersome and clumsy machine into po-

101

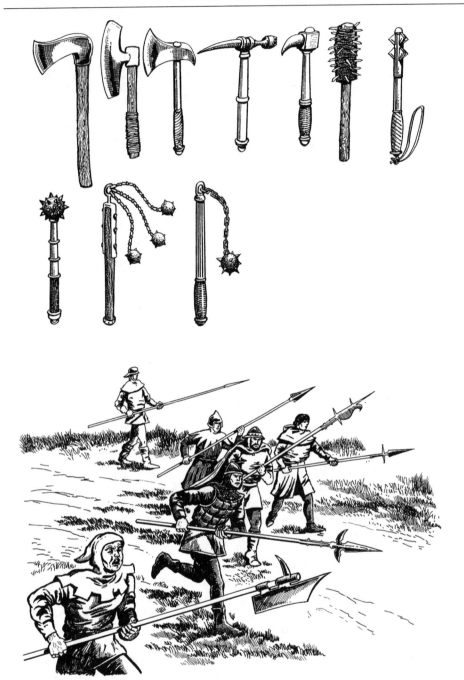

sition. To build the track it was sometimes necessary to fill in a deep ditch, an operation being effected under a rain of projectiles. Furthermore, the preparation of the rolling track clearly revealed the intention of the besiegers and the point where the attack was going to take place.

Assaulting by making a breach required destroying a portion of the defensive wall. To do so, the attackers used a so-called mine, digging a tunnel under the wall, removing masonry and cutting away at the foundation, resulting in the collapse of the wall. (See illustration, page 94.) Undermining was a long, arduous and dangerous operation, but its great advantage was discretion. The defenders did not suspect the mine's existence, or if they did, it was difficult for them to know its precise position. When the mine had been detected and located, the besieged might react by digging a counter-mine gallery to meet their opponents for dreadful underground combat.

Another means to make a breach was sapping, in which stones at the base of the wall were individually picked off, dislodged and torn out until the wall collapsed. Sapping, too, was a very dangerous operation because the defenders dropped stones, threw incendiary materials and spears, and shot down arrows on the exposed sappers. To protect themselves, the besiegers might con-

Top: *Various medieval offensive weapons. Besides the heavy sword with a double-edged flat blade, offensive weapons included the spear, the lance, the battle-axe, the war-hammer, the combat-mace and the morning star, a baton with a short chain at the top attached to a metal ball covered in spikes. Bottom: Infantry armed with various medieval spike-weapons. Spike-weapons, also called staff-weapons, were composed of a long wooden haft and a metal end with spikes, blades or hooks. Generally developed from agricultural implements, they allowed men on foot to engage mounted combatants. Along with their varied shapes came a variety of names, including holy-water sprinkler, boar-spear, guisarme, oxen-tong, sponton, pole-axe, two-bills and halberd.*

Mounted knight in the 14th century. All of medieval weaponry was marked by a tactical arms race. The chief problem was the struggle between missile power and mobility, and protection from missiles combined with shock effect. This was exemplified by the increasingly heavily armored knight on his armored warhorse, armed with thrusting spear and sword.

struct a cat. A cat (also called rat, chasteil or tortoise) was a strong movable timber gallery covered with a solid roof. Like a belfry, a wooden cat was vulnerable to fire and revetted with rawhide and wet turf.

Another ancient method of making a breach was using a battering ram. The ram was a strong beam with a metal point at one end. It was maneuvered by a party of men moving it backwards and forwards against a gate or a masonry wall. The violent shocks worked by direct percussion but also by vibrations, which loosened the stones. The defenders might react by interposing between the wall and the metal head to absorb the force of the blows. They could also try to deviate the ram by catching its end with a rope fitted with a slip-knot, and of course they could riddle the attackers with various missiles. Therefore rammers were also protected by a cat in which the battering ram was hung from the roof by means of solid ropes or chains. (See illustration, page 95.)

Obviously, assaulting by ladder or belfry or through undermining, sapping or ramming was very difficult, even impossible, if the fortress was surrounded by a broad ditch filled with water. In that case the attackers had the choice of ferrying assaulting troops by boats or constructing an improvised bridge, a kind of dike across the wet moat, with fascine, earth, brushwood, tree-trunks and whatever materials they could find. Another method was to get rid of the water by digging a derivation canal, leaving the defenders high and dry.

As soon as the breach was practicable, the frontal assault was effected. In the meantime, however, the besieged might have hastily built another improvised defensive wall behind the breach to prolong the resistance. If the attackers succeeded in penetrating the castle or the town, combat might continue if the defenders had withdrawn behind a second line of defense, in the castle keep or in the urban citadel.

German Landsknechte, 15th century

The assault was a confused and bloody hand-to-hand battle. It was a crucial confrontation for both parties and the turning point of the siege. Individual factors, such as physical fitness and bravery, played a central role, but pugnacity was not enough against overwhelming numbers. A repulsed assault generally cost a lot in casualties and could sometimes turn to harrowing defeat by loosening all the bonds of discipline, generating fear and a spirit of *sauve qui peut*, resulting in mass retreat. A successful assault might result in pillage, rape, destruction, fire and massacre. To avoid this terrible predicament, the defenders might choose to pay a ransom or negotiate an honorable capitulation before things got worse.

To conclude, it is important not to overestimate the spectacular and dramatic aspects of siege warfare just described. It must be kept in mind that medieval armies were heterogeneous, temporarily raised, not very mobile and never numerous. The attackers did not generally have enough time to lead an attrition operation; they had only a few hurling machines or none at all; and they had insufficient numbers of troops. Only the large wars involving realms, large duchies or coalitions, such as the wars between the French Capetian kings and the English Plantagenet sovereigns, the crusade against the Albigenses, the Reconquista in Spain, the Crusades in Palestine, and the conflicts during the Hundred Years' War, saw the deployment of huge armies and exceptional operations. Large-scale siege warfare was actually rare, for practical reasons: lack of time, combatants and military means.

GARRISON AND FIGHTING FORCE

The exact number or total strength engaged in a siege or a battle was difficult to estimate as medieval sources were always inaccurate or gave figures that were obviously exaggerated. As a general rule, the garrison of a castle was never numerous; it included the lord, his sons, a few mounted men of arms, a provost, and a few squires and pages. The Truce of God, an edict of the Church, clearly defined the non-combatant (women, children, peasants, traders and clergymen), but the institution was never fully respected; some lords encouraged their peasants to train with bows and arrows, giving them an opportunity for leisure and a game of skill, but with the intention of having additional troops in case of war. All men living in the castle were obliged to serve as guards. In case of a siege, all inhabitants were involved—some actively, with arms in hand, and others indirectly by supplying ammunitions. The defense of a free town was secured by a municipal militia, an armed force raised among the citizens.

As previously pointed out, the ost was the base of military organization. When a suzerain went to war, he levied his vassals for a period of forty days; most troops raised by ost were consequently temporary and disorganized. The ost service had other aspects, though; a vassal might be asked to remain neutral or to allow troops to cross his estate, or to furnish various supplies.

Medieval conflicts, at least until the Hundred Years' War, never lasted for long. Battles were fought within hours; most campaigns and sieges lasted for days or weeks, the longest for a matter of months. Only kings, high princes, dukes and rich free cities could afford to maintain a permanent militia or a small armed force.

Again, medieval armies were never numerous. Between the years 600 and 1500, the greatest battles rarely involved more than ten thousand men in each camp. This figure was considerable in the Middle Ages, but today it corresponds to two military divisions. A state capable of raising such strength mobilizes, in doing so, all its potential and finance. Even the Crusades and the great medieval coalitions rarely include more than thousands of soldiers. During the Third Crusade in 1198, the French king Philippe Auguste had 650 knights and 1,300 infantrymen. The king of England, Richard Lion-Heart, had an equal number of troops. The Seventh Crusade, headed by the French king Louis IX in 1248, counted 12,000 footmen and 2,500 horsemen, an imposing force for the time. In 1467 for the siege of Dinant, the powerful duke of Burgundy had 30,000 men. By that time a lance was composed of a fully equipped and armored knight, three mounted archers, a page on horse, a crossbow man and three pikemen on foot.

As a general rule, medieval troops lacked coherence. They were merely irregular groups of vassals raised by feudal ost—rounded-up peasants with little warlike spirit and heteroclite armament. They formed low-value and ill-disciplined contingents that retained their individuality, independence and even rivalries right into the thick of the battle. Therefore, in the 14th century, kings, dukes, princes, and rich free cities encouraged their vassals to pay a special tax instead of submitting to the inconvenient ost. With the funds raised, they paid mercenaries and maintained permanent armed forces. Professional soldiers cost a lost, however, and their loyalty and determination in combat depended on the amount and regularity of their pay.

Mercenaries were recruited in the low gentry, among the homeless, social outcasts and adventurers. They were grouped in loose companies headed by a gang-leader proclaiming himself captain. During the Crusades, the Christians employed Turcopoles, who were autochthonous mercenaries forming units of light cavalry. Mercenaries were on the whole not reliable; they did not hesitate to pass into the opposite camp if conditions were better there.

In peacetime, mercenaries were dismissed and unemployed. They then formed gangs of bandits surviving by marauding the countryside, pillaging villages, robbing merchants and ransoming travelers—even in some cases by attacking castles. These unchecked gangs were particularly active in the 14th century. By that time, the Genoan crossbowmen were reputed for their skill. In the following centuries Swiss mercenaries were especially appreciated for their bravery. Certain Italian mercenaries (condotierri) were celebrated; some of them achieved high position, such as the famous Francesco Sforza, who became duke of Milan in 1450. The German Landsknechte were formidable mercenaries in the beginning of the 16th century.

The logistics of the marching army were completely improvised. Soldiers shifted for themselves, procuring food and supplies on the lands they crossed. Plunder and pillage were often the only means of survival, sacking a castle or a town the most convenient way to reward troops and pay mercenaries. The passage of an army, friend or foe, was always a calamity for the local population because the concept of indemnifying civilian victims was totally unknown.

This being said, it is important to underline a few points regarding medieval violence. It must be kept in mind that the period under consideration lasted a thousand years, and accordingly, times of peace and relative quiet were numerous. The frequency and intensity of medieval war are difficult to measure as they vary considerably in time and space. We who have witnessed and experienced industrial conflict, general mobilization, total war, mass extermination and nuclear fire can easily imagine how rudimentary and small-scale medieval warfare must have been.

Medieval Europe suffered many dark and disastrous periods, notably in the 9th, 10th and 14th centuries. However, it is very questionable to assert that the Middle Ages on the whole were more violent than any other period of history. Proportionally, how barbarous were the Middle Ages compared to the massacres during the wars of religion in the 16th century, the killings in the time of Louis XIV, the Napoleonic butchery and the two World Wars in the first half of the 20th century?

3

The Evolution and Apogee of Medieval Castles in the 13th and 14th Centuries

THE EVOLUTION OF CASTLES IN THE 13TH CENTURY

The 10th and 11th centuries by and large were a period of uncertainty, impetuousness and reorganization after the chaos of the early Middle Ages. In the 12th century, the boisterous feudal society seemed to expand and mature. The 13th century marks a period of balance and prosperity considered the apogee of medieval civilization and the golden age of castles. In France, for example, royal authority was greatly restored, the feudal independent local lords were on the decline, and the political and financial situation was more or less stabilized, allowing the Capetian sovereigns to integrate fortifications in a wide state strategy.

The Crusades enabled the West to learn much of eastern military engineering. Intercourse between European and Arab civilizations was constant, and new ideas developed there were used at home. Both siege warfare and European fortifications underwent a significant evolution in the 13th and 14th centuries.

Royal creations in the 13th and 14th centuries were astonishing in their scale and sophistication. The introduction of coherent systems marks a radical transformation. The most significant evolution was the development of the external wall, called the enceinte, increasing space within the castle for a larger garrison and providing more combat emplacements. While bulky but passive donjons had been the main defense works in the previous centuries, castles of the 13th and 14th centuries were more often homogeneous and comprehensive sophisticated fortresses composed of right walls flanked by cylindrical towers. Though irregular ground-plans were in some cases imposed by natural sites, the tendency was to build castles following a regular, symmetrical, geometrical and rigorous layout; the castles of Vitré and Poitiers (France) and Caerlaverok (Great Britain) were triangular. But the most commonly used outline was a regular rectangle as seen in the Tower of London and in the castles Harlech, Bodiam and Beaumaris (Great Britain), Muiden (Netherlands), and Villandraut, Dourdan and Vincennes (France) just to mention a few. This kind of regular rectangle fortress was sometimes called a yard-castle. Defense was improved with passive obstacles, easy communications, efficient flanking, and active combat emplacements spread out in better positions that gave them more autonomy, increasing the defensive capability of the castle.

These great improvements, reviving the essential principles of fortification, permitted the building of castles in sites totally deprived of natural defenses. The rectangular disposition of the regular fortress created an open ground, a bailey or bascourt, allowing rapid movement for the garrison and the placing of war machines for hurling projectiles over the walls. Ancillary buildings—residence or palace, chapel, huts for servants, quarters for soldiers, stables for domestic animals, storehouses and other elements related to the castle community's life—were placed against the walls, leaving space for a central courtyard and even a garden.

As previously discussed, the curtain was the portion of wall between two towers. Curtains were mostly straight, rather than curved or zigzagged, in order to reduce blind spots. To oppose assaulting by scaling-ladder and belfry, castle builders made walls higher; to thwart undermining, sapping and ramming, they made them thicker. The thickness was particularly large at the base of the wall. Strength was provided by giving the lower portion of the wall a sloping apron or plinth. This compact mass of large stones, called a batter or talus, was not only too wide to be tunneled under and weakened, but it also increased the stability of the construction. Another advantage of the talus was that when the defenders dropped stones upon it, the stones splintered and ricocheted with a shrapnel effect on enemies at the wall.

The main active combat emplacement on top of the wall, the crenellated parapet, was improved. Merlons were often fitted with observation slits which also served as arrow-splits. Crenels were furnished with wooden panels (huchet) hanging upon swivels in the merlon on either side; when required, these shutters could be pushed open far enough to allow the archer to command his target below, while the sloping shelter afforded him overhead protection from a falling arrow. Not infrequently the wall-walk had a rear- as well as a fore-parapet with crenels and merlons, so that the curtain wall could be held even if an enemy obtained access to the courtyard. The inside of the thick curtain might also be fitted with a corridor, occasionally called a gaine. This was a kind of vaulted gallery allowing troops to move rapidly and undercover from one place to another. The gallery was not only an easy communication but a combat emplacement if furnished with arrow-splits.

Curtains were reinforced by towers, of which there were two sorts: wall-towers and corner-towers. These often carried individual names and were strongholds arranged for active defense with crenellated parapets, hoardings and arrow-splits; they projected from the walls in order to flank the curtains and ditch. In plan they were square, rectangular, almond-shaped or more frequently cylindrical or semi-cylindrical. As with the curtains, the tower base was often strengthened by a sloping apron and a buttress. These features provided stability, offered protection against scaling, undermining and ramming, and had something of a deterrent effect simply through their appearance of strength. The batter might have different forms: triangular, angular, almond-shaped, or similar to a bridge-fender, the prow of a ship or a bird's beak.

In height towers varied considerably. They were always higher than walls, allowing observation and command of the curtains. With this construction, if enemies conquered the wall-walk, they remained under fire coming down from the tower. On some occasions the communication between the tower and the wall-walk could be interrupted by a small drawbridge. The height of a tower was sometimes calculated in order to send and receive optical signals: For example, in the enclosure of the abbey of Cluny (France), the high Tour Ronde allowed communication with the castle of Lourdon via the church bell-tower of the hamlet of Cotte and a tower built near the village of Lournand.

The summit of the tower was either covered with a roof or arranged as an open crenellated terrace where hurling machines could be placed. The top might also be fitted with an échauguette or a watchtower.

The inside of the tower was divided into a various number of stories arranged as living accommodations, supply-stores, arsenal, prison and so on. In some cases a half-cylindrical tower accommodated the projecting apse of a chapel—in Colchester Castle (Britain) or Avila (Spain), for example. Access to the rooms was by means of ladder or masonry spiral staircases; it is worth noting that most medieval staircases and passageways in castles were deliberately narrow, so that one man could hold a passage against many. Small and narrow grated windows were pierced to let light come in and also to be used as observation points and arrow-splits. With all these features, each and every castle tower formed an isolated stronghold that could be independently defended, even when other parts of the castle had fallen.

As previously mentioned, the distances between corner- and wall-towers were calculated according to the range of bow and crossbow. In some cases towers were replaced by overhanging watch-turrets called pepper-pot towers. A pepper-pot was a kind of big échauguette resting on corbels or buttresses. Pepper-pots had the same flanking combat function as normal towers, but they were much cheaper to build.

The main walls and towers, the enceinte forming the core of the castle, might be defended by one or more external enclosures or concentric walls. These walls were part of the so-called concentric castle, an eastern invention. An external wall, called a lice or list, created an additional obstacle, a delaying line of defense. Depending on the natural features of a site, the list either embraced the whole castle or protected only a particularly exposed or weak façade. In some mountainous sites, lists often formed a succession of fortified points spreading out on the steep access road. In other cases the walled area was further enlarged so that it came to enclose two or more yards, each defended by a wall.

The list was frequently a stone wall with flanking towers similar to the main enclosure. However, the list

Curtain. Staircases provided access to the wall-walk. The wall-walk might also be covered with a tile roof to shelter sentries from rain and to protect combatants from enemy projectiles.

was always lower than the main enceinte, according to the principle of command. This basic principle of fortification allowed superposed and simultaneous shooting from both the external and the main walls. Owing to the disposition, height and profile of the works, archers on the main enceinte could shoot out over the heads of their comrades on the outer. Thus both enceintes were in action for both combined and successive defense. Consequently a tower's elevation (called the gorge) was sometimes a straight wall or more frequently omitted, leaving the work open on the inside. That way, if the external tower was seized, the attackers were vulnerable to projectiles hurled by the defenders deployed on the main enceinte.

Communication between the main and the external walls was by means of posterns. Posterns, also called sally-ports, were fortified gateways having two functions. In peacetime they were doorways permitting people to enter and leave the castle without opening the main gate. In wartime, from posterns the defenders could undertake a sally. Especially intended for this military purpose, some sally-ports were hidden or at least well concealed.

The space between the main enceinte and the lists

was usually fairly broad. If wide enough, this belt of land was used in time of war as an emplacement for hurling machines and as a campground where peasants of the vicinity could find refuge. In peacetime it was used as pasture, as a training ground for soldiers, as a place where tournaments and jousts were held, and as a fairground or market for traders and merchants.

Keeps, towers and walls were fitted with shooting niches narrowing into vertical arrow-splits through which archers could shoot. Though used in earlier castles, from the 13th century onwards these active combat emplacements were more numerous, better designed and more conveniently placed in order to turn the land surrounding a castle into a dangerous killing ground by reducing or preferably eliminating all blind spots (angles below and beyond which the ground cannot be seen and defended). Arrow-splits had many designs combining protection of the archer and angle of fire. Many forms were experimented with to find the broadest view and the widest field of shooting.

The shooting niche or chamber could accommodate one or more combatants, generally one shooting archer or crossbowman and a varlet or garçon loading a spare

Cross-section of curtain fitted with talus and gallery

Merlons fitted with arrow-splits and crenel with shutter

bow. In its simplest form the arrow-split or loophole was a long narrow vertical slit, perhaps 2 m long. In some exceptional cases, arrow-splits were very long (6.80 m in Najac castle and 8 m in Aigues-Mortes): in such cases, the niches were fitted with two levels for two archers. In other castles one chamber or niche might be fitted with more than one arrow-split or loophole, allowing one archer to shoot in various directions. As a general rule, however, large and numerous openings were to be avoided as they weakened the building and form targets for the besiegers.

A loophole might terminate in a fish-tailed base, and this was often plunged, or sloped downwards, the better to enable the archer to command the ground below. In other cases, the loophole ended at the bottom in a round hole called an oilette, like an inverted keyhole. Or there might be two oilettes, at top and bottom, in which case the loophole assumed a dumbbell shape.

Originally designed for use with bows, loopholes were eventually adapted to accommodate the crossbow. This ancient weapon was revived in the 12th century and, though forbidden by the Church in the council of Latran in 1139, was widely used in the 13th, 14th and 15th centuries. The crossbow shot a short metal arrow

called a bolt with good accuracy and great power of penetration, enabling an archer to pierce armor and giving him a range up to 150 m. To use the crossbow with its small horizontal bow, vertical loopholes became cruciform, meaning that they were fitted with one or more transverse horizontal slits allowing the archer to observe, aim and shoot with efficiency. These loopholes were called crosslets.

In the so-called yard-castle and concentric castle, the keep lost a part of its significance, being no longer the lord's dwelling place. It seems, however, that the medieval castle-builders could not renounce this symbol of power, and in many cases the donjon already existed before the concentric enceinte was constructed around it. Generally the keep played only a military role as a retreat where resistance could go on even when the rest of the castle had fallen. The weakness of such a scheme lay in the purely passive concept of defense that it represented. In the last analysis, such castles proclaimed the gospel of defeatism, the lurking conviction that in the long run the attack was always superior to the defense, that the gateway would eventually be forced or the curtain walls mined, breached or scaled, and that if then the garrison were lucky enough to withdraw into the don-

Corner-tower, Castle of Maqueda (Spain). Maqueda Castle was situated southwest of Madrid. An ancient Roman fort, the castle was rebuilt in 981 by the Arab architect Fatho Ben Ibrahim. Reconquered by king Alfonso de Castilla in 1083, Maqueda became the domain of Don Fernando Yañez in 1153, then a possession of the military order of Calatrava, and then a royal residence for Queen Isabella. Note the typical Moorish merlons.

Wall-tower with échauguette and pepper-pot turret

jon, they would have naught to expect therein save the slow agony of starvation.

So we see that in some castles (Coucy in France, for example, or Harlech in Britain), the donjon was superseded by what might be called a keep-gatehouse. The lord of the castle came forwards from the retired position and jealous isolation of the older donjons. Instead, he assumed the defense in the fore, combining his residence and combat quarters in the gatehouse. This radical change, transforming the entire castle theme, was however the exception rather than the rule, and keeps were also placed in the middle of the yard-castle as can be seen in the royal palace of the Louvre in Paris (France). In other designs, Dourdan (France) for example, the keep was incorporated within the enceinte and became a part of the defense as a remote corner-tower; it had, however, its own ditch and drawbridge, and its monumental dimensions made it noticeable. In many other designs, the integration of the keep in the defensive system was such that it no longer constituted a noticeable element. In

other castles, Carcassonne (France) and Muiden (Netherlands) for example, the keep was simply omitted and the castle consisted of a powerful enceinte.

When natural conditions were suitable, notably in flat sites, fortresses were surrounded by moats. Here again, dimensions were extremely variable, but a width of 12 to 20 m and a depth of about 10 m were rather common. The inner edge of the ditch (at the foot of the wall) was called the scarp, and the outer side was called the counter-scarp. The counter-scarp was often masonry, too, in order to hold the ground and to prevent the ditch being filled in either by natural erosion or by hostile enemy action. The middle of the bottom of a dry ditch was usually furnished with a narrow draining canal called a cunette. In some rare cases the bottom of the ditch was tiled.

A great majority of medieval moats were dry, but depending on the natural situation, some were filled with water. A wet moat, called a douve or wet ditch, formed a very efficient obstacle against the assaulting party. However,

Corner tower

Aigues-Mortes (France). The door leading from the wall-walk to the wall-tower is defended by an overhanging brattice.

Forms of loopholes and crosslets. Shapes of loopholes, both for bow and crossbow, were extremely varied in length and width.

Crossbowmen. The man on the left uses a weapon with an iron stirrup; he loads it with a hooked strap attached to the girdle by spanning and straightening his body. The man on the right is aiming through the arrow-split.

wet moats could be something of a mixed blessing; they were inconvenient in peacetime, which meant that unofficial bridges were often erected—with subsequent argument and indecision about the right moment to chop them down in an emergency. Besides, water might dangerously erode the base of the wall, and stagnant water might be a year 'round health hazard for the inhabitants of the castle.

The water for a douve could simply be collected from rain, but because this source was unreliable, the wet ditch was very often supplied with fast-flowing water coming from a river or sea by means of dikes, sluices, watergates and derivation canals. In certain cases, wet ditches took on the proportions of a lake, a marsh or even an intentional flood.

In all fortification, in all periods, the gate was the weakest point. As a general rule, a castle included only one main entrance and possibly one postern or a few side-gates. The main entrance was heavily defended by a gatehouse. Throughout the 13th century the gatehouse was gaining in importance over the donjon. The gatehouse was usually an imposing structure, and as the 13th century drew to a close it became the dominant feature of the castle.

The portal of the gatehouse was a Gothic arch either pierced in a tower or deeply recessed between two strong flanking towers. Dimensions of the portal were variable but always large enough to let a cart or a group of horsemen through. The portal included a stout wooden fold-

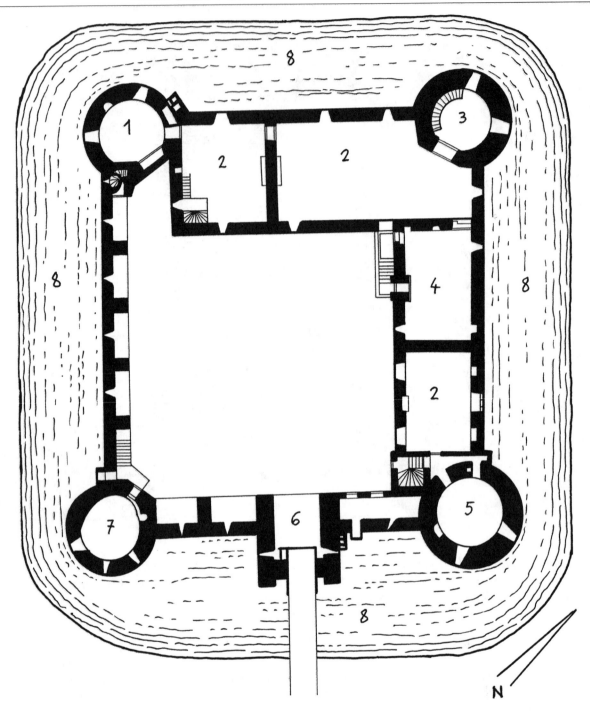

Ground-plan, Muiden (Netherlands). The castle of Muiden (Muiderslot in Dutch) is situated east of Amsterdam in the province of North-Holland. The castle, originally a 10th century tower, was built about 1285 by the earl of Holland, Floris V. Muiden was deprived of keep and displays a regular rectangular plan 32 x 35 m with (1) the West-tower, (2) living quarters and chapel, (3) the North-tower, (4) the kitchen, (5) the East-tower, (6) the gatehouse, (7) the South-tower and (8) the wet moat. The Muiderslot was restored in 1955, and today is perfectly preserved.

Muiden castle (Netherlands)

ing door composed of two heavy leaves reinforced with nails and iron parts. In closed position it was locked by heavy transverse mobile beams that fitted into oblong slots or bar-holes in the side walls. One of the leaves was often fitted with a wicket, a small door allowing the passage of a pedestrian without having to open the main door.

As previously mentioned, many castles were enclosed by moats. If the moat was wide, it was spanned by a fixed timber bridge resting on piers of wood or stone. This bridge did not, however, extend across the moat, but stopped short of the portal, from which it was reached by a drawbridge. In its simplest form this would be a wooden roadway, pushed backwards and forwards horizontally upon rollers or just manhandled into position. More elaborately, the drawbridge was raised by chains, taken into the gatehouse through sloping holes and wound upon a windlass for closed position.

The weight of the drawbridge and chains and the friction of the winching mechanism made the closing operation a complicated, rather slow and laborious ma-

neuver. Consequently, to close the access instantaneously, a portcullis was installed. The portcullis was a vertical metal grating or a heavy wooden grill framed and shod with iron. It moved up and down in slots or chases in the side walls of the entrance passage. The portcullis was hoisted by a windlass for open position and quickly slid down by its own weight for rapid closed position. There might be a second portcullis and a pair of folding gates at the inner end of the passage. The windlasses for both the drawbridge and the portcullis were placed in a chamber situated above the causeway on the first floor of the gate-building.

The passage through the gate was not necessarily straight, but sometimes angled or even zigzag to create obstacles. These obstacles were reinforced by active combat emplacements. The gatehouse was always heavily guarded and included a guard-room and shooting-chambers fitted with arrow-splits and crosslets placed on both sides in the towers. Overhead, the portal was defended by an overlooking brattice or hoarding, or in late examples by a stone corbelled balcony with machicolations

119

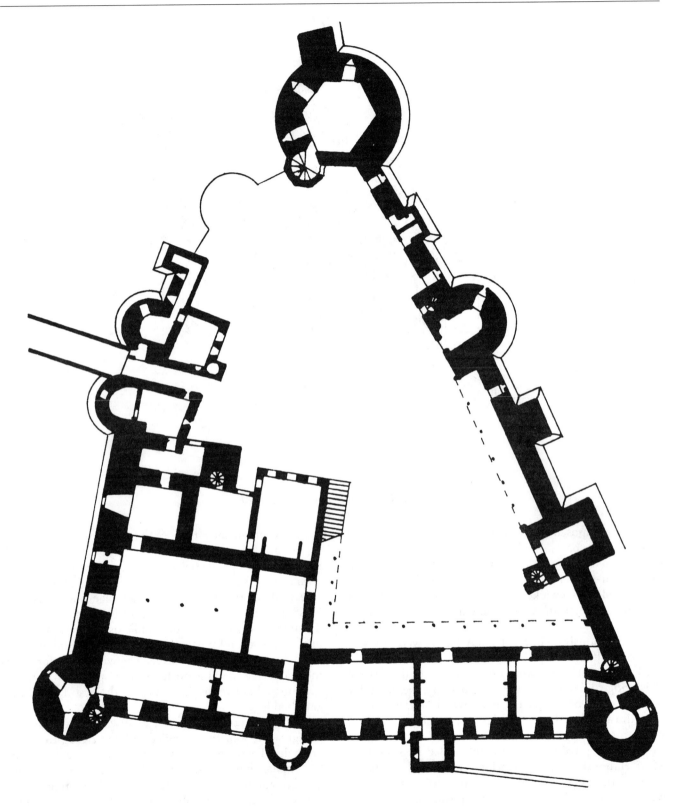

Ground-plan, castle Vitré (France). Situated in Ille-et-Vilaine in Brittany, Vitré castle was created in the 11th century and enlarged with a triangular plan in the 14th century.

allowing plunging fire. The vaulted ceiling of the passage was often fitted with meurtrières (also called assommoirs or murder-holes), apertures or voids through which projectiles and offensive materials might be cast down upon assailants who had penetrated thus far. Some sophisticated castle gatehouses were furnished with deceiving elements and cunning traps concealed in unexpected places such as hidden pits in floors, dead-end staircases, fake posterns, genuine secret passages from which the defenders might sally forth upon intruders, labyrinthine corridors, and rearyard or chicanes where confused attackers were ambushed and delayed. All the main doors of the castle—not only those of the gateway and posterns, but also those admitting passage from the courtyard to the wall-towers and the domestic buildings—were secured by draw-bars.

The sophisticated masonry yard-castles were so expensive that they were within the reach of only kings, princes, dukes and rich earls. The arrangements just described apply to merely a few fortresses. Besides, each castle had its own development depending on natural site, strategic situation, and owner's wealth. Regular rectangular yard-castles were difficult to build in a mountainous site where natural conditions imposed an irregular outline and where

Louvre castle in Paris. The Louvre castle was built by King Philippe Auguste. Completed about 1202, the Louvre included a central cylindrical keep 31 m high and 18.5 m in diameter, with walls about 4 m thick. The donjon was hemmed with a wet ditch and a broad square enceinte 100 m x 100 m with buildings, wall and corner-towers, two defended gatehouses and an external wet ditch 13 m wide. The Louvre was at one and the same time a military stronghold, a citadel, a safe for the royal treasure, one of the king's residences, an arsenal, a place for receptions and feasts, a law-court, and a prison. The grand donjon was demolished in 1529, and the Louvre was reshaped and enlarged by François I, Henri II, Catherine of Medici, Henri IV, Louis XIII, Louis XIV, Napoleon and Louis XVIII as a royal palace. Today it is used as a museum.

steep slopes prevented flanking. Furthermore, individualism, particularity and tradition were very strong in certain regions, and many 13th century works were erected following traditional designs. Moreover, many castles were modest because of financial restraint; many local lords simply could no longer afford the burden of building and maintaining huge fortifications. At the same time, many noblemen refused the system of ost and preferred to pay the suzerain in money rather than in military service. In the 13th century vassals were gradually beginning to change into tenants. Feudalism, the use of land in return for armed service, was beginning to weaken; but it would take hundreds of years to disappear completely.

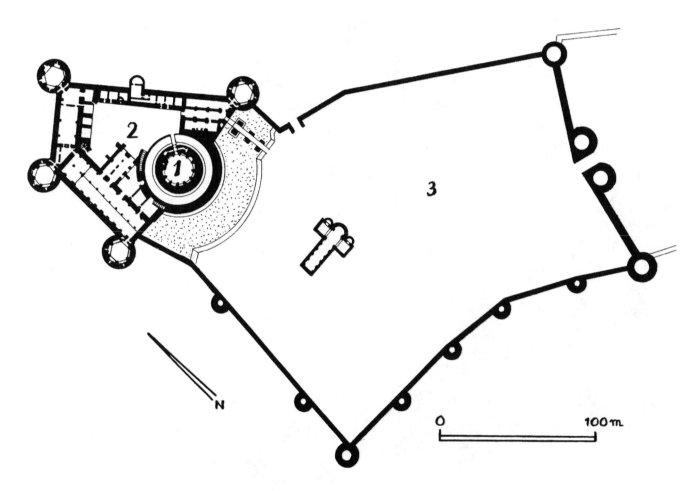

Ground-plan, castle Coucy (France). The castle Coucy is situated near Laon (department of Aisne) on a spur dominating the river Ailette. The circular donjon (1) was the highest and biggest in Europe. Built between 1225 and 1242 by the baron of Coucy, Enguerrand III, it measured 31 m in diameter and 54 m in height with walls 7 m thick. The donjon was placed at the front, so Coucy might be called a keep-gatehouse castle. The donjon was surrounded by an enceinte (2) flanked by four corner-towers (30 m high and 20 m diameter) including the residential house, a large hall (58 m x 14 m) and a chapel. South of the castle there was a wide ditch and a large bailey (3) enclosed by walls, eleven wall-towers and one gatehouse. The castle Coucy became in 1396 the property of Louis of Orléans, brother to King Charles VI, and was turned into a fortified palace. Coucy donjon was destroyed by the Germans in 1917, but many ruins are preserved today.

Angers castle (France), the porte des Champs (Fields Gatehouse)

THE INTERNAL ARRANGEMENT OF CASTLES

The internal disposition of castles depends on many factors such as the dimensions of the bailey, the natural environment, and the rank and wealth of the owner, to mention just a few. All castles, however, included a certain number of common elements that allowed inhabitants to carry on with daily life. Today some medieval castles—transformed for modern purposes, or totally in ruins—evoke dreams, incite romanticism, or appear terribly bleak and depressing places, but even the best preserved are but empty shells of their former selves. In their heyday, castles and baileys were busy, noisy and smelly places of life with a pronounced prosaic and rural character.

Under influences brought home from the Crusades, living conditions in castles were greatly improved. Comfort and luxury were introduced, at least for the rich lords. Masters, families and servants no longer dwelled in cold, dark and inconvenient donjons but in comfortable houses constructed in the baileys. Public function and private life were separated in specialized spaces on a scale impossible to confine within the narrow limits of a keep.

Kings, princes, dukes and high prelates received their guests in a large decorated room, the hall (also called palatium, aula, palais in French, Palast or Pfalz in German), showing off their rank, prestige, authority and wealth. In some cases the great hall emerged as a structure independent in its own right, a hall-house as we might call it. There, wearing their crowns and regalia, the persons of state sat upon cushioned and ornamented thrones placed on a dais, a sort of platform or tribune. In the great hall or the hall-house were held feasts and banquets, ceremonial meetings and social gatherings, receptions and dubbings, official military councils and hearings of the court of justice.

Some royal halls were built after the fashion of a church with nave, aisles and arcades. Dimensions of the halls varied considerably, but generally they were about 15 to 20 m long and 5 to 10 m wide. In Britain, Winchester Castle's hall, built by King Henry III between 1220 and 1236, was 33 m × 17 m. By far the noblest medieval hall in Europe was Westminster Hall in London; built by Rufus and remodeled by King Richard II between 1394 and 1399, this astonishing structure measures internally no less than 72 m × 20 m. The hall of the French royal palace of the Cité in Paris is 70 m × 25 m or 1,750 square meters.

Chinon castle (France), Tour de l'Horloge (Clock Tower)

Daroca in Aragon (Spain), La Puerta Baja (Low Gatehouse)

125

Gatehouse, Carisbrooke Castle, Isle of Wight (Britain)

Eilean Donan Castle (Scotland). Eilean Donan is situated east of Kyle of Lochalsh in the Highlands. A modest fortress, it was constructed on a small island about 1220 in order to protect the Loch Duich from pirates. Abandoned in 1719, the castle was fully restored in the 20th century and linked to the mainland by a stone bridge.

The center of private daily life was the camera or solar (sleeping-chamber) and the bower (also called suite, the lady's apartment). In these rooms lords and ladies received their intimates, took meals and slept. The private room was pleasantly furnished with precious tapestries and various luxury and ornamental items such as mirrors, chests and coffers inlaid with enamel or precious metals. The private chamber included a bed with elaborate structures, sometimes with testers and hangings. The bed was furnished with quilts and pillows (both stuffed with feathers), linen sheets, and coverlets or fur rugs. Night lights were used to dispel evil spirits. Servants and lesser folk slept in straw or huddled in bunks in the outbuildings.

Frequently the camera had more specialized items such as a wardrobe for clothes, a closet with privies, sanitary and washing facilities, a meeting-room for private audience and intimate council, a study with a library counting a few books and precious family archives. These rooms were divided by stone or wooden walls in rich houses or by curtains in modest manors.

The higher a person's place in the hierarchy, the more spacious and luxurious his living quarters, being in some cases palaces with large individual apartments. Double or triple rows of narrow grated windows, fitted with painted glasses and wooden shutters decorated in Gothic style, replaced the inconvenient loopholes. At night lighting was provided by candles and torches fixed on ornamental chandeliers. Heating was provided by large fireplaces and additional charcoal-stoves in winter; thick hangings prevented draughts around the doors. Halls and living quarters often had brightly painted wooden coffered ceilings. Walls were plastered and painted, decorated with drapes, tapestries, paneling, trophies, statues and heraldic devices that added interest to the scene. Tales of great apartments and halls ankle-deep in soiled straw can be discounted as untypical; straw being a dangerous fire hazard, it was more likely that floors (sometimes fashioned of wooden boards, tiles or even marble) were left bare or covered with rugs and skins. The façade of the lord's house might be furnished with galleries resting on timbers, masonry arcades and columns allowing horizontal circulation with other buildings. The gallery was a kind of patio, too, a pleasant lobby or promenade for conversation and rest.

The private lord's warriors made use of a special guard-room, a so-called knights' chamber or a tower where they lived and trained. Next to it there was frequently an arsenal arranged in a tower to store weapons and ammunitions. The arsenal was completed by a smith-workshop to fabricate, maintain and repair weapons and armor.

Horses demanded specialized manpower such as hostlers, lads and stablemen to see to their daily feeding, watering, cleaning and exercising. There had to be a constant back-up for health checks and veterinary care. The harness and equipment had to be manufactured and maintained. To serve all these needs there were various workshops for blacksmiths and harness and saddle makers.

Hurling machines (catapults, trebuchets and others) as well as hoardings were made by carpenters, stored piecemeal in sheds and reassembled in time of war. Arrows

View of castle Roquetaillade (France). The château Roquetaillade is situated 7 km south of Langon in the Gironde. Constructed in 1306 by the cardinal Gaillard de la Mothe, it is composed of a massive square donjon enclosed in walls with four corner-towers and a gatehouse.

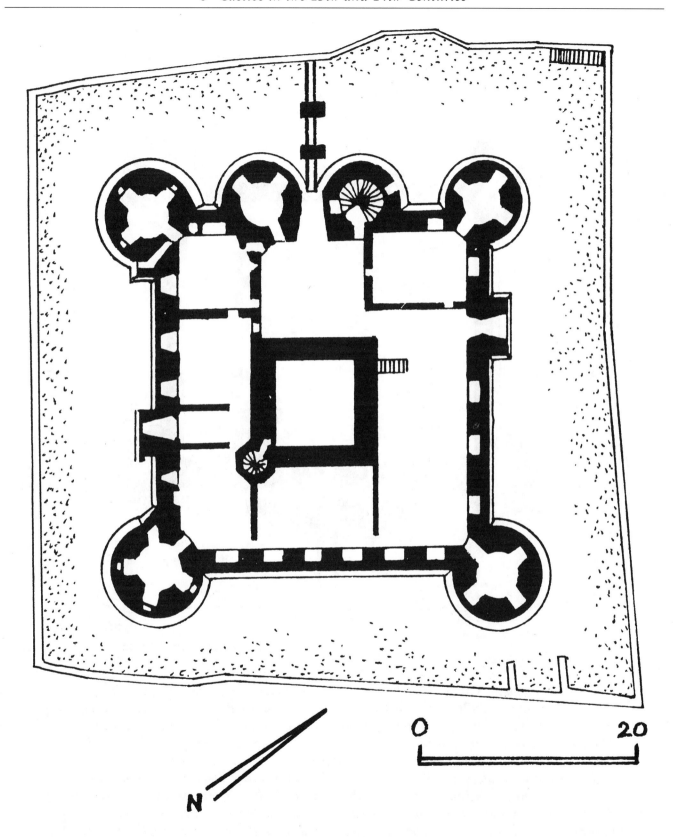

Ground-plan, Roquetaillade

129

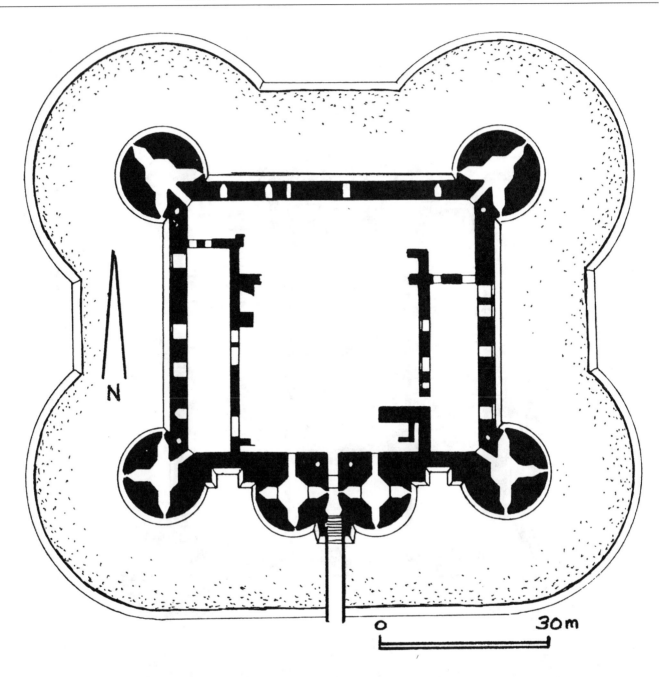

Ground-plan, castle Villandraut (France). Villandraut, situated near Langon in Gironde, was erected between 1305 and 1314 by the archbishop of Bordeaux, Bertrand de Goth (the future pope Clement V, who was involved in the dissolution of the Templar order). The castle, deprived of donjon, was a typical gothic design composed of a regular rectangle 52 m x 43 m. The curtains were 11 m high and 2.20 m thick. They had thick taluses and four corner-towers 20 m high, 11 m in diameter and 2.70 m thick. The gatehouse, placed between two strong towers on the south wall, had a drawbridge to cross the 15 m wide and 6 m deep moat. The inner yard included a chapel, a palace for the pope and various service buildings. Villandraut's design was directly influenced by the English castles Beaumaris, Harlech and Caerphilly built in Wales by King Edward I.

130

were made by fletchers, and there would be a dog-handler and a falconer training hounds and falcons for hunting.

Besides the domestic, military and logistical personnel, some rich and powerful lords maintained a numerous court with musicians, poets, artists, astrologers and so on.

Castle communities always included a place of worship served by one or more chaplains. The chapel was very often beautifully decorated in Gothic style. It might include an oratory heated by a fireplace for the master and his intimates and connected to the living quarters by means of a gallery. The chapel-bell put rhythm in the daily life. Following the Roman tradition, the medieval day was composed of twelve hours of daytime and twelve hours of night, divided in subperiods of three hours beginning with *prime*, corresponding to sunrise at 6:00. *Terce* was 9:00, *sixte* or Angelus was midday at 12:00, *none* was 3:00 in the afternoon and *vespers* corresponded

to the end of daytime at 600; at night *compline* corresponded to 9:00, *matins* was midnight, *laude* was 3:00 in the morning, and a new day began again at the next prime.

The castle was often fitted with a pigeon-house. Colombophilia was an ancient oriental art brought to Europe during the Crusades. Carrier-pigeons were tamed and used to send messages (during a siege, for example). Pigeon-houses were of diverse design, but generally they were more or less ornate towers inside which the walls were arranged with nests.

Every castle required considerable storage space for water, food, munitions, weapons, fodder for animals, fuel for heating and lighting, and timber for hoarding, siege machines, maintenance and vehicles. All of these supplies were necessary if a castle was to withstand a prolonged siege or act as a springboard for offensive operations. The reserves were accommodated in separate buildings or accumulated in the lower stories of the castle. Such

Obidos (Portugal). Situated north of Lisbon in Estramadura, the city Obidos was on the seashore in the Middle Ages, but due to filling in of the gulf, it is now 10 km inland. Obidos was originally a Celtic oppidum, then a Roman fort, then a harbor fortified by the Moors. The city was reconquered in 1147 by King Afonso Henriques, who undertook a wide program of fortifications around the town. The castle, placed on a 75 m high hill dominating the town, had a rectangular plan with four corner-towers. In 1282, King Dinis offered the town and castle to his wife, Isabella. From then until 1833, Obidos was traditionally the residence of the Portuguese queens and greatly decorated and enlarged.

rooms were fitted out with shelves and racks and kept as clean, cool and dry as possible.

Careful attention was paid to reserves of water, well and cistern. Wine and beer were kept in casks or in bottles. Obviously, there were always problems with storage of food, particularly meat. Animals such as chickens, geese, doves, ducks, and pigs were reared, and slaughtered when required. Stored food was usually in the form of grain, which could be expected to keep longer than flour. Naturally the corn had to be ground into flour before baking and therefore many castles were equipped with a mill.

From the 13th century onwards, cooking was done in a special kitchen distinct from the eating-room so that lords and guests were not troubled by smells and smoke. The influence of the Crusades was present in sophisticated dishes with spices, aromatic herbs, sauces, sweetmeats, oils, dried fruits and others exotic products. The kitchen was usually large because it was used to prepare food for the whole community. It included one or more fireplaces, ovens, sinks, a bakery, and pantries as well as storeplaces for food and fuel. A palace also possessed kitchen-gardens, orchards, cattle-sheds, poultry-houses, and rabbit-hutches as well as a butchery and a buttery. The latter has nothing to do with butter; the word comes from the French *bouteillerie*, the place to keep bottles. In other words, it was the room from which wine and ale were issued.

Manners and customs had evolved since the early Middle Ages, and castle dwellers were particularly refined in their habits. As a matter of fact, rich people and rulers were cleaner in the late Middle Ages than in the 18th century. It was difficult to imagine a mighty lord accepting filthy living conditions, and jobs had to be found for the servants to do, if for no other reason than to keep them busy. Sanitary and washing facilities were primitive, but they did exist. Before and after meals, the guests washed their hands (the table-fork was not introduced until the Renaissance; until then, one ate with the fingers). The great master and his intimates were massaged, perfumed and given depilatory care by chambermaids and barbers. They bathed in tubs that were carried into the bedroom, and as there was of course no running warm water, the water for the bath had to be heated and carried in by servants. Castles were fitted out with latrines and apartments with night-commodes and chamber pots which were emptied by servants.

The lord had the right of justice over his subjects, and penalties and punishments were various according to the offense: lashing, fine, pillory, branding, mutilation, temporary or permanent exile, death by hanging. Therefore, castles often had a pillory—a wooden carcan fixed on a pole where the shameful condemned was exposed to all in the middle of the bailey. Without a doubt there was also a prison intended for high-ranking prisoners waiting to be liberated against ransom. It was unlikely that such a prison was used to hold rebellious peasants; even feeding them on bread and water was considered a waste of resources. As for the famous oubliette (from the French verb *oublier*, to forget), which supposedly was a dark cell arranged in the deepest cellar of the castle in which prisoners should be intentionally forever forgotten, it is in most cases merely a creepy legend to frighten tourists. The same applies to dreadful torture-rooms, which were far from standard castle equipment.

Again, not every baron in the 13th century lived within such a castle as described above. Many of the smaller landowners continue to inhabit moated homesteads, timbered earthworks and modest manors.

THE DESIGN AND CONSTRUCTION OF FORTIFICATIONS

The building business was the only large scale medieval industry. From the 11th century onwards, the use of masonry was stimulated by religious architecture, and building techniques were greatly improved. The building business developed many new specialized crafts and trades. However, projects were often thwarted by lack of manpower and financial restraints. Whatever the locale, it was always extremely costly to conceive, construct and maintain fortifications. Waste, therefore, was to be avoided. Materials of any demolished building were systematically reused for the construction of a new one. Finances were secured by various taxes, tolls and fines. Further funds might be provided by a marriage with an advantageous dowry, a lucky ransom, a fruitful booty after a victorious war, financial support from the suzerain or a loan contracted to a Jewish or a Lombard financier. For want of something better, the lord had to moderate his ambition and try to reduce expenses by exploiting his own stone-quarry, providing timber from his own forest, and fabricating bricks on his own estate.

In the 13th century, construction techniques were still based on experience, passed down orally or by means of primitive manuals to the next generation. Gradually, new ideas began to appear, and although these were not based on established principles—many principles of engineering and methods of construction had yet to be discovered—they proved rational and were improved upon. Masterbuilders and ingeniatores were all-round specialists who not only designed churches, siege-machines and fortresses, but also directed and organized working sites. Most of them were anonymous, but some were known, even famous: James of Saint George under the reign of the English king Edward I (1272–1307); Sicard de Lordat, serving the count of Foix Gaston III Phébus (1331–1391); Raymond du Temple under the reign of Charles V of France (1364–1380); and Antoine de Chabannes under Charles VII (1422–1461) were competent engineers developing their own styles. Master-builders gradually acquired a high social status and were well paid.

Schools of engineering and architecture did not exist, so master-builders learned their skills through the transmission of techniques and knowledge from one generation to another. Some of them experimented with new techniques and searched for new solutions to construction problems. Nevertheless, the lack of means of construction, the unreliability of calculation, the weakness of methods and the improvised technology sometimes resulted in the disastrous collapse of towers, walls, church bell-towers and cathedrals. In the popular imagination, medieval constructions have a reputation for sturdiness, but this reputation is somewhat ill-founded; many works preserved today have survived only because of later repairs and reinforcements.

In the Middle Ages, a lord planning to build or enlarge his own castle or even to crenellate a wall had first to obtain the right to do so from his suzerain or from the king. It need hardly be said that such regulation, in times when the central government was weak, was apt to be more honored in the breach than in the observance. Hundreds of castles were erected without obtaining royal or ducal permission. Called "adulterine castles," these works were sometimes dismantled when central authority was restored.

Whether a brand new creation or a renovation or enlargement of an older place, every castle was a unique undertaking with its own problems, which were solved by various adaptations depending on many factors, including the natural site, the local traditions, the architect's skills and the owner's resources. The architect and the lord or trustee would decide together the best place to build the castle. Their choice was influenced by various strategic, technical and financial considerations, and nearly always involved a site favoring defense such as a high ground, a spur, a hill, an island or a marsh.

The master-builder, often assisted by a team of master-masons, would then make a design and present to the lord a specification of work to be done (explained by means of a drawing, a map or a model), along with an estimate of the cost and time required for completion. After discussion, negotiation, and bargaining, an agreement was reached and both parties signed a contract. The master-builder himself recruited all specialized workers. Carpenters and tool-makers as well as quarrymen, masons, and stone-hewers were organized in hierarchical associations of free-masons. The common workers were furnished by the lord and raised among his estate's peasantry according to various feudal rights and fatigues.

As a general rule, activities were possible only during good weather, which usually meant from the beginning of spring until the end of autumn. The number of working personnel involved and the time for completion varied considerably according to many factors, such as the volume of the work, sudden difficulties, bad weather, later modifications, unexpected financial problems or lack of manpower. The formidable Château-Gaillard was completed in only two years, from 1196 to 1198; most castles, however, took many years to build. Too, once finished they needed maintenance and even modernization in order to adjust to improved assaulting methods. Today it is hard to establish an accurate date of completion for most castles because of the number of later modifications.

The work site required an important infrastructure. Stones were extracted in a quarry usually created in the vicinity; the diversity of the construction material was thus as large as the geological grounds and contributed to each castle's individuality. Stones had to be transported to the work site by road or by boat, which in some cases required the creation of a track or a canal. A brick factory, a chalk-oven, stores and other facilities had to be built; tools, materials, wood and timber had to be gathered; workers had to be accommodated in camps and huts.

The ground-plan of the castle was prepared by marking off points and distances with stakes and chains, until gradually the whole outline of moats, towers and walls was pegged out. Crowds of workers then dug ditches or heaped up the motte, removing huge volumes of soil with means which today look ridiculous: shovels, picks, baskets, hampers, wheelbarrows and tip-carts.

When a portion of ditch was dug, masons built strong wall foundations (remember that castles were vertical buildings demanding stability). In good ground conditions large flat stones were tilted inwards to take the thrust of the wall above. When the ground was less stable, masons start with a framed-up timber raft; on marshy ground they had to install timber piles driven deep.

Once the foundations were made, the masons began to build towers and walls. Timber scaffolds were gradually raised as work proceeded, and stones, bricks and other materials were carried up by men or by hoisting devices. Roofs of towers and buildings were made by carpenters, tilers and slaters.

Constantly, the master-builder had to supervise all of the construction, control alignments, check material quality and so on. To all these tasks were added the construction of échauguettes, gatehouse, houses, chapel, lord's residence, dungeon, and more. And the conception and construction of the castle were even more complicated in mountainous sites where transport was difficult and weather unpredictable. Spectacular difficulties were met in wet or marshy sites.

Religious and military medieval constructions had some techniques in common, but the main concerns in building a castle were durability and the ability to withstand a siege. Foundations and aprons at the base of walls and towers were made of huge stones from 60 cm up to 3 m high. Walls were made of stones usually between 20 and 60 cm high. Building stones varied greatly. Millstone grit and granite were very strong but not easily worked; sandstone was rather friable; chalk was burnt for lime to make plaster; but the best material between these extremes was limestone. It was one of the finest building stones, and masons took advantage of its good weathering qualities, its ease of working, and its consistent texture.

The walls of the castles in southern European countries, especially Spain, Italy and Sicily, were built of adobe (unfired brick dried in the sun), or of a cement made of pressed soil mixed with stone, which formed a hard, resistant material. Bricks about 20 cm high made of baked clay were another common material especially employed in northern Europe where stone was scanty.

Walls were generally made by blocage or blocking-up in the Roman tradition: They were composed of two skins of masonry, one external wall, and one internal revetment, and the space between both was filled with rubble, earth, mortar, pieces of stones, gravel and so on. This technique did not produce as strong a wall as larger and properly fitted stones, but it allowed relatively cheap construction of massive and resilient walls. The stones of the external wall were frequently masonry of squared and carefully dressed blocks called ashlar; they might be also made of bossage, which meant that their external surface was rather rough or hewed with projecting patterns. The bossage may have been intended to make projectiles ricochet or to break the point of a battering ram, but probably its main function was decorative—or possibly deterrent, since it gave an impression of strength.

To increase wall resistance various techniques were used. Tyings and clampings were placements of larger stones within a masonry wall. Clamping might be vertical to form stable columns, or it might consist of horizontal rings or layers in order to strengthen a wall or increase the stability of a tower. The coherence of the wall was reinforced by iron clamps firmly fastening stones together.

A blind arch was a semicircular bow of stones embodied in and supporting a wall. It was also used as relieving vault above any openings that typically weaken a wall such as posterns, gates, windows, loopholes, embrasures and so on. Buttresses were deep pilasters or vertical strengthening masonry applied to places in the wall where pressures and thrusts were the greatest; they were also used to support échauguettes and pepper-pot turrets. The standard medieval staircase was the ordinary spiral sort with a vertical central shaft. Each step was built into the wall at one end, leaving a round lump at the other which became the shaft. This sort of staircase was universal and in general use for hundreds of years. Drainage of rainwater in open spaces such as wall-walks, terraces and platforms was managed with gutters, weepers (holes) and gargoyles (spouts, often fancifully or grotesquely carved).

The main purpose of a fortress was to be sturdy, strong and resistant, but attention was always paid to aesthetic considerations, since fortifications were also prestige objects reflecting the authority and the wealth of their owner. Bossage, clampings, bricks and stones of different colors formed more or less elaborate patterns decorating walls, towers and buildings. The rhythm and style of corbels accentuated the light-and-shadow effects. On top of the walls, the slender silhouettes of échauguettes, chimneys and pinnacles—contrasting with the regular outline of merlons—contributed to the embellishments. The elevation of donjon, gatehouse, towers and walls conferred strength, originality and majestic grandeur. Protective religious items (such as statues of saints and the Holy Virgin) as well as coats of arms and other heraldic ornaments were placed above portals, gates and doors.

THE EVOLUTION OF CASTLES AND FORTIFICATIONS IN THE 14TH CENTURY

By the end of the 13th century, Europe was affected by economic disorganization and the beginning of a crisis. The conquest of cultivated grounds ceased; the construction of cathedrals stopped; economic and demographic growth were on the decline. The general situation went from bad to worse in the 14th century because of plague, disorder and war. Famines, provoked by bad harvests, and epidemics—notably the terrible plague called the Black Death, which began in 1348 and lasted for years—killed probably one-third of the European population. Whole villages disappeared, fields returned to fallow lands, and many towns were almost deserted. Depopulation, economic disorganization, social collapse, and moral and religious crises resulted in troubles, revolts of the poor and repression.

These calamities were worsened by an unprecedented large-scale conflict called the Hundred Years' War, fought from 1337 to 1453 between Europe's two most powerful realms, France and England. More than by

Buttress

decisive large pitched battles, the Hundred Years' War was characterized by siege warfare, regional expeditions, local operations and ambushes. In France, villages were raided, looted or burned by passing armies who practiced scorched-earth destruction.

The Hundred Years' War was actually a tangling up of Franco-English wars, civil conflicts between Frenchmen, large-scale banditry and popular insurrections. Hostilities were actually interrupted by truces and long periods of relative peace, because neither the English nor the French could sustain the war effort. Permanent armies, fortifications and ransoms being very expensive, both belligerents rapidly became financially exhausted and neither was ever able to gather enough means, money and men to allow a decisive strike that would bring the war to a victorious end. The official time of real war was about 30 years, but the habit of violence created a new class of armed men, and unchecked gangs, wandering private armies and unemployed mercenaries brought additional insecurity, murder and pillage to the devastated countryside.

The Hundred Years' War resulted in enormous growth of fortifications. Although few new fortresses were built, many older works were rearmed, many castles were modernized, and many existing structures were embellished. In addition, many points of importance were fortified—not only military strategic strongholds but places important to the economy, such as towns, villages, hamlets, farms, mills and bridges, as well as religious buildings such as isolated monasteries, churches and chapels. Simultaneously, the vicissitudes of the Franco-English war resulted in the destruction of many places both by military operations and by intentional dismantling: A castle might be destroyed if strategically vulnerable, hard to defend, or too advanced in territory held by the enemy, for example.

The technical evolution of military architecture occurring during this period of war, plague and disorder was mainly characterized by continuation of traditional methods, minor improvements and a few innovations. Everything previously described was still employed, and

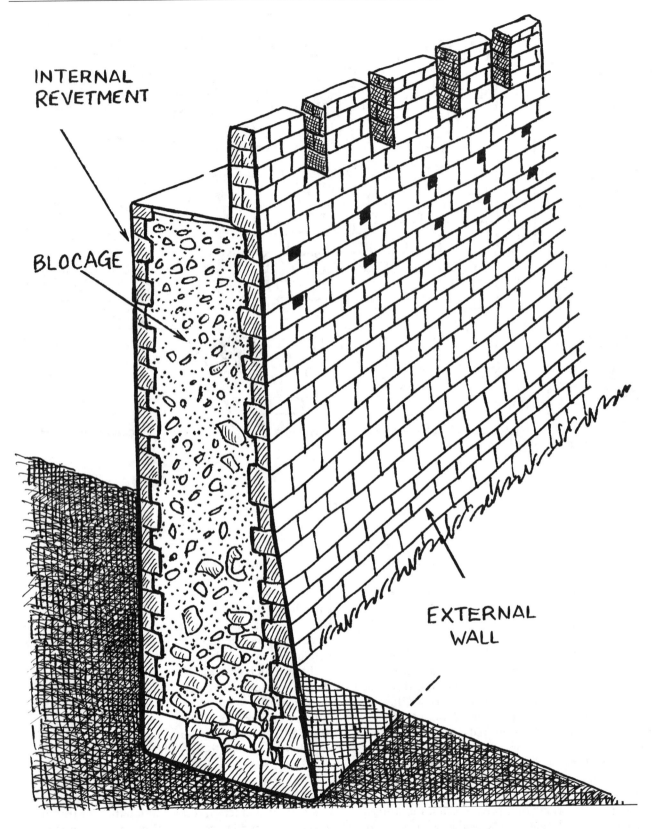

INTERNAL
REVETMENT

BLOCAGE

EXTERNAL
WALL

Cross-section of a wall made of blocage

Blind arch

fortifications evolved at the mercy of circumstances, without rule or guideline.

The militarization during the Hundred Years' War resulted in the growing practice of retaining soldiers in service. Rapid movement of the garrison around the walls in time of siege was hindered by the multiple defensive obstacles that castle planners had hitherto favored. Hence there was a strong tendency to reduce the size of castles and to simplify their ground-plans. Accordingly, the 12th century concept of the rural great-tower was revived. This was generally composed of a single rectangular enclosure of moderate size or a high rectangular dwelling tower with thick walls flanked by four cylindrical corner-towers and a simplified gatehouse. Examples of such tower-houses can be seen in castles Alleuze, Anjony and Sarzay in France.

Other changes reflecting the military situation were castles with deeper moats and walls and taluses, enceintes, towers with aprons and donjons of greater height and thickness. One of the main innovations was the double wall-walk crowning the summit of certain cylindrical towers, allowing more firepower.

Another innovation was the use of so-called machicolation. Towards the end of the 13th century, the inconvenient timber hoarding, vulnerable to fire, began to be replaced by projecting masonry parapets on great stone brackets known as corbels. The space between each pair of corbels was open to the wall-walk, forming a machicolation, an opening through which materials could be cast down upon the besiegers. Machicolation, which originated in the Middle East, was constructed on top of walls, towers and dungeons, and often added to older works

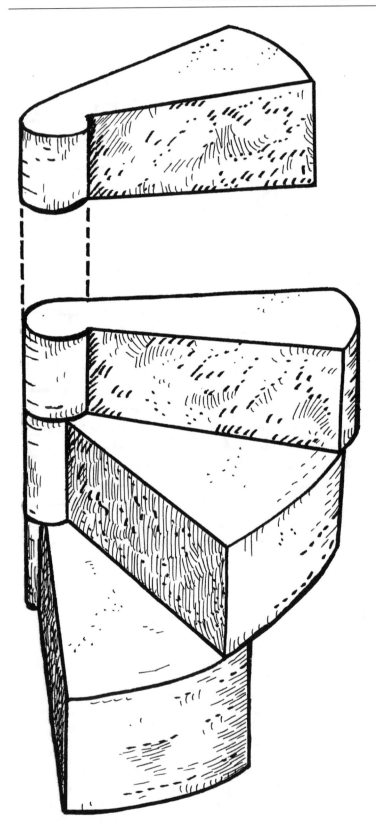

Schematic view of a spiral staircase

(which complicates attempts at accurate dating of structures). This disposition allowed each combatant a medium range combat emplacement (shooting down with bow from the crenel) and a close range emplacement (dropping projectiles through the hole in the floor for plunging fire). Machicolation represented important progress, but it was very expensive to build; consequently many modest lords continued to use old-fashioned hoardings. A significant economy might be realized when machicolation was placed only above an access, a gate, a door, or a portal in the form of a projecting balcony, called a brattice or moucharabieh. The installation of machicolation allowed a widening of the wall-walk, which might be covered with a timber structure or even a permanent tiled roof to shelter sentries from cold and rain and protect combatants from enemy projectiles.

When firearms begin to play a significant role in end of the 15th century, machicolation lost a great deal of military efficiency. However, having a formidable appearance, it remained, together with échauguettes, crenels, merlons and other medieval features, a decorative element used in residential palaces and civilian architecture.

In the 14th century significant improvements were brought to the defense of the gatehouse. Still more elaborately, the drawbridge was raised by cables or chains hung from a pair of rainures or gaffs (timber beams received back into long chases or slots in the gatehouse). If the castle ditch was far out, the drawbridge might span a stone-lined or rock-cut pit immediately in front of the portal. Whether raised by cables taken directly into the gatehouse or by means of gaffs, such a lifting bridge could only be handled with much labor. A solution to this problem came in the 14th century with the devising of the counterbalanced drawbridge, or turning bridge as it was sometimes called. This spanned a carefully constructed stone pit, in the sides of which were sockets for the axles (called trunnions) upon which the drawbridge turned, more or less midway in its length. With each half acting as a counterweight to the other, much less effort was needed to set the bridge in motion. When raised, the inner half was received into the pit, while the outer half fell back against the portal, to which it formed an extra barrier, while in front the pit yawned, impassable. The wicket (pedestrian door) was then often independent from the main portal and fitted with its own drawbridge and windlass. Simultaneously, the moat was deeper and broader and even doubled with a second ditch (filled or not with water) to complicate the enemy's approach.

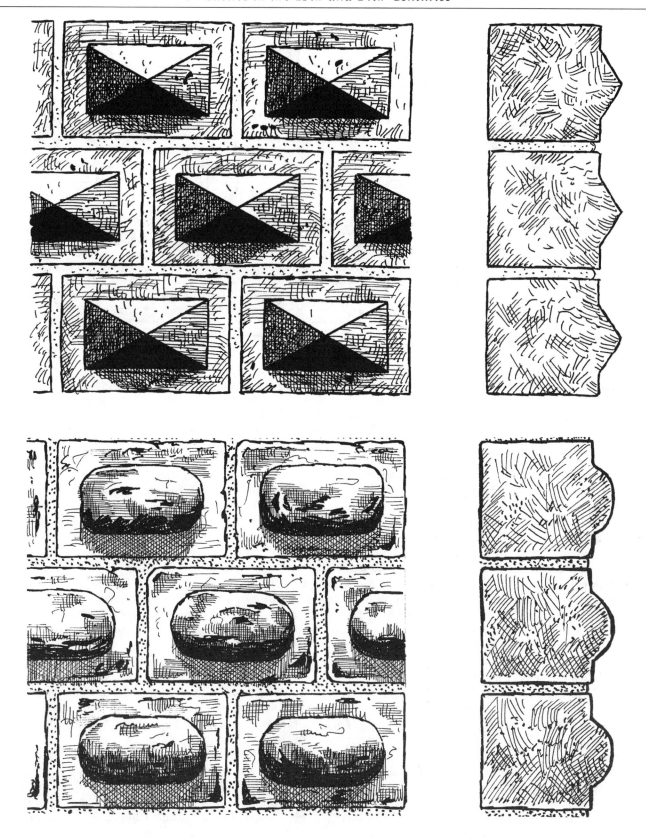

Front view and cross-section of two forms of bossage

Vertical clamping and horizontal clamping

Beyond the drawbridge, the entrance to the castle was further defended by outer works. The barbican, originating in Arabian fortification, was placed on the far side of the moat in front of the gate. It concealed the entrance and protected it from enemy strike; it worked as a filter and formed an additional defense line. Usually a fortified outer ward, a low square stronghold or a masonry U-shaped tower, it was always fitted with crenellated parapet, its own ditch and its own gatehouse with drawbridge. As an exception, the barbican might be a round tower connected to the main enceinte by a double crenellated wall as can be seen in Carcassonne (southern France). The gatehouse to the barbican was usually placed not in line with the main portal but on a flank, so as to check a direct rush upon the latter. Possibly a barbican was fitted with sluices and water-gates allowing control of the water level in a wet moat.

Another outer-work was the so-called bastille. This was a large barbican which might have the dimensions of an independent castle with walls, towers, gatehouse, drawbridge and sometimes even its own garrison. It was usually built at the gate of a town. An example is the castle Saint-Antoine (the famous Bastille stormed in 1789), constructed over the period 1370–1382 (during the reign of Charles V) to defend the eastern access to Paris.

The Hundreds Years' War was also marked by the drawing together of broad fortified fronts composed of castles, isolated watchtowers, strongholds, tower-houses, fortified farms, hamlets, villages and towns. Entrusted to loyal vassals, these fronts enabled both sides to conduct a wide strategy with supply-bases holding passages and controlling whole regions.

A significant innovation at the end of the 14th century was the creation of the so-called block-castle. This kind of stronghold was characterized by the absence of external walls, the abandonment of isolated combat emplacements, and the construction of a massive core in which towers were at the same level as the enceinte, creating a vast terrace on the summit of the fortress. This design facilitated communication from one part of the castle to another and allowed defenders to deploy their hurling machines (later firearms). Examples of this sort of disposition were to be seen in the Bastille in Paris and in castle Tarascon.

If 14th century castles were military strongholds, they were dwelling places, too. There was an increasing emphasis on the more domestic aspects of the accommodations. Castles had always been domestic to some degree, but domestic considerations came in a poor second to those of defense from the 11th to the 13th century. In the 14th and subsequent centuries, however, the demand for more space and greater comfort was quite evident in the plan of new castles and the additions to existing ones. In the new structures the appearance was still very much that of a fortress, but internally they were houses. New foundations in the 14th and 15th centuries fully reflected the period's attitudes with regard to domestic comfort in fortified premises. Such new castles were, however, greatly outnumbered by existing ones where, for simple economic reasons, it was not possible to build entirely afresh. In such cases the demand for greater domestic

Machicolation on arch and buttress

141

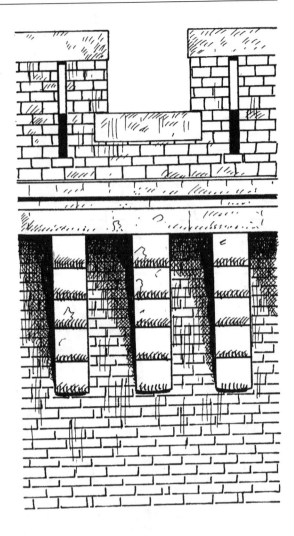

Cross-section and front view of machicolation. Machicolation was made of a series of stone brackets at the top of the wall, serving to widen the wall-walk and thrust the parapet outwards until it overhung with holes left between the brackets.

space and comfort was met by additions to the existing structure, and this practice goes a long way toward explaining the great variety in the appearance of European castles as we see them now. Most frequently the additions took the form of a new wing with walls, towers and new houses with many floor levels adding greatly to the amount of accommodations available. By this time the keep was largely abandoned as the principal living-place of the owner and was relegated to the comparatively less important role of prison, storehouse, and arsenal.

Throughout Europe, fortresses built by emperors, kings, dukes, earls, barons, noblemen or prelates included—within their towered enceintes, large baileys and courtyards—huge vaulted halls, beautiful chapels and luxurious gothic palaces intended for the pleasure of brilliant courts. The increased height of the walls was accompanied by the construction of houses with several stories and elaborate suites of stone rooms leaning on the enceinte. The residential house became more profuse in decoration, better lit and more lavish in its proportions; the accent was on gaiety, refinement and elaboration. Usually occupying a whole wing in the castle, the house was divided in spacious, comfortable and decorated apartments. The façades, pierced with elegant windows as glass had become far more common, opened on a yard or a garden. Highly decorative coats-of-arms, crests and blazons adorned walls, gate, galleries and staircases. As brilliantly displayed in the illustrations of the book *Les Très Riches Heures du Duc de Berry*, towers, échauguettes, pignons, gables, pinnacles, chimneys, dormers

Italian machicolation. Note the typical Italian Gibelin dovetail-shaped merlons.

and mullioned windows, staircase-turrets and high pitched roofs enhanced the majestic verticality of the 14th century castle.

The splendid fortresses of the 14th and early 15th centuries were the last realizations of medieval fortification. Having reached its apogee, military architecture gradually entered a period of crisis caused by the inven-

tion and utilization of firearms. Guns and permanent armies announced the end of the Middle Ages; they reinforced the centralized power of the state, they quickened the definitive disappearance of private castes, and they dictated for the following centuries a totally new kind of fortification.

Cross-section of a wall fitted with machicolation

Vitré (France): the gatehouse. Vitré was situated on the border of the duchy of Brittany and the realm of France. The entrance to the castle shows a good example of 14th century gatehouse.

Front view of a gatehouse with barbican

Top: *La Brède castle (France). Situated in the Gironde near Bordeaux, castle La Brède was constructed probably in 1285 and enlarged in 1306. La Brède was a modest fortress whose main defenses were the wide wet moat and the two barbicans giving access to the living quarters and the circular donjon. La Brède belonged to the French philosopher Charles de Secondat, baron of La Brède and Montesquieu (1689–1755), author of "L'Esprit des lois."* Bottom: *General view of a 14th century castle, showing the various parts.*

Saint-Denis gatehouse in Paris, built within King Charles V's enceinte at the end of the 14th century

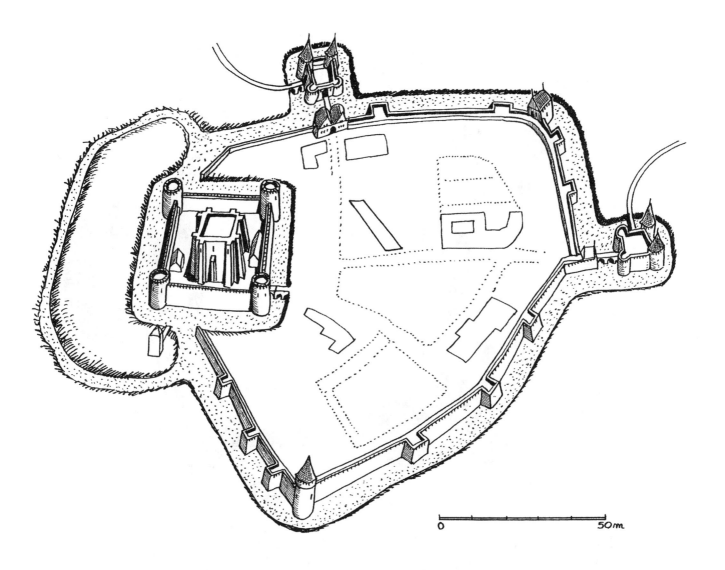

Caen castle (France). Caen developed as the capital of Normandy when the duke Guil-laume (the future king of England, William the Conqueror) decided to install his resi-dence in 1060. Caen castle was composed of the Norman donjon, constructed about 1120 by England's Henry I. It was a massive square building 25 m x 25 m with walls 4.30 m thick reinforced with buttresses. After the fall of Château Gaillard in 1204, the French king Philippe Auguste seized the province Normandy and Caen. Large works were un-dertaken: The donjon was enclosed by a square chemise with four corner-towers and a ditch. A stone enclosure with towers was built to protect the large oval bailey (266 m x 233 m) in which today the Saint-Georges church and the Salle de l'Echiquier (justice hall) are preserved. The subject of dispute between the French and the English from 1350 to 1450 during the Hundred Years' War, Caen was many times besieged, taken and retaken, and both occupiers reshaped the defenses, notably the two main gates (the southern porte de Ville and the porte des Champs in the east). Both were fitted with gatehouses and bar-bicans.

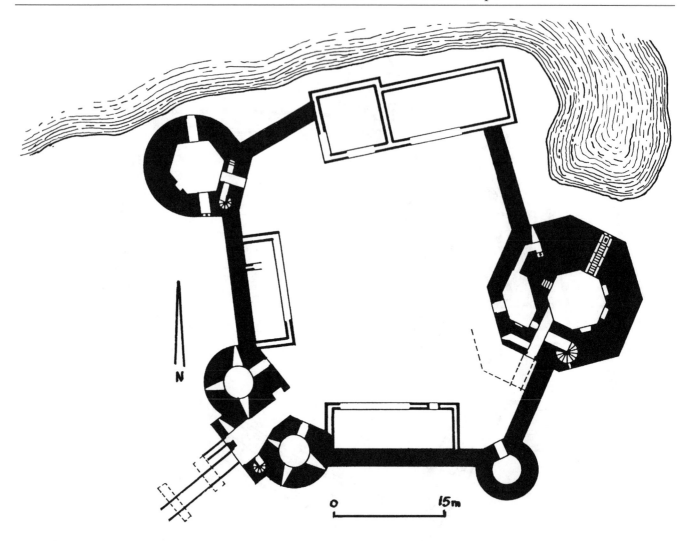

Ground-plan, castle Largöet-en-Elven (France). The castle Largoët-en-Elven is situated near Vannes (Morbihan) in Brittany. It was built between 1374 and 1394 by the lord of Malestroit. The castle includes a moat, a walled bailey with towers, a gatehouse and living accommodations. The donjon, placed on the eastern curtain, is particularly impressive: It is an irregular octagon 57 m high divided in five vaulted stories with walls 6 to 10 m thick.

Opposite: *View of donjon Largöet-en-Elven (France)*

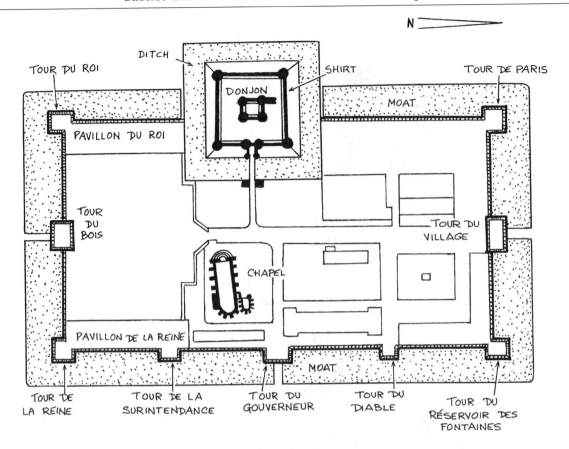

Ground-plan, castle Vincennes (Paris). The creation of the royal castle Vincennes was directly connected to the Hundred Years' War. The safety of the king of France being no longer guaranteed in Paris, the sovereigns decided to establish a fortress outside the city walls in the forest of Vincennes east of the capital. The construction began during the reign of King Philippe VI de Valois in 1337, the donjon was built in 1361 by King Jean II le Bon, and the fortress was completed during the reign of King Charles V in 1373. Vincennes was a large regular rectangle 175 m x 334 m enclosed by a dry ditch 24 m broad and 12 m deep. The walls were 15 m high, flanked by nine square towers 42 m high with wall 3 m thick. The enceinte included three gatehouses. The inner surface measured more than 6 hectares with various service buildings, accommodations, and a chapel. In the middle of the western curtain there was the formidable keep, forming a castle within the fortress. The donjon had its own ditch 22 m wide and 14 m deep; the keep was hemmed with a shirt with machicolation, crenellation and a strong talus, four corner pepper-pot turrets, and a barbican and a gatehouse both fitted with drawbridges. The donjon was a massive square 16 x 16 m, 52 m high with walls 3 m thick; it was reinforced with four half cylindrical corner-turrets. At the beginning of the 17th century, the castle lost a large part of its military value, and cardinal minister Mazarin had two royal houses built: one for the king (Pavillon du Roi) and one for the queen (Pavillon de la Reine). In the meantime the southern curtain was demolished and replaced by a decorated portico with columns. The donjon was then used as a state prison. During Napoléon's reign, the castle was used as barracks, the towers were lowered and flanking artillery casemates were established. Today Vincennes castle is a museum and houses the archives of the French ground forces.

Cross-section, donjon of Vincennes. The donjon was divided in six vaulted levels. The ground floor was the kitchen, the first floor was the royal hall, the second was the royal chamber, the third was the royal children's apartment, the fourth was the royal officers' chamber, the fifth was the arsenal and the sixth was a combat platform with crenellation and machicolation. All rooms were decorated, heated by fireplaces, lit by windows and accessible via a spiral staircase. The keep included a well 19 m deep and latrines installed in the northwest turret.

153

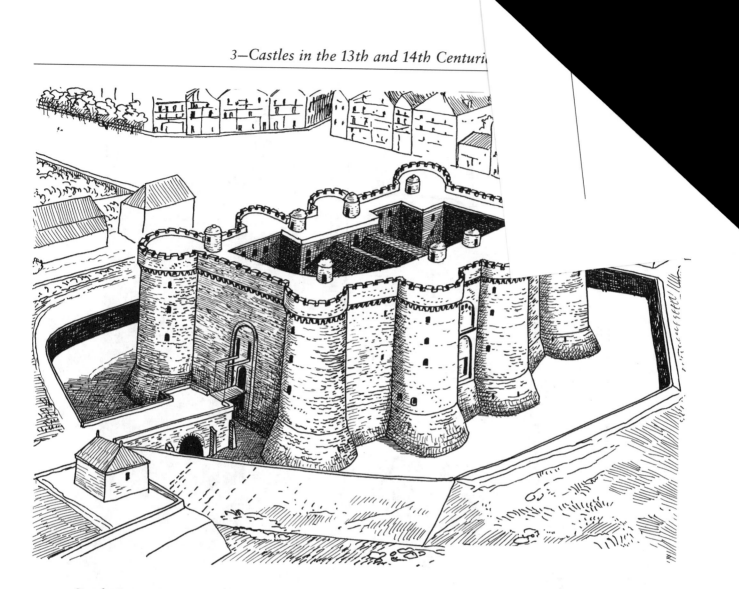

Castle Saint-Antoine, Paris. The castle Saint-Antoine, better known as Bastille, was built between 1370 and 1382 to protect the main gate east of Paris. The Bastille, ordered by Charles V, was also intended as a refuge for the king. It included curtains as high as the eight powerful towers (20 m high and 2 m thick). The citadel was later used as a prison. A hated symbol of the monarchy, the Bastille was taken and destroyed during the French revolution in 1789.

Opposite: *View of the donjon of Vincennes castle*

Castle Alleuze (France). The castle Alleuze was situated near Saint-Flour (province Auvergne, department of Cantal). The château, standing on a steep hill dominating the river Ternes, was built in the 13th century by the constable of Auvergne and belonged later to the bishops of Clermont. During the Hundred Years' War, it was occupied by a gang of brigands headed by the chief Bernard de Galan, who ravaged the region from 1383 until 1395, when the fed-up inhabitants of Saint-Flour assaulted and burned the place. Alleuze, rather similar to the castle Anjony, was a rectangular two-story donjon with four small corner-towers.

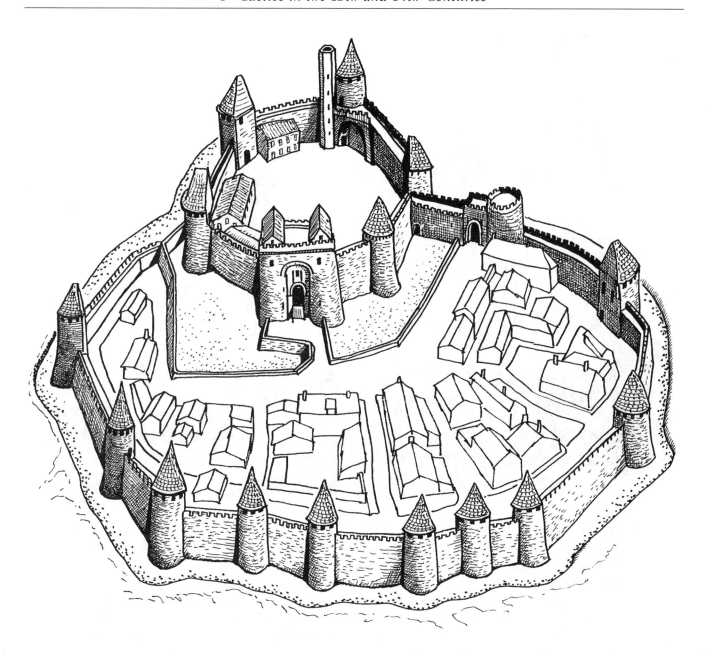

Castle Billy (France). The domain of Billy, situated near Vichy in the department Allier, was given by King Louis VIII (1223–1226) to the lord of Bourbon, Archambaud VIII. He and his son Archambaud IX built the castle on a high ridge dominating river Allier. The castle, probably completed by 1247, was composed of two parts: the high castle and the bailey, which became a small village. The Bourbonnais—corresponding today to the department Allier—was established as a duchy in 1328. Between 1356 and 1410, the castle was reshaped by Duke Louis II de Bourbon. After the treason of the duke constable Charles III of Bourbon, the duchy, which had passed over to the king of Spain and Germany, Charles V, in 1523, was reattached to the crown of France by King François I in 1531. The Château Billy is today partly preserved.

Castle Foix (France). The castle Foix in the Ariège is situated on a 60 m high rocky spur dominating the town at the junction of rivers Arget and Ariège. Founded probably in 1002 by the count Bernard de Carcassonne, the castle played a significant role during the crusade against the Albigenes (1208–1229) but was finally forced to surrender to the king of France, Philippe III, in 1272. The county of Foix passed into the domain of Albret, then submitted to Antoine de Bourbon and united with the realm of France under Henri IV's reign in 1589. The castle, built between the 11th and 15th centuries, is composed of three main towers enclosed by two walled enceintes.

Opposite: Chillon (Switzerland). Chillon castle is situated on a small rocky island on Lake Geneva, near Montreux canton of Vaud. Originating from a square donjon built by the bishop of Sion in the 11th century, the castle was rebuilt about 1150 by the counts of Savoy. Further enlargements happened in 1255 with walls, towers, a covered bridge, a palace called Fürstenberg, various service buildings and courtyards. Until the 16th century Chillon was one of the residences to the dukes of Savoy, then a prison. Today it is a historical monument.

Schattenburg in Feldkirch (Austria). The castle Schattenburg is situated in the town of Feldkirch on the river Ill in the Voralberg. The castle, constructed in the middle of the 12th century by the count Hugo von Montfort, is composed of a rectangular berchfrit and a palas (residence) as well as various buildings and towers later added. About 1500 the castle was adapted to firearms by the addition of an artillery bulwark. Looted and burnt by the Swedes during the Thirty Years' War (1618–1648), today Schattenburg is a restaurant and a museum.

Opposite: *Mariastein (Austria). The castle Mariastein is situated in Tyrol. Strategically placed on a hill dominating the river Inn, it was built about 1362 by the lord of Freundberger and yielded to the duke of Bavaria in 1379. The castle includes an imposing berchfrit (donjon) and various accommodations. Mariastein was a place of pilgrimage in the Middle Ages and today has been converted into a museum.*

161

Gutenberg (Liechtenstein). The small principality of Liechtenstein is situated on the right bank of the Rhine between Switzerland and Austria in the Voralberg mountains. The territory was formed in 1699 by the reunion of the domains Vaduz and Schellenberg. Annexed by Germany (1815–1866) then by Austria (1876–1918), Liechtenstein has been an independent state since 1924. The principality has two castles: Gutenberg, dominating the Rhine near the village Balzser, was built by the count of Fauenberg in the 13th century. The second castle, Schoßberg in the capital Vaduz, is the prince's residence.

Top right: *Riegersburg (Austria). The fortress Riegersburg was situated on a steep hill in the valley of the river Grazbach in the province Styria. Occupying a strategic position at the border with Hungary, the site has been fortified since the Celtic and Roman times. The actual fortress, one of the most powerful of Austria, was composed of the reunion of two 13th century castles, Liechtenegg and Kronegg. Often attacked by the Hungarians and the Turks, the Festung was adapted to firearms and enlarged in the 16th century. The fortress was turned into a residence in 1648; since 1822 Riegersburg castle has been the prince of Liechtenstein's property. Bottom right: Gutenfels castle (Germany). Gutenfels castle is situated near the village of Kaub in the Rhine valley, 35 km south of Coblence. Gutenfels castle was built in the first half of the 14th century by the lord of Falkenstein. It was a typical German mountain castle with a high bergfried dominating a crenellated dwelling house and a walled bailey.*

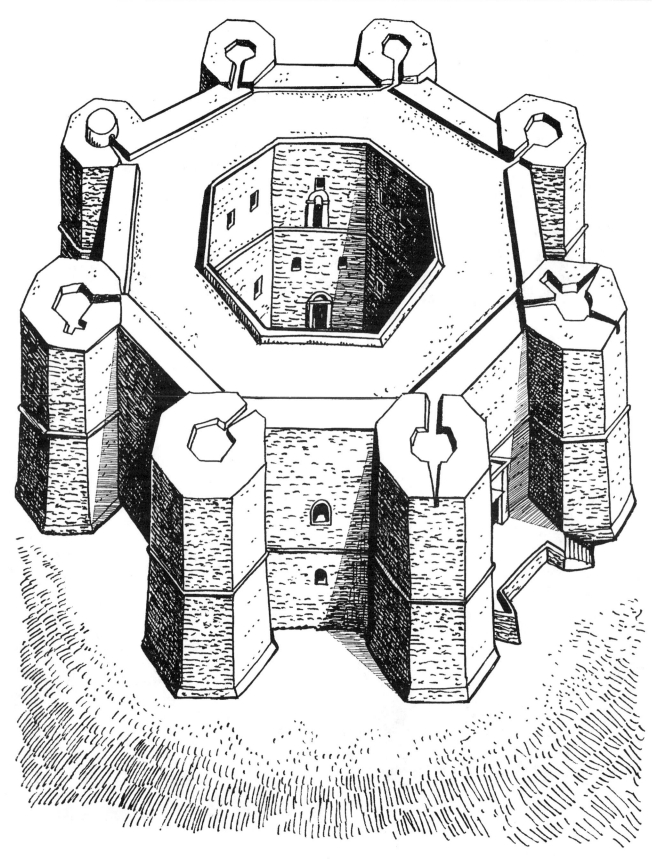

Castle Beersel (Belgium). The castle Beersel is situated south of Brussel in Brabant. It was erected between 1300 and 1310 as an oval work defended by a large lake. It was adapted to firearms in 1491 by the construction of three massive horseshoe-shaped artillery towers. The castle Beersel was profoundly transformed at the end of the 17th century and turned into a residence.

Opposite: *Castel del Monte (Italy). The Castel del Monte is situated south east of Barletta in Apulia. The fortress was built on a hill between 1240 and 1250 by the German emperor Friedrich II Hohenstaufen. Probably designed by the emperor himself, the castle is very original; deprived of donjon, it is a regular octagon with eight towers as high as the curtains (24 m) enclosing a small inner yard. Behind its imposing military appearance, Castel del Monte was a luxurious residence inspired by Arabian architecture, with a richly decorated hall, rooms and apartments, a portal in ancient style, and a cunning water supply.*

Helmond castle (Netherlands). The castle Helmond is situated east of Eindhoven in the province Northern-Brabant. Originating from an ancient work built in the beginning of the 13th century, the actual castle was constructed about 1400. It is a typical yard-castle with four curtains, four corner-towers and one gatehouse. From the 16th century onwards, the castle lost its military function and was turned into a residence. Note that because of the low ground level in the Netherlands, most Dutch and Flemish fortresses were fitted with a wide wet ditch—what the Dutch call a waterburcht.

Opposite: *Middelburg in Alkmaar (Netherlands). Alkmaar is situated north of Amsterdam in the province of Northern-Holland. The dynasty of Holland was founded by a warrior, Gerulf, who gained fame by successfully fighting against the Scandinavian Vikings, and who became the first count. From the 11th century onwards the counts of Holland, through an aggressive policy, achieved domination of the archipelago of Zeeland and the Frisian country. In 1256, they conquered the region of the river Amstel and its main town, Amsterdam, and established their capital in the Hague. Holland became the most significant political power in the Low-Countries in the 14th century. The castle of Alkmaar, built about 1287 by Count Floris V, was one of the strongholds intended to deter and repulse any Frisian aggression.*

Castle Ewssum (Netherlands). The waterburcht Ewssum was situated near the village Middelstum in the north of the province Groningen. The castle, built about 1278 by the local lord Ewe in den Oert, was the center of a small domain. Note the typical bulb roof and the special drawbridge, which were characteristic in northern Europe. In 1472, a low artillery tower was added by the lord Onno van Ewssum to provide shelter to firearms. Today the castle has disappeared and only the artillery tower remains in the middle of the wide wet ditch.

Windsor Castle (Britain). Windsor, situated west of London in the county of Berkshire, has been the royal residence since its creation in 1070 by William the Conqueror. In the Middle Ages many English monarchs contributed to its embellishment and enlargement: Henry II between 1165 and 1179, Henry III in the 13th century, Edward III in the 14th century and Henry VIII in 1511.

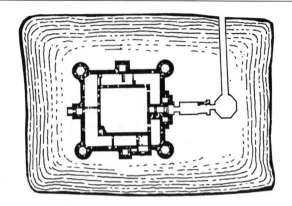

Ground-plan and view of the castle Bodiam (Britain). Bodiam, situated north of Hastings in Sussex, is a good example of military architecture at the end of the 14th century. The castle was built under the reign of King Richard II between 1385 and 1388 by Sir Edward Dalyngrigge. It was intended to defend the river Rother from French pirates. Regular and symmetrical, its conception was influenced by the castles Harlech and Beaumaris. It was a rectangle with walls 12 m high and 2 m thick, four corner-towers 18 m high and 9 m in diameter, and square wall-towers. Access was via a gatehouse and a barbican with drawbridges to cross the wide wet moat. Bodiam was a fortress but also a comfortable residence.

Caernarvon (Britain). Caernarvon, situated on the north coast of Wales, was a bastide created in 1283 by King Edward I, on an ancient Roman site called Segontium. Caernarvon castle, dominating the town, was completed in 1323 and was a citadel intended to control the boisterous Welsh. Profoundly modified in the 19th century, since that time the castle has housed the palace of the prince of Wales.

Guadamur (Spain). Castle Guadamur is situated about fifteen kilometers west of Toledo in Castilla. Retaken by the Christians in 1085, Guadamur constituted a strategic post overlooking the river Tago. The 30 m high Torre del Homenaje (donjon) forms the core of the castle to which two concentric quadrangular enceintes were added. In its present appearance, Guadamur is the result of arrangements made in the 15th and 16th century by the family López de Alaya. The castle was purchased in 1887 by the count of Asalto, Carlos Morenes y Tord. Damaged during the Spanish Civil War (1936–1939), Guadamur is today private property.

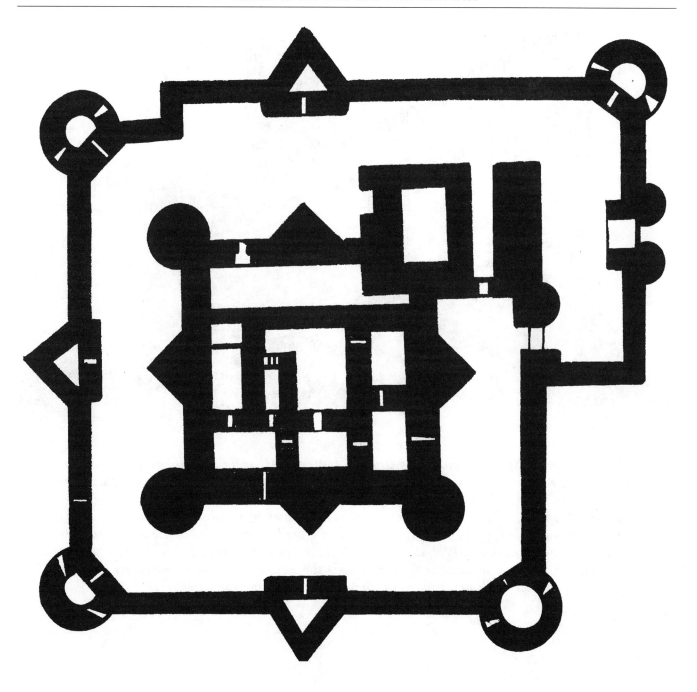

Ground-plan, castle Guadamur (Spain)

Castle Almansa (Spain). Almansa is situated between Albacete and Alicante in Castilla. An ancient Roman fortress and Moorish stronghold called Al Manxa, the castle was rebuilt by the Knights Templars in 1248. In 1310, it became the possession of the king of Castilla-Aragon, Jaime Alfonso I. The actual castle dates from modifications made at the end of the 14th century by King Enrique III of Castille-Leon. The fortress was threatened with destruction in 1919, but fortunately it was classified as an historical monument in 1921. Since then, restored and maintained, the castle Almansa proudly displays its square donjon, its walls and towers on the spur dominating the town.

Opposite: Alarcón (Spain). Alarcón is situated in a bend of the river Júcar south of Cuenca in Castilla. Probably founded by the son of the Visigoth king Alaric, the fortress was taken in 784 by the Moors and used as a stronghold by the chief Mohammed-el-Fehri. Alarcón was reconquered by King Alfonso VIII in 1184 and given to the military order of Santiago. Alarcón castle, rebuilt between 1194 and 1203 by the Knights Templar, includes a massive square donjon, external walls and a triangular bailey down the hill.

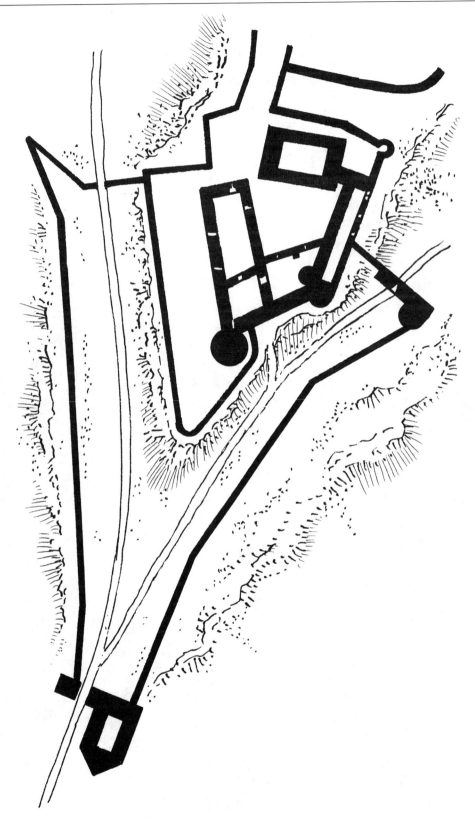

Ground-plan, castle Alarcón (Spain)

Estremoz (Portugal). Situated west of Elvas in province Alentejo, the town has kept its donjon from the 13th century and its bastioned enceinte from the 17th century.

4

TRANSITIONAL FORTIFICATIONS IN THE 15TH AND 16TH CENTURIES

GUNPOWDER AND EARLY GUNS

Gunpowder or black powder is composed of 10 percent charcoal, 15 percent sulfur and 75 percent saltpeter. The origin of this substance is totally unknown, but it seems that the Chinese were the first to use it—for fireworks and perhaps as a psychological weapon—in the 10th century. Gunpowder was brought into Europe by the Arabs, who had commercial contact with both the Far East and the West. The formula of gunpowder was mentioned for the first time in Europe in a book entitled *De Mirabili Potestate Artis et Naturae* (On the Marvelous Power of Art and Nature), written in 1242 by the English Franciscan monk Roger Bacon (1214–1294).

Who first used the substance to propel a missile, and when and where, is completely unknown. The first illustration depicting a weapon that looks unquestionably like a primitive gun is to be seen in a book entitled *De Officiis Regnum*, written in 1325 by Walter de Milimete, chaplain to the English king Edward III. However curious and primitive this pictured gun may appear, it nevertheless presents the main basic features of all guns until the second half of the 19th century.

A gun is composed of a metal tube or barrel (the inside of the tube is called the bore), closed at one end (called the breech), in which the explosion of the propelling charge happens. The charge is ignited through a small hole, the vent. The other end of the bore is open and called the muzzle. Until the last half of the 19th century, guns were loaded through the muzzle, and of course it is from the muzzle that the projectile is expelled. The

tube is mounted on a carriage for stability, aiming and transport. The explosion of gunpowder produces a tremendously strong thrust with loud noise and heavy smoke composed of hot toxic gas. Powder gives a source of energy thousands times stronger than that of human muscular force.

With the coming of gunpowder and artillery, a new and irreversible kind of warfare was introduced. Firearms begin to appear in Europe in the 14th century. As early as 1304 reports of their use were made in Lombardy; in Florence in 1315; in Rouen in 1338. In 1343, the Moors employed guns at the siege of Algesiras, and tradition holds that the first battle featuring artillery was Crécy on 26 August 1346.

The main advantage of those primitive weapons was the dramatic and terrifying effect caused by noise, flames and smoke. In fact, they were often more dangerous for the gunner himself than for the intended target. Technical difficulties were worsened by the fact that firearms were regarded as devilish weapons in complete opposition with the chivalric ideal of gallantry. Captive early gunners were sometimes put to death as criminals breaking the traditional laws of war. Another reason firearms were frowned upon was lack of profit: Firearms were more lethal than conventional weapons of the time, and a dead enemy was worth only the price of his armor and possessions, while a live prisoner was a potential source of ransom money.

The technical troubles with early cannons were numerous. They were subject to incidental explosion because they were built by assembling longitudinal bars of metal and binding them with hoops, a technique based on the system used in cooperage. The projectile had to be round as possible so as to fit the bore as perfectly as existing technology would permit: Too large and the shot either refused to enter the muzzle or jammed on firing and exploded the piece; too small and it lost range and accuracy. Gun bores were not standardized, so each gun needed its own adapted ammunitions. Range was poor—not superior to that of traditional hurling machines—and gunners were exposed to enemy arrows and bolts, therefore they had to be sheltered behind mantlets. The contemporary gunpowder was weak stuff, with a low grade of purity and much uncertainty of action. The substance, if ground and mixed before use, gradually sifted all the grains back into three layers of saltpeter, charcoal and sulfur. Early artillerymen preferred to transport the three dry ingredients separately and mix them on arrival in the siege or in the battlefield—not an easy task on a wet day, and positively hazardous and highly dangerous in combat conditions. Early cannons big enough to do damage to castle walls at a safe distance were heavy, cumbersome and not fitted with wheels; they had to be transported on wagons and erected in position on timber-framed beds, resulting in poor maneuverability. The rate of fire was low because of the dangerous, complicated and time-consuming loading procedure. Some unknown early gunners experimented with breech-loading by using a removable loaded breech-piece, but due to loss of propelling gas, this method was not very successful and thus not widely used until the second half of the 19th century. Before then, the majority of European guns were smoothbore brass muzzle-loaders.

Anyone can imagine the chances taken in transporting and manipulating dangerous substances like gunpowder as well as putting into action primitive and not always reliable guns. Tragic accidents were common; the weapons were already dangerous in exercises, and the problems were even worse in the middle of the stress of a battle. Obviously, artillery crews had to be courageous, cool and collected, well drilled and disciplined.

The successive steps of loading the gun were carefully carried out on a gun-commander's order. The propelling gunpowder (carried in kegs) was poured into the barrel with a long-hafted spoon and pushed down with a ramrod. Next, a gunner drove the cannonball into the bore with a wooden rammer. The projectile was wrapped in a wad (old cloths, paper, mud, grass or hay) to avoid gas dispersion and to keep the round shot from rolling out.

Once the piece was loaded, it had to be aimed. This happened horizontally by manually moving the gun to the right or to the left with heavy handspikes and vertically by adjusting one or more wooden wedges (called coins) under the breech. Aiming was done by direct sight or with the help of primitive instruments, but accuracy was poor, especially in the case of a moving target. Ignition of the propelling charge was accomplished with a linstock brought close to the ignition vent pierced in the upper side of the gun. Flashing through the vent, fire ignited the gunpowder charge, which exploded, expelling the shot with flames, an awful noise and such violence that the gun brusquely moved backwards. This sudden movement, called recoil, made reaiming necessary. Firing also produced toxic, bad-smelling clouds of smoke which soon hung thickly over batteries and obscured gunners' view on windless days. Right after every shot the barrel had to be scraped with a spiral (a sort of large corkscrew fixed on a staff) to remove fouling, and swabbed out with a wet sponge attached on a wooden staff in order to extinguish all burning residues of wad.

Because of the slowness of loading, aiming and cleaning, the rate of fire was rather low: ten to twenty shots per hour depending upon the caliber of both gun and crew. Moreover, after a while the gun began to get overheated, and it was necessary to cool down the barrel with water or with wet sheep-skins or stop firing. Otherwise, the gun could get damaged with cracks and even explode, with disastrous consequences for the crew.

The range (distance between the gun and its target) depended on the quantity of propelling charge, the weight of the cannonball and the type of the gun. To make a breach in a fortification wall, close range fire of 50 m (or even less if possible) was required. Cannons shot direct fire in a flat trajectory with a grazing angle of 5 to 15°.

THE DEVELOPMENT AND INFLUENCE OF FIREARMS

After countless unsuccessful experiments, lethal accidents and ineffective trials, firearms research and techniques gradually improved, and chroniclers report many types of guns—mainly used in siege warfare—with numerous names such as veuglaire, pot-de-fer, bombard, vasii, petara and so on. In the second half of the 14th century, firearms became more efficient, and it seemed obvious that cannons were the weapons of the future. Venice successfully utilized cannons against Genoa in 1378. During the Hussite war from 1415 to 1436, the Czech Hussite rebels employed firearms in combination with a mobile tactic of armored carts (wagenburg) enabling them to defeat German knights. Firearms contributed to the end of the Hundred Years' War and allowed the French king Charles VII to defeat the English in Auray in 1385, Rouen in 1418 and Orléans in 1429. Normandy was reconquered in 1449 and Guyenne in 1451. Finally, the battle of Châtillon in 1453 was won by the French artillery. This marked the end of the Hundred Years' War; the

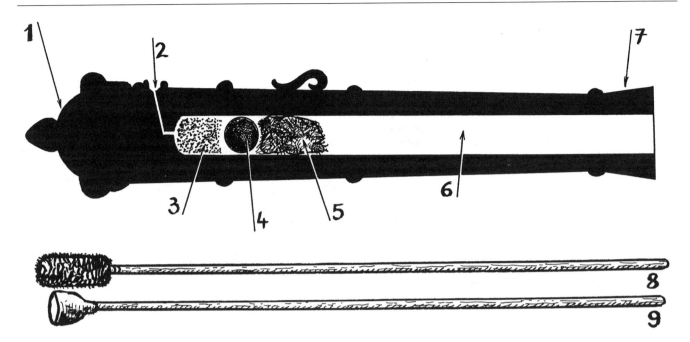

Cross-section of a loaded gun ready to fire: (1) breech (2) vent (3) powder, propelling charge (4) shot (5) wad (6) smooth bore (7) muzzle (8) cleaning sponge (9) rammer

Bombarde

English, divided by the Wars of the Roses, were driven out of France, keeping only Calais. The same year saw the Turks taking Constantinople, which provoked consternation, agitation and excitement in the whole Christian world.

In that siege and seizure of the capital of the Eastern Roman empire, cannon and gunpowder achieved spectacular success. To breach the city walls, the Turks utilized heavy cannons which, if we believe the chronicler Critobulos of Imbros, shot projectiles weighing about

500 kg. Even if this is exaggerated, big cannons certainly did exist by that time and were more common in the East than in the West, doubtless because the mighty potentates of the East could better afford them. Such monsters included the Ghent bombard, called "Dulle Griet"; the large cannon "Mons Berg" which is today in Edinburgh; and the Great Gun of Mohammed II, exhibited today in London. The latter, cast in 1464 by Sultan Munir Ali, weighed 18 tons and could shoot a 300 kg stone ball to a range of one kilometer.

A certain number of technical improvements took place in the 15th century. One major step was the amelioration of powder quality. Invented about 1425, corned powder involved mixing saltpeter, charcoal and sulphur into a soggy paste, then sieving and drying it, so that each individual grain or corn contained the same and correct proportion of ingredients. The process obviated the need for mixing in the field. It also resulted in more efficient combustion, thus improving safety, power, range and accuracy.

Another important step was the development of foundries, allowing cannons to be cast in one piece in iron and bronze (copper alloyed with tin). In spite of its expense, casting was the best method to produce practical and resilient weapons with lighter weight and higher muzzle velocity. In about 1460, guns were fitted with trunnions. These were cast on both sides of the barrel and made sufficiently strong to carry the weight and bear the shock of discharge, and permit the piece to rest on a two-wheeled wooden carriage. Trunnions and wheeled mounting not only made for easier transportation and better maneuverability but also allowed the gunners to raise and lower the barrels of their pieces.

One major improvement was the introduction in about 1418 of a very efficient projectile: the solid iron shot. Coming into use gradually, the solid iron cannonball could destroy medieval crenellation, ram castle-gates, and collapse towers and masonry walls. It broke through roofs, made its way through several stories and crushed to pieces all it fell upon. One single well-aimed projectile could mow down a whole row of soldiers or cut down a splendid armored knight.

About 1460, mortars were invented. A mortar is a specific kind of gun whose projectile is shot with a high, curved trajectory, between 45° and 75°, called plunging fire. Allowing gunners to lob projectiles over high walls and reach concealed objectives or targets protected behind fortifications, mortars were particularly useful in sieges. In the Middle Ages they were characterized by a short and fat bore and two big trunnions. They rested on massive timber-framed carriages without wheels, which helped them withstand the shock of firing; the recoil force was passed directly to the ground by means of the carriage. Owing to such ameliorations, artillery progressively gained dominance, particularly in siege warfare.

Individual guns, essentially scaled down artillery pieces fitted with handles for the firer, appeared after the middle of the 14th century. Various models of portable small arms were developed, such as the clopi or scopette, bombardelle, bâton-de-feu, handgun, and firestick, to mention just a few.

In purely military terms, these early handguns were more of a hindrance than an asset on the battlefield, for they were expensive to produce, inaccurate, heavy, and time-consuming to load; during loading the firer was virtually defenseless. However, even as rudimentary weapons with poor range, they were effective in their way, as much for attackers as for soldiers defending a fortress.

The harquebus was a portable gun fitted with a hook that absorbed the recoil force when firing from a battlement. It was generally operated by two men, one aiming and the other igniting the propelling charge. This weapon evolved in the Renaissance to become the matchlock-musket in which the fire mechanism consisted of a pivoting S-shaped arm. The upper part of the arm gripped a length of rope impregnated with a combustible substance and kept alight at one end, called the match. The lower end of the arm served as a trigger: When pressed it brought the glowing tip of the match into contact with a small quantity of gunpowder, which lay in a horizontal pan fixed beneath a small vent in the side of the barrel at its breech. When this priming ignited, its flash passed through the vent and ignited the main charge in the barrel, expelling the spherical lead bullet.

The wheel lock pistol was a small harquebus taking its name from the city Pistoia in Tuscany where the weapon was first built in the 15th century. The wheel lock system, working on the principle of a modern cigarette lighter, was reliable and easy to handle, especially for a combatant on horseback. But its mechanism was complicated and therefore expensive, and so its use was reserved for wealthy civilian hunters, rich soldiers and certain mounted troops.

Portable cannons, handguns, harquebuses and pistols were muzzle-loading and shot projectiles that could easily penetrate any armor. Because of the power of firearms, traditional Middle Age weaponry become obsolete; gradually, lances, shields and armor for both men and horses were abandoned.

The destructive power of gunpowder allowed the use of mines in siege warfare. The role of artillery and small firearms become progressively larger; the new weapons changed the nature of naval and siege warfare and transformed the physiognomy of the battlefield. This change was not a sudden revolution, however, but a slow process. Many years elapsed before firearms became widespread, and many traditional medieval weapons were still used in the 16th century.

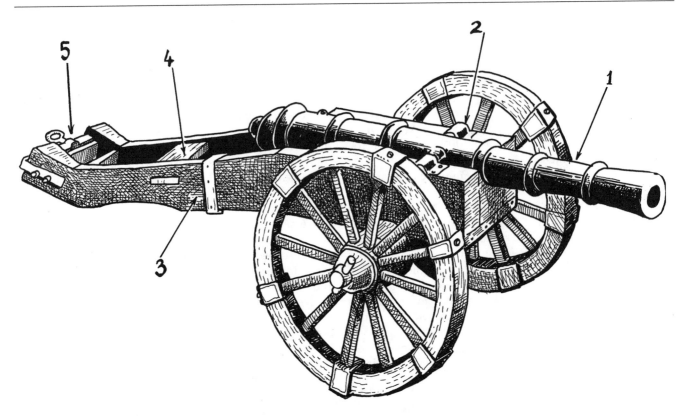

View of a gun. A piece of artillery is composed of two main parts. The gun (1) is fitted with trunnions (2) allowing it to be fixed firmly on a strong timber carriage composed of two cheeks (3) linked by cross-bars (4), fitted with a cross (5) and a hook, and two heavy wheels with axle-tree for transport. This kind of field gun did not undergo major change until the second half of the 19th century.

One factor militating against artillery's advancement in the 15th century was the amount of expensive material necessary to equip an army. Cannons and powder were very costly items and also demanded a retinue of expensive attendant specialists for design, transport and operation. Consequently firearms had to be produced in peacetime, and since the Middle Ages

Italian culverin. Dating from the latter half of the 15th century, this gun displayed an interesting mounting, complete with a system of regulating elevation.

Aiming the gun. The illustration shows German Landsknechten aiming their heavy gun with a handspike in the end of the 15th century.

had rudimentary ideas of economics and fiscal science, only a few kings, dukes and high prelates possessed the financial resources to build, purchase, transport, maintain and use such expensive equipment in numbers that would have an appreciable impression in war.

Conflicts with firearms became an economic business involving qualified personnel backed up by traders, financiers and bankers as well as the creation of comprehensive industrial structures. The development of firearms meant the gradual end of feudalism. Firearms also brought about a change in the mentality of combat because they created a physical and mental distance between warriors. Traditional mounted knights, fighting

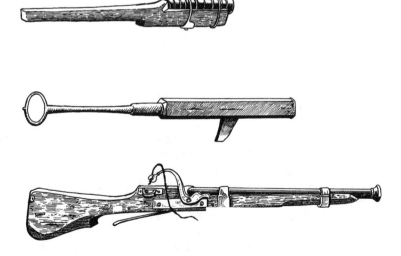

Evolution of small arms. Top: handgun, about 1400. Middle: harquebus from the 15th century. Bottom: match-lock harquebus, about 1500.

Handgun. While aiming, the shooter ignites the propelling charge with a glowing match. The weapon would rest on a pavis or on a parapet.

each other at close range within the rules of a certain code, were progressively replaced by professional infantrymen who were anonymous targets for one another, while local rebellious castles collapsed under royal artillery's fire. Expensive artillery helped to hasten the process by which central authority was restored.

SIEGE WARFARE WITH FIREARMS

At the end of the Middle Ages, guns and portable firearms progressively played a more and more important role. Though primitive and unreliable, these new weapons were far more effective and less cumbersome than ancient medieval hurling machines. Siege warfare was now dominated by the deadly clash of artillery, unless a small and stealthy commando party could infiltrate and open the portal to the rest of their comrades. (Everything previously said about treason, blockade and psychological siege-warfare is of course still applicable.)

In the actual storming of a place, the advantages of firearms lay with the defenders. The attacker up on a scaling ladder was in no positio₁ to reload his weapon once he had discharged it, while one marksman behind the battlements could keep firing away as fast as comrades could reload and hand fresh weapons to him. In the meantime, cannons placed in the castle towers could smash belfries, battering rams and tortoises. If the besiegers did gain a foothold on the wall-walk, they could be swept from it by a single charge of grapeshot or langrage (small balls, nails and miscellaneous hardware forming a sort of shrapnel).

Firearms, then, obliged the assailing party to develop methods of shielding their attacking forces and concealing them from view. They improvised by using earthworks as temporary fortifications, concealing themselves behind masses of earth working as shields or breastworks, or placing their artillery in trenches. The useful range of siege-cannons being about fifty meters, attacking methods consisted of bringing artillery as close as possible to the defensive walls by digging a network of trenches to which zigzag patterns were given in order to avoid enfilade fire. These earthworks were made by

Rampart harquebus

civilians and peasants of the neighborhood, who were arbitrarily rounded up because men-of-arms (until the 17th century) would feel dishonored to handle shovels, picks and wheelbarrows.

Siege warfare was commonly led in an unskillful and clumsy way. Because of careless and foolhardy leaders, ill-disciplined soldiers and lack of systematic methods, siege operations cost many lives; engineering officers and workers were particularly exposed. Success was generally achieved more through the defenders' weakness than through the besiegers' merit.

The first phase of the siege was an artillery duel. Besiegers arranged their guns in batteries. They bombarded the defenders deployed on towers and on walls. Mortars launched bombs (explosive devices), carcasses (incendiary projectiles) and shrapnel. Mortar-gunners tried to smash food and water storage and powder-magazines whose destruction would hasten the defenders' decline. They also fired at random to create panic and terror by blind destruction.

Batteries were installed on "cavaliers" (also called cats), artificial earth embankments raised above ground level, in order to have a dominating firing position. They could also be sunken by being placed in a trench. If necessary, siege guns were installed on wooden platforms made of thick planks resting on beams to avoid sinking in loose ground. Guns were sheltered behind earth embankments, palisades, fascines and gabions. Fascines were large cylindrical bundles of brushwood used to hold back the earth of a parapet, to strengthen a trench or to fill up a moat. Fascines could also be laid together on a wooden frame (called a chandelier) to make a sort of wall that protected the besiegers during sapping operations. A gabion, also called a corbeil, was an open-ended cylindrical basket made of poles and woven brushwood. Gabions were widely used in fieldworks until the end of the 19th century. They were put in rows and filled with earth to form a protective screen, to revet or reinforce the sides of excavations.

The defenders riposted with counter-fire aiming at workers and batteries. They could also launch a surprise counter-attack to disorganize the besiegers and drive them back. As ever, sorties and counter-attacks were quite important for the morale of the defenders; the psychological benefit could even turn the tide of the siege.

Batteries of the besiegers were linked together by trenches and communication saps in order to supply them with men and ammunitions. Fortlets and redoubts were built to serve as supply-magazines, regrouping points, command posts or field hospitals. In the thunder of explosions and the thick smoke clouds, the approach sector was aswarm with activity, the coming and going of workers and suppliers and the bringing of dead and wounded who were evacuated while fresh troops moved onto lines. This zone could become a bloody battlefield when the besieged launched a counter-attack.

As always, the aggressor had to make a breach to penetrate the location by force. To do so, two standard methods were used. The first one consisted of grouping guns in a breach-battery, which meant concentrating a number of guns on one section of the wall and delivering an uninterrupted series of hammering blows until the stone-work collapsed. The second method, possible only if the nature of the ground was favorable, consisted of digging a mine, that is, an underground tunnel under the city or castle walls. In this mine the besiegers would place kegs of gunpowder. The explosion of the powder would blast away a part of the solid wall. In reaction, the defenders might dig a counter-mine, tunneling under or alongside the attackers' work, entombing and sealing the mine.

Mines were more and more frequently employed for breaching walls, so much so that in the terminology of war, a mine eventually came to be regarded as the explosive device rather than the tunnel in which it was laid. Mines were reported in Orense in 1468, in Malaga and Sarzanello in 1487, in Naples in 1503, and in Padua in 1509. A specialized refinement of the explosive mine was the petard, a conical metal cask filled with gunpowder ignited by a fuse used to blow up gates, doors or sally ports.

Once the breach was made, foot soldiers would storm in and fight in bitter hand-to-hand combat in the smoking ruins. This assault could be more difficult if the defenders had had time to construct a temporary work, called a lodgement or retirade, to seal the breach from inside, or if they decided to continue to fight in the castle-donjon or in the urban citadel. As previously mentioned, the final assault was a crucial confrontation for both parties and the turning point of the siege. A repulsed assault cost a lot of casualties and might result in the collapse of the attacking party. On the other hand, a successful assault might result in pillage, rape, destruction, fire, and the massacre of the defenders. To avoid either catastrophe, a party might choose to negotiate an honorable capitulation.

TRANSITIONAL FORTIFICATIONS

In the 15th century, vertical medieval military architecture entered into a progressive crisis. High walls and huge towers intended to be impassible obstacles become vulnerable targets. However, it is important to repeat here a point mentioned previously, that changes brought by the use of artillery did not strike like a sudden revolution but constituted a gradual evolution. The remarkable castles, urban enceintes and citadels of the 13th and 14th centuries did not become obsolete overnight. Thick masonry, high walls and huge towers were targets for only those few attackers—kings and dukes—who were rich enough to afford a powerful artillery. The invention of gunpowder and artillery in no way diminished the role of medieval castles, citadels and fortified cities as strongholds, bases for operations, quarters for troops, armories and supply stores.

Nevertheless, it was obvious that castle-builders had to do something. It was proving impossible to meet the needs of artillery warfare with immediate and efficient solutions, partly because of the lack of experience and partly because of traditionalism and conservatism. Master-builders' theoretical considerations and practical realizations in the second half of the 15th century were essentially aimed at adapting and modernizing preexisting fortresses. So-called transitional fortification (between the medieval vertical system and the horizontal bastioned system) developed without basic principles or clearly defined theory, each stronghold being individually adapted to firearms as far as its design would allow. Transitional fortification, covering approximatively the period from 1450 to 1530, tried to reconcile two essential demands: to resist the destructive effects of heavy artillery and hand-held guns by passive means, and to allow for the most efficient use of defensive firearms with active elements.

Passive Elements

To resist artillery, castle builders did their best to improve the quality of masonry, and their first reaction was to increase the thickness of existing works. The walls of the Dicke Turm in the castle of Friedberg (Hesse in Germany) are 5.70 m thick, those of the Dicke Zwingen tower in the castle of Goslar (Germany) 6.50 m, and those of the Navarre tower in the enceinte of Langres (France) 7 m. The Kaiserturm in the castle of Kufstein (Tyrol in Austria), built between 1518 and 1522, is an impressive four-story tower with 7.40 m thick walls. In the château of Ham (Somme in France), the walls of the Tour du Connétable, erected in 1480, are 11 m thick at

Siege devices. Top: fascines. *Middle:* frizzy horse. *Right:* gabion

ground level. The Spanish fort of Salses (near Perpignan in southern France) was built between 1497 and 1504; its walls were 10 m thick, and after the siege of 1503, they were enlarged to the incredible thickness of 14 m.

The tendency to increase thickness was, however, not new. To resist battering ram and undermining, some previous works had impressive dimensions. The walls of the Constance tower in Aigues-Mortes (southern France), completed about 1250, measured 6 m thick. Those of the donjon Largoët-en-Elven (Brittany in France), improved about 1390, were 6 m thick on the top and 10 m at the base.

This solution seemed logical, but in practice its effectiveness was questionable. Those masoned carapaces were extremely expensive and of dubious efficiency. Indeed, the thick-walled fortresses were blind and deaf enclosures that could not easily be fitted with active defense elements and living accommodations.

To increase the thickness of walls a new method was created: the rampart. A rampart was composed of a thick layer of earth heaped up between an ancient wall and a new rear wall. This disposition was relatively cheap and very efficient; earth was readily available, and its smothering elasticity allowed it to absorb the shock of cannonballs just like a cushion. Moreover, the rampart was rather wide, allowing the placement of defensive artillery pieces. The invention of the rampart was very important;

in fact, the rampart became one of the basic features of subsequent bastioned fortification.

Guns shoot with a grazing trajectory, which means that the projectile follows a horizontal course. It was therefore possible to defend vast spaces around a fortress provided that no house or vegetation stood in the way. The vicinity of the stronghold had to be bare and flat. This wide stroke of land around a fortress is called the glacis.

Analyzing the principle of grazing fire, castle builders came to the conclusion that height was a mixed blessing. High curtains and elevated towers were convenient targets for enemy gunners. To diminish exposed surfaces and to maximize grazing fire, master-builders began to reduce the height of the works. Towers were cut down to the same level as the curtains and ramparts. To keep the place inaccessible, ditches were made deeper. Reduction of wall height and increase of moat depth resulted in a half-sunken fortification, another characteristic of later bastioned fortification.

Another method of opposing cannonballs was to give parapets, merlons, battlements, walls and towers rounded angles, oblique faces, curved outlines, and receding and streamlined surfaces in order to deviate enemy projectiles. This tendency to use curved surfaces and cylindrical towers was not new; its origins are evident in 12th century donjons.

Siege battery. A battery is several guns of the same kind firing in the same direction, towards a common target.

Active Gun Emplacements

To utilize firearms defensively, master-builders brought adaptations and improvements to existing castles, citadels and urban enceintes. They made a distinction between small arms and heavy cannons.

Traditional arrow loopholes and crossbow crosslets were numerous in previously built castles, but they were narrow and thus unsuitable for small arms, portable guns, pistols, harquebuses and other long-barreled musket-type weapons. To allow the discharge of those firearms, loopholes and crosslets were adapted. The adaptation usually took the form of a round hole at the base

or in the middle of the arrow-slit, which became known as a cross-and-orb. This rudimentary adaptation allowed for the use of both firearms and bows—necessary because both sorts of weapon remained in the late-medieval arsenal. Over time, however, shooting openings developed for the exclusive use of firearms, and vertical splits were reduced in size or even omitted. In ground-plans, shooting openings widened out or were given an X-shaped plan to increase traverse. For larger artillery the firing chambers were opened out into full-scale embrasures. Blocked with wooden shutters when not in use, the inward part had to be made splayed very wide, to enable gunners to move their weapons laterally.

Active elements for heavy cannons posed complex

Opposite: View of a siege in the 16th century

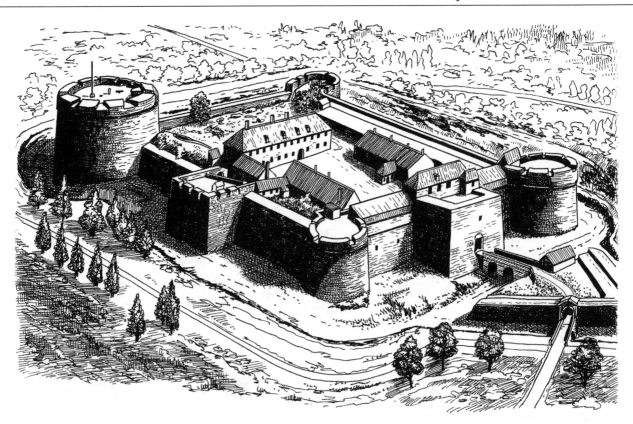

Castle Ham (France). Castle Ham, situated near Péronne in the Somme, was completed by 1480. Adapted to firearms, it was a regular rectangle characterized by a deep ditch, low and thick walls, massive casemated artillery towers and a huge donjon called the Tour du Connétable with walls 11 m thick. The fortress was still in military use in the 17th century and became a state prison in the 19th century. The most famous prisoner was prince Louis-Napoléon Bonaparte (the future emperor Napoléon III), who managed to escape in 1846. The fort of Ham was destroyed by the Germans in 1917.

problems and demanded structural arrangements. A large gun was heavy and cumbersome and required a rather large emplacement that not only provided enough room for ammunition and accessories, but also allowed freedom of movement for muzzle loading and accommodated the recoil force of the gun. Release of toxic smoke was also a problem, and gun emplacements had to be easily accessible for supply purposes. Obviously not all citadel, town or castle combat emplacements were suitable for mounting cannon. The curtain wall-walk might be too narrow to permit safe recoil, or tower floors might be too weak to bear the considerable weight, or the stoutest roofed and easily strengthened part of the building might not command a good field of fire. For these reasons and more, new and suitable artillery emplacements had to be created.

The question was, where to do so? Not all towers could be cut down (those for example serving as living accommodations, or those made necessary by high ground in the vicinity), and transforming a wall into a rampart was sometimes impossible because of lack of space inside the stronghold. In many cases such problems resulted in the creation of artillery emplacements outside the place in gun platforms called bulwarks.

The term bulwark is a corruption of the Dutch word *bolwerk*, which originally meant an earth entrenchment. Called boulevard in French, bollwerk in German and balovardo in Italian, the bulwark might be either an earth rampart or a masoned wall around the whole ancient medieval enceinte, or a simple entrenchment reinforcing a vulnerable point. In whatever material, shape, size and dimension, it presented many advantages. Its dimensions were calculated for the placement, supply and firing of artillery. Situated outside the enceinte, the bulwark created an additional line of defense and increased the range of the guns. Its profile was generally low in order to maximize grazing fire. It offered space where the besieged might regroup for withdrawal or a sally. It worked as a shield protecting the escarp of the main enceinte, and it put the inside of the castle—or the suburb of a city—out of range of enemy artillery. The bulwark was relatively cheap to build if constituted of rampart (thin masonry retaining thick earth).

When urban fortifications were dismantled in a later period, the bulwark got its modern meaning: It was turned into a boulevard or an avenue, a wide lane with trees alongside.

The bulwark might also be an ancient tower that had been lowered, or a totally new work constructed to reinforce a weak part of the wall. In that case the bulwark was a low, strongly masoned artillery tower. This work was occasionally circular but more often U-shaped, and projecting in order to flank curtain and ditch. It was called a roundel, rondelle, Bastei or basteja in northern Europe, bastillon in France and torrionne in Italy. Its summit was arranged as a platform with gun embrasures and sometimes fitted with crenellation and machicolation (reflecting the strength of earlier medieval traditions).

The artillery tower included one or more stories fitted with flanking casemates. A casemate was a vaulted, closed gun-chamber pierced with a firing embrasure. It gave an excellent protection to guns, gunners and ammunition, but the

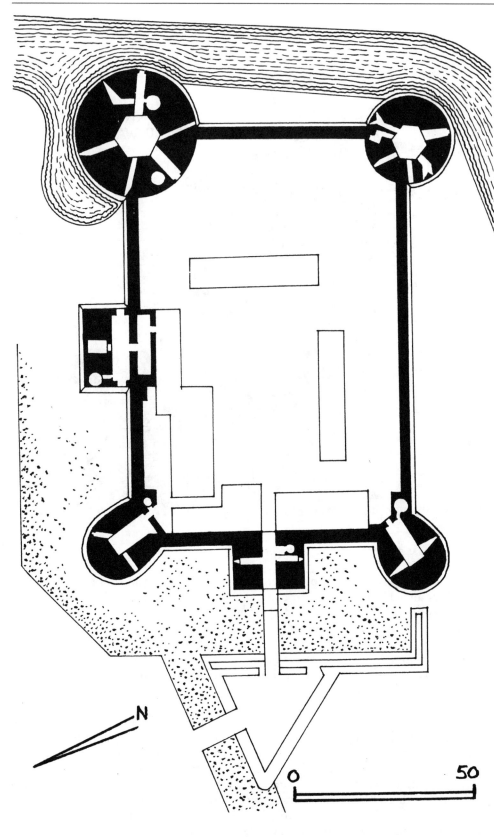

Ground-plan, castle Ham (France)

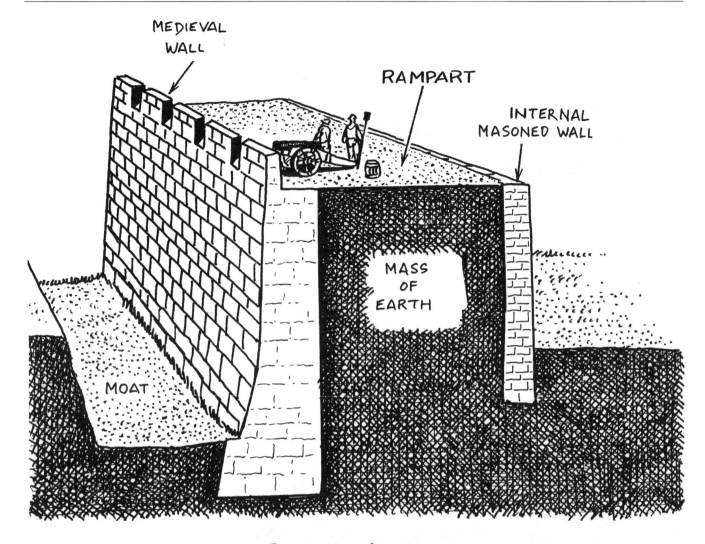

Cross-section of a rampart

thickness of its wall might allow only limited observation and a reduced field of fire—a problem compounded by the fact that the roundish shape of the 15th century artillery tower left blind spots at its foot. The major drawback of the casemate, however, was ventilation. In spite of aeration via drafts, chimneys, vents and shafts, after a few shots the chamber was full of choking smoke. In peacetime, the casemate was generally an obscure, humid, musty, drafty and unhealthy place.

For a better flanking of the ditch, master-builders of the transition time designed two special works: the fausse-braie and the caponier. The fausse-braie was a kind of low bulwark, an under-wall constructed outside and alongside of the main enceinte, generally between two towers. It was often open and fitted with embrasures.

The caponier, also called moineau, was a small, low-profiled work running at right angles across a dry moat.

It projected from the foot of a wall or a tower and was usually concealed by the counter-scarp. The caponier usually included only one story, with closed, vaulted casemates fitted with small firing-holes through which musketry fire could be directed against any enemy crawling about at the very bottom of the wall. The work might be continued across the moat up to the counter-scarp to form a covered passage. Widely used in the second half of the 15th century (Bonaguil, Blaye, Toulon, Bayonne and Rhodes, for example), the caponier was still used in the bastioned system and became the main flanking element in the 19th century polygonal fortification.

The entrance to a town or a castle was also influenced by the new weaponry. Gatehouses were fitted with embrasures, arrow-splits were modified, bastilles and barbicans were adapted to firearms. The 15th century barbican tended to be a powerful bulwark, a formidable artillery tower with strong masonry, ramparted walls,

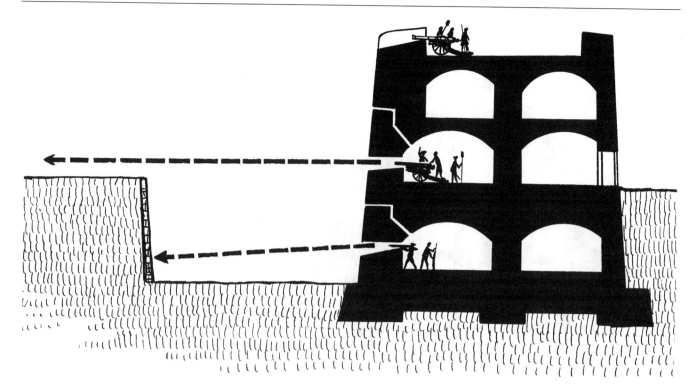

Schematic view of grazing fire and glacis

terre-plein fitted with gun emplacements behind thick parapets, and stories furnished with gun casemates. The barbican's shape varied, but it was often a huge U-shaped work projecting into the moat ahead of the gatehouse. As medieval traditions still remained strong, the work was commonly fitted with machicolation and crenellation. Numerous examples can still be seen, such as castle Montreuil-Bellay (Maine-et-Loire in France), Ranrouet (Loire-Atlantique in France) or Elburg (in the Netherlands) to mention just a few.

The barbican was always open in its gorge (the side toward the gatehouse) so that if it was taken, the invaders were exposed to the defenders' fire. The barbican allowed a withdrawing or sallying party to regroup. It was always surrounded by its own outer ditch and fitted with its own drawbridge.

Active and passive elements of transition fortification were added to existing works, resulting in arrangement, adaptation, and even amputation and destruction of ancient parts. In many cases, modifications, modernization and mutilations complicate the dating of these structures today. It is not uncommon to see an 11th century motte with a 12th century masonry donjon, hemmed with 13th century outer walls with towers equipped with 14th century machicolation, to which are added 15th century gun-holes and bulwarks and 16th century bastions.

ARTILLERY FORTIFICATIONS IN THE EARLY 16TH CENTURY

From the end of the 14th century onwards, the art of war and fortification became a popular subject for study. Treatises, guidebooks, and manuals were written and spread widely through a revolutionary method: printing with movable type. Invented in the mid–14th century by Johann Gutenberg in Mainz, Germany, printing came rapidly into use throughout Europe. Great names of the Renaissance are not only artists and architects, but also early military theorists developing fortifications entirely adapted to firearms.

Leonardo da Vinci (1452–1519) was a painter, sculptor, architect, engineer, and scientist involved in anatomy, botany, geology, mechanical engineering, armaments and fortifications. In 1483, he entered the service of the duke of Milan, Louis-Maria Sforza (nicknamed Ludovic the Moor), and worked for him as civil architect and military advisor until 1499. Leonardo designed weapons (giant crossbows, steam-guns, machine guns, mortars, breech-loading guns) as well as military engineering devices (an assault bridge, a wooden armored vehicle, a submarine and even a parachute). He studied ballistics and made many theoretical designs of fortresses, including round forts with several rows of casemates, caponiers,

193

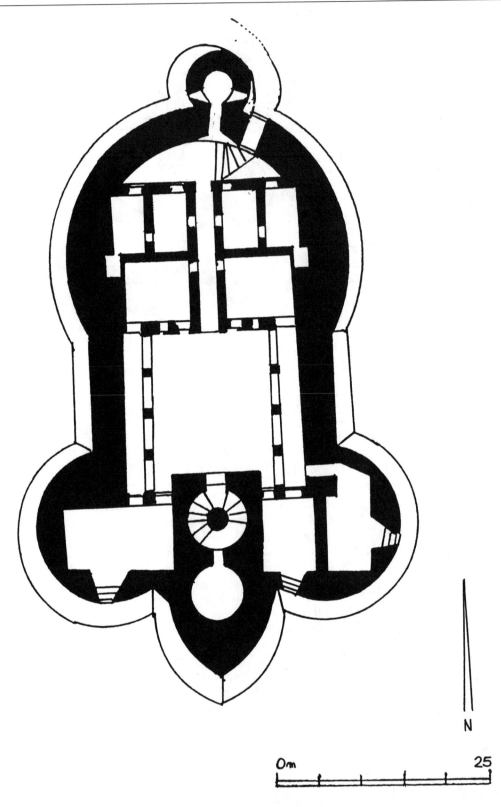

and ravelins with rounded parapets.

Between 1502 and 1504, Leonardo was engaged by the republic of Florence as military counselor. He participated in the construction of the castle Imola in 1502, the fortress La Verruca in 1503, the fortifications of Piombino in 1504 and the castle of Milan between 1506 and 1513. From 1515 until his death in 1519, he was in the service of the king of France, François I.

Francesco di Giorgio Martini (1439–1502) of Sienna was a civilian architect and an early theorist of fortification. In 1480, he published a treatise on that subject titled "Trattati dell'architectura ingegneria e arte militare" ("Treatise on Architectural Engineering and the Military Art") in which he presented interesting forms for forts and experimental shapes for towers, donjons and caponiers in order to improve flanking. From 1480 to 1486, the creative Giorgio Martini was in the service of the condottiere-duke Federico di Montefeltro, for whom he designed a palace and fortifications in Urbino. Francesco di Giorgio Martini participated in the construction of the fortress rocca of Mondavio, completed in 1492. In 1494, he entered the service of king of Naples and Sicily, Alphonso II, and designed fortifications in Naples.

N

0m   25

Ground-plan, castle Sassocorvato (Italy). The roundish castle Sassocorvato, situated near Urbino, was completed about 1474.

Castle Rambures (France). Castle Rambures in the Somme, completed about 1470, is composed of four circular towers and round curtains.

More than by his realizations, which are rather classical and traditional, Giorgio Martini is important for the influence of his theoretical work.

Painter, sculptor and architect Michelango Buonarotti (1475–1564) is a major figure in the history of art. To make a living, Michelangelo was engaged as military advisor in Florence in 1529. Some of his preserved designs and drawings show curious fortified defenses evoking the shapes of monstrous lobsters. In 1547, Michelango worked on new fortifications around the

195

Bellver (Palma de Majorca, Spain). Situated west of Palma on the Balearic Island Majorca, Castle Bellver was built in the 15th century to serve as a summer residence for the kings of Spain. Bellver is a curious fortress adapted to firearms with round ramparts, three flanking towers, a circular donjon and a low artillery bulwark. The castle was used as a prison until 1915.

Rocca de Senigallia (Italy). The castle Senigallia displays a low profile typical of the fortresses built in the end of the 15th century. Note however the presence of the old-fashioned medieval machicolation.

Fort Salses (France): west front with donjon. Salses, situated near Perpignan in the department Pyrénées-Orientales, was built by the Spanish between 1497 and 1504, by the order of Fernando of Aragon. It was designed by the artillery grand-master Francisco Ramirez. Salses is an excellent example of late 15th century heavy masoned fortification with a very low profile.

Vatican. In 1557 he completed the castle of Civitavecchia which bears his name.

Albrecht Dürer (1471–1528) is one of the most significant artists of the Renaissance. In Nuremberg in 1527, he published a book about fortification titled "Etliche Unterricht zu Befestigung der Stett, Schloß und Flecken" ("Several Instructions for Fortifying Towns, Castles and Small Cities") in which he proposed the use of huge artillery towers called bastei or basteja. Dürer, who was also an urbanist, designed an ideal city defended by wet moats, earth bulwarks and corner caponiers.

With the restoration of royal authority in the fifteenth century came a new system of fortification in which urban walls and the private fortifications of local lords were progressively integrated into a national military defense, financed and controlled by the central state. However, most of the designs of the early transition period were temporary, improvised and makeshift solutions to the problems of the time. Many proposed designs represented an evolution without a future. Not until the 16th

century does one see fortifications efficiently designed for and against artillery.

A new concept of military defense appeared as private castles were replaced by forts. Forts were not royal, ducal or baronial residences in which the high-born castle owner shared the rigors of siege with his own personal body-guards, civilian servants and family; rather, they were strongholds garrisoning only professional soldiers. Forts included living accommodations (barracks) of greater or lesser comfort for soldiers and officers. In peacetime, they housed a few professional soldiers (headed by a governor) who were full-time experts in artillery, engineering and logistics, a select cadre who could be relied on to discipline and train common soldiers in time of war. Meanwhile kings, dukes, emperors and princes resided at their capital, directing the grand strategy of the whole war, as hard-riding messengers ensured that their armies would be in the right place at the right time.

The royal forts marked out the board upon which

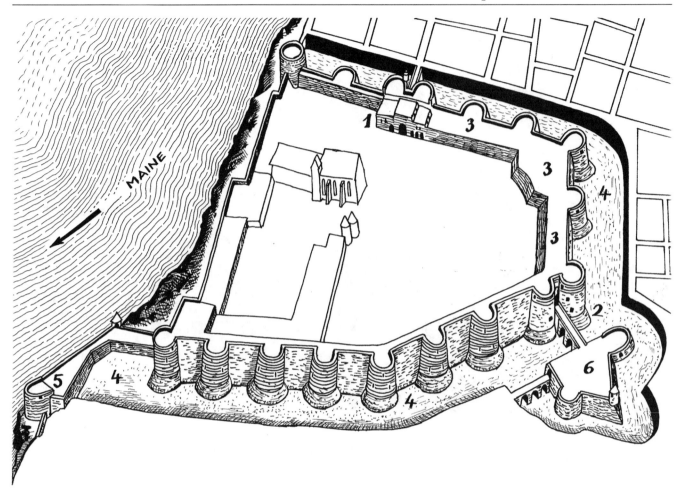

Castle Angers (France). The castle of Angers in Maine-et-Loire was built between 1228 and 1238 by the regent Blanche of Castille during the minority of King Louis IX as a stronghold against the boisterous dukes of Brittany. Placed on a cliff overlooking the river Maine, it was composed of a vast enceinte 660 m in perimeter including seventeen towers and two gatehouses. The castle was embellished by the duke of Anjou, Louis II, in 1384, and reshaped by the duke René of Anjou between 1450 and 1465. At the end of the 15th century, the castle was radically changed, turned into a fortress adapted to artillery by the royal governor Donadieu de Puycharic. All towers were cut down to the level of the curtains (the average height remained 18 m), and walls and towers were fitted with casemates. The part of the fortress between the Porte de Ville (1) up to the Postern des Champs (2) was thickened by a wide rampart (3); the dry moat (4) was made much deeper; and two artillery outworks were created: the tower Guillon (5) and the huge barbican des Champs (6). Completed about 1592, Angers castle eventually became a prison, and remained such until 1817, after which it was an army administrative center. Today the castle is an imposing historical monument housing the Saint-Laud chapel and the remarkable tapestry of the Apocalypse from 1373.

Various types of firearms openings. Top: arrow-splits adapted to small firearms. Middle and below: embrasures for small and medium guns.

Cross-section of a firing chamber. The gun placed in the firing chamber is an early breech-loader.

the great game of war was played. Concentrated essentially on land and sea borders, military architecture became a state monopoly in the 16th century. The kings of France fortified their borders, and the German emperors and the regional princes did the same to contain the Turks. In Britain, King Henry VIII broke with the pope and, as a result, was faced in 1538–1539 with the possibility of an invasion by both France and Spain. His answer was a string of coastal forts in the southeast of England.

In this increasingly centralized context, private medieval castles were militarily out of date and politically suspect, being the seat of potential rebellion. Some were abandoned, others were handed over to demolishers and became stone quarries; some underwent voluntary amputations and were reshaped into residences. In such case, defensive elements were transformed: crenellation, machicolation, échauguettes, and towers became mere

symbolic decorations, and wall-walks became terraces for pleasure. The residence was considerably embellished, with large windows replacing arrow-splits and embrasures, monumental staircases leading to brilliant halls and sunny apartments, and ditches and glacis turned to yards, flowery gardens, esplanades and parks.

THE BASTIONED SYSTEM

The crisis of fortification and all problems generated by firearms were finally solved by Italian inventions, the bastion and the bastioned system.

In 1495 the French king Charles VIII led an absurd expedition in Italy, claiming Naples and the south of the peninsula to be annexed to the French crown. Armed with a powerful and modern wheeled artillery, Charles

Castle La Motta (Spain). Castle La Motta, situated near Medina Del Campo in province Valladolid, was founded by the Moors. The castle was reconquered in 1077 and rebuilt by King Alfonso VI. It was built in red bricks and composed of a corner donjon called La Monta, a large walled enclosure with towers and outwork. Castle La Motta was adapted to firearms in the 15th century.

obtained significant success, which opened a series of conflicts known as the Italian Wars in the first half of the 16th century.

By now the Renaissance had made scholars and military engineers well aware of the mathematics and geometry necessary for their trade. Significant military engineers and architects such the family San Gallo or Michele San Micheli further developed the early theorists' works, devoting themselves to military study and experimenting with new fortification methods. The result was the introduction of the bastion. Who invented the effective bastion is not clearly known, but it is without doubt an Italian invention that appeared in the beginning of the 16th century.

A bastille is an outwork; a bastillon is a small bastille; and the word bastillon was bastardized to bastion, meaning a protruding terraced platform generally as high as the main wall. It is distinguishable from any previous artillery tower by two essential characteristics: a low ramparted profile (recall that a rampart consists of two masonry walls, called revetments, retaining between them a thick mass of earth to absorb the impact of cannonballs) and a pentagonal arrow-headed ground-plan.

The bastion was rather low above the ground in order not to be an easy target. The depth of the moat prevented scaling. Bastions and curtains included a thick breastwork with embrasures protecting gun emplacements, a banquette for infantry soldiers fitted with small

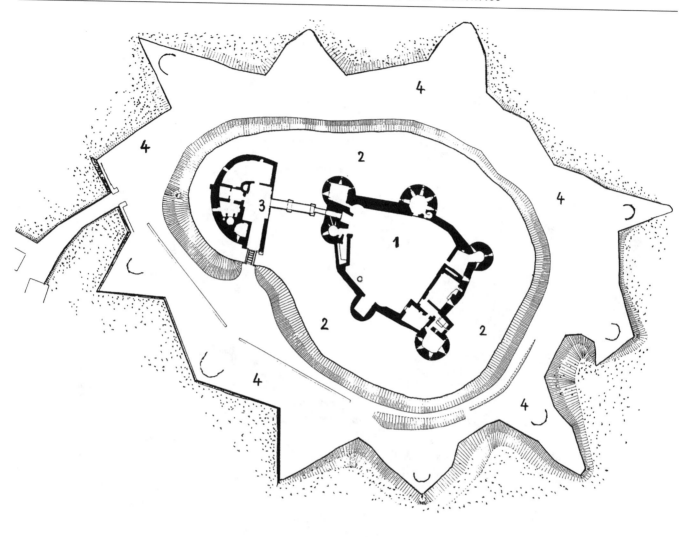

Ground-plan, castle Ranrouët (Brittany, France). The château Ranrouët is situated near Herbignac between Guérande and La Roche-Bernard in the department Loire-Atlantique. The origin of the castle was a Roman coastal watchtower. The castle was constructed by the lords of Assérac about 1125, rebuilt in the second half of the 13th century, then taken and destroyed by the king of France, Charles VIII, in 1488. About 1500 the castle (1) was reconstructed and profoundly reshaped by the lord Jean IV de Rieux, with a wide wet moat (2) and a D-shaped barbican (3). In 1585 during the wars of religion, Ranrouët was occupied by the Spaniards, and the duke of Mercœur had a large earth bulwark (4) built all around the castle to house artillery. The château was disarmed in 1619 on Louis XIII and Richelieu's order, and severely damaged in 1793 during the French Revolution. Since then the castle has stood abandoned, but the vestiges are particularly interesting and imposing.

Opposite top: *Bulwark.* Opposite bottom: *Cross-section, bulwark.*

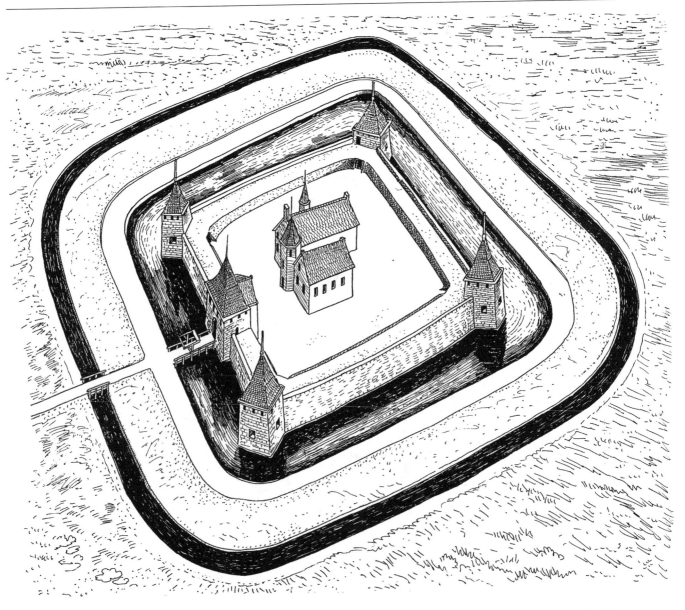

Castle Wedde (Netherlands). The castle Wedde, situated west of Groningen near the border with Germany, was originally a rural stronghold built in 1370 by the local lord Van Addinga. About 1460, the small castle was considerably enlarged with a ramparted bulwark flanked with four square corner artillery towers, a wet moat, a glacis and a second external wet ditch. The border castle played a significant military role in 1478, in 1593, in 1665 and in 1672. Occupied by the French in 1795 and partly demolished in 1814, the castle was abandoned until 1955, when it was restored.

arms and a wall-walk suitable for supplying and firing artillery.

The bastion's pentagonal outline included two faces turned outward to the enemy. Both faces joined at the outward-thrusting salient. They were connected to the curtain by two portions of wall called flanks; the meeting point of face and flank is called the shoulder. The gorge is the back-space turned to the inside of the city or fort. The surface enclosed by those five lines is called terre-plein.

To increase the defenders' safety, Italian bastions were often fitted with an orillon (ear), composed of a recess and

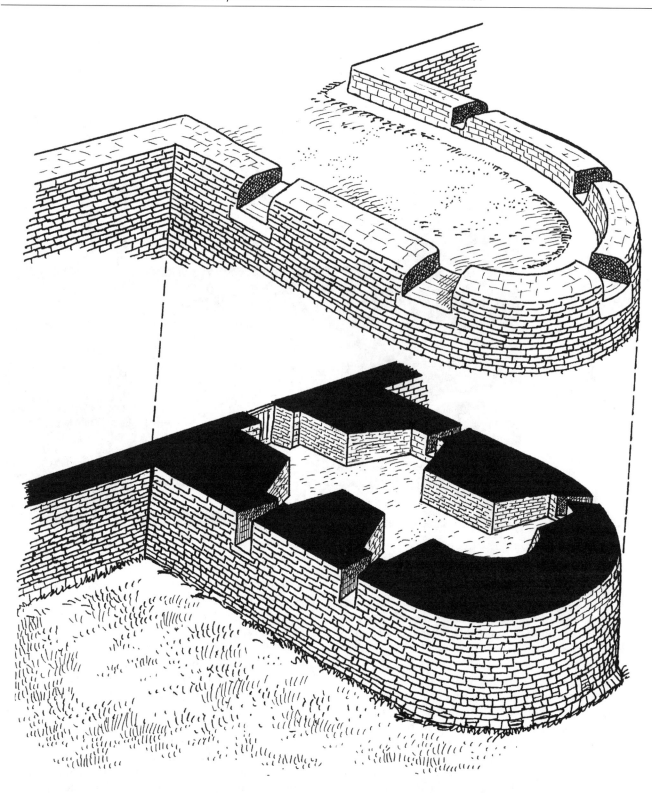

Schematic view of an artillery tower. Also called bulwark, boulevard, rondelle, bastillon, basteja, bastei or torrionne, the artillery tower was protruding and fitted with a top platform with embrasures in a round parapet and one or more casemated stories.

Cross-section of a casemate

a protruding screen built on the shoulder, protecting the defenders in the flank from oblique enemy bombardments but allowing them to enfilade the ditch. This protective element was either round or square. These shapes gave bastions their characteristic arrowhead or "ace of spades" form.

The so-called old Italian bastioned system was characterized by a curtain flanked by two bastions with ears replacing medieval corner- and wall-towers. No assault party could approach the curtain without being fired at from the side. A development was the so-called cavalier (also called cat), a raised structure higher than the rampart whose outline was similar to that of the bastion. The purpose of this inner work was to gain observation points and to give additional firepower and increased height to the bastion so as to command the surroundings. The cavalier also acted as a kind of huge shield, preventing enfilade-fire and protecting buildings in the town

or fort. On the other hand, because of its height, the cavalier could be an easy target.

To increase flanking possibility, the cavalier might also be placed in the middle of the curtain to form an additional flat bastion, called piatta-forma. This variant is called Venetian bastioned fortification.

The new Italian bastioned system, largely resulting from experiments led by military engineers Jacomo Castriotto, Girolame Maggi and Francesco de Marchi, was a great improvement. Its practical base was the so-called bastioned front; composed of one curtain and two projecting larger half-bastions, the bastioned front allowed the housing of more guns. But the main improvement was in the flanking. Each bastion flank protected not only the curtain but also each face of the neighboring bastion. The new bastioned system all but eliminated blind spots, every part of the fortress being always covered by fire coming from neighboring parts. The new Italian bastion

View from the inside of a casemate within an artillery tower. Note the thickness of the wall, the limited view and arc of fire.

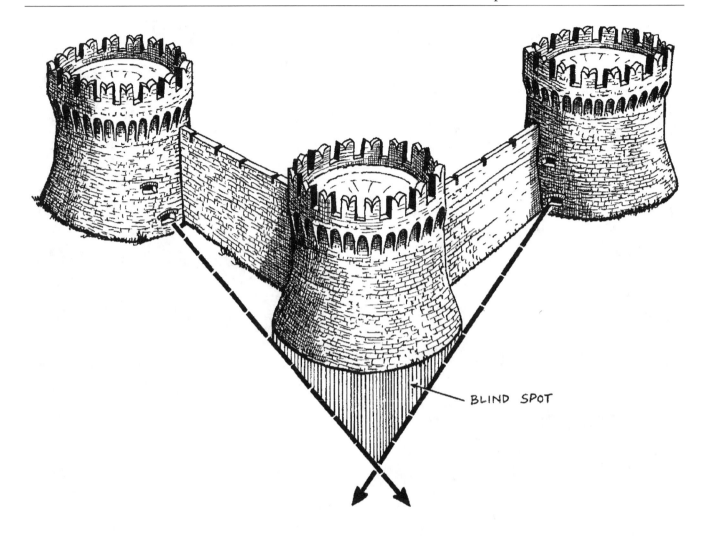

Schematic view of blind spot

outline restored the balance of arms in favor of the be-sieged, permitting maximum defense with relatively few defenders.

The new Italian system was further improved by the creation of an outer work called a ravelin (also named demi-lune or half-moon), which was placed in front of the curtain as a triangular independent island. Another important feature was the creation of the covered way, a continuous broad lane placed on top of the counter-scarp all around the fortress. It formed a first line of combat because the alley was "covered" by an uninterrupted breastwork. The crest of the parapet was aligned on the slope of the glacis to give grazing fire; defenders posted on the covered way gained a fire-range equal to the breadth of the ditch. The idea of protecting this outer lane beyond the ditch is attributed to the Italian military engineer Nicolo Tartaglia.

The Italian bastioned front was thus an ensemble of

elements related by rules and geometric ratios. The unit could be repeated at will to form a fort or an urban enclosure. The outline of the front could vary endlessly in length and be connected according to various angles. Engineers dreamed up infinite variations, partly according to local circumstances (the need to adapt fortifications to the site) but also according to a sort of fashion created by currents, schools or movements. The latter phenomenon, particularly in 16th century Italy, gave birth to uncountable theoretical bastioned fronts and endless sterile disputes between engineers of opposing cliques.

The bastioned system was very costly and demanded a specialized corps of engineers with knowledge in artillery, geometry and mathematics. The art of fortification had become a science, resulting in the definitive disappearance of medieval private fortification and signalling the standardization of military architecture.

Once owners of their walls and towers, medieval

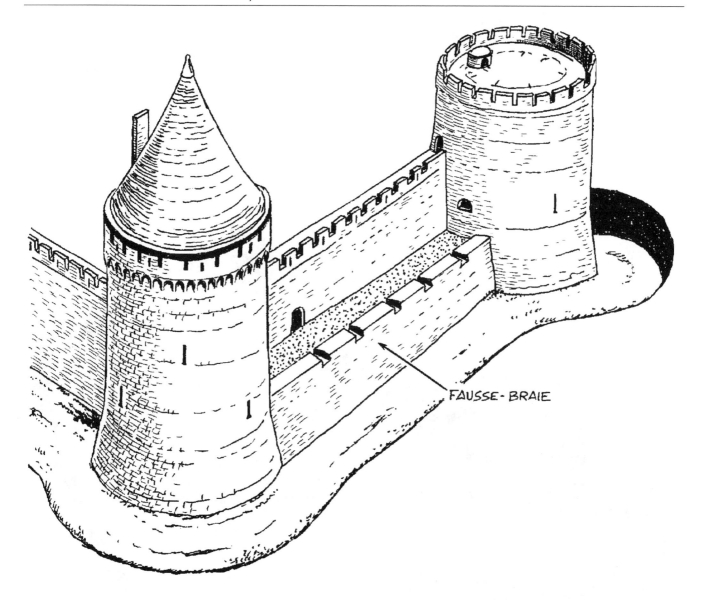

FAUSSE-BRAIE

View of a fausse-braie

towns now found that with the arrival of expensive guns and bastions, they could no longer afford their own fortifications. For funds, they turned to the central authority. In return the rulers demanded control, tutelage and then exclusive rights over defenses; they allowed fortification only of places with a strategic value for the security of the state.

In the 16th, 17th and 18th centuries, the bastioned system had a large impact on urbanism. The great developments in the spaces of bastions, moats, outworks and glacis were of such massive, impenetrable scale and required such a wide open field of fire around them that the formation of suburbs farther out was discouraged.

During the 16th century, European fortification was dominated by Italian engineers. François I and Henri II in France, the Holy Roman emperor Charles V in Spain, Germany, Italy and the Low-Countries, and Henry VIII in Britain relied upon Italian architects to build citadels, forts and urban enceintes. Example of Italian influence in Europe are numerous, but the bastioned system spread worldwide with European colonization. The development of the Italian monopoly was accelerated by printing; many treatises and books about fortifications were written and spread all over Europe.

By the end of the 16th century, however, the Italian monopoly was in decline. Too obsessed by theory and geometry, selling their experience as mercenaries, Italian engineers were replaced by national military architects.

During the war of liberation in the Netherlands from 1568 to 1648, a new generation of Dutch engineers created a new bastioned style, and the apogee of the bastioned fortification was reached in the second half of the 17th century with the French engineer Sébastien Le Preste de Vauban. This bastioned system was universally adopted and proved its worth until the first half of the 19th century.

Note: The museum of the French Army in Paris, in the Hôtel des Invalides, contains in its attic (Musée des Plans-Reliefs) fantastic models of 17th century bastioned towns and forts. Anyone with an interest in fortifications should consider a visit.

Above: *View of a caponier*

Opposite top: *Ground-plan of a caponier.* Opposite bottom: *Ground-plan, castle Lassay (Mayenne, France). The castle Lassay was constructed in the 12th century, destroyed during the Hundred Years' War and rebuilt in the 14th century. In the 15th century the count of Vendôme, Jean II, obtained the right to adapt the fortress to firearms and had a powerful horseshoe-shaped barbican built between 1457 and 1459 in front of the gatehouse.*

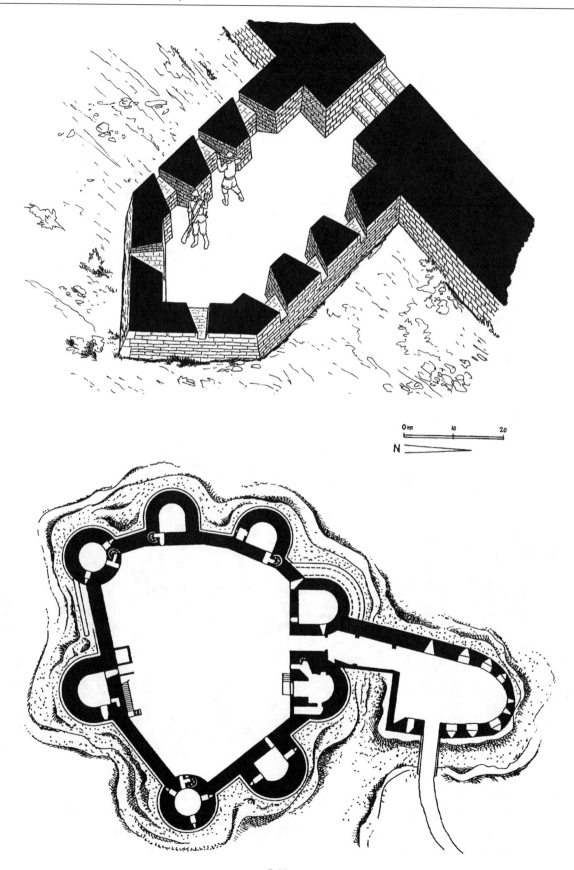

Top: *Barbican in Krakow (Poland)*. Bottom: *Civitavecchia (Italy). Artillery tower in the castle Michelangelo. The castle Michelangelo was designed about 1508 by Bramante. It was completed by Michelangelo, whence its name. The castle is square with four heavy circular artillery torrionne.*

Minceta Tower (Dubrovnik, Croatia). Dubrovnik—in the Middle Ages called Ragusa—is a port on the Adriatic coast. The town was founded by the Greeks and became in the 1st century BC a Roman harbor called Epidaurum. Ragusa, devastated by the Ostrogoths and the Avares, belonged successively to Byzantium (867), to Venice (1205), and to Hungary (1358). In the 15th century Ragusa became a free city, and its previous defenses were enlarged to face the Turkish menace. The imposing Minceta artillery tower was built in 1461 by the Florentine engineer Michelozzo.

213

Artillery tower in castle Roverto (Italy), built about 1488

Belem tower (Portugal). The Belem tower, situated near the river Tago in Lisbon, was planned by King João II and designed by his friend Garcia de Resende. The death of the king in 1495 resulted in the cancellation of the project, but the tower was built between 1515 and 1519 by King Manuel I and engineer Francisco d'Arruda. The tower was 35 m high with five stories, richly decorated with shield-shaped merlons, statues, heraldic ornaments, balconies, galleries, windows, columns and échauguettes. But the tower was also a powerful stronghold, with casemates defending the entrance of the Portuguese harbor. The Belem tower was demolished by the French during the Napoleonic wars and rebuilt in its original form in 1845.

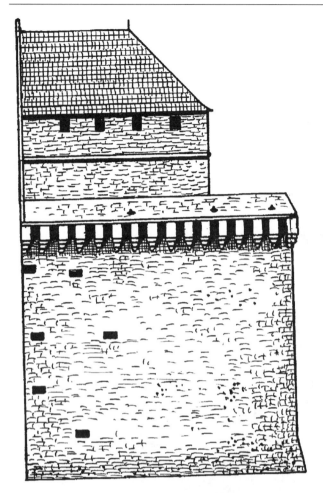

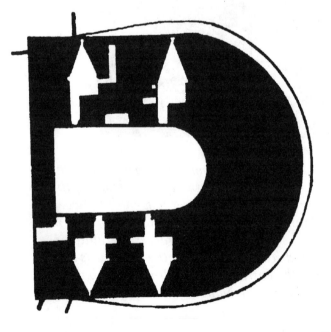

Top right: *Mont-Saint-Michel (Manche, France). Tour Boucle, built in 1440.* Bottom right: *Clisson (France), southwest boulevard. Castle Clisson, situated near Nantes in the department Loire-Atlantique, was built in 1217, with many additions throughout the Middle Ages. Between 1460 and 1480, the duke of Brittany, François II, had an external enceinte built with three casemated artillery towers. Severely damaged in 1793, castle Clisson has kept its imposing ruined vestiges.* Left: *Fougères (Ille-et-Vilaine), France. Side view and ground-plan of the Surienne casemated artillery tower, built about 1480.*

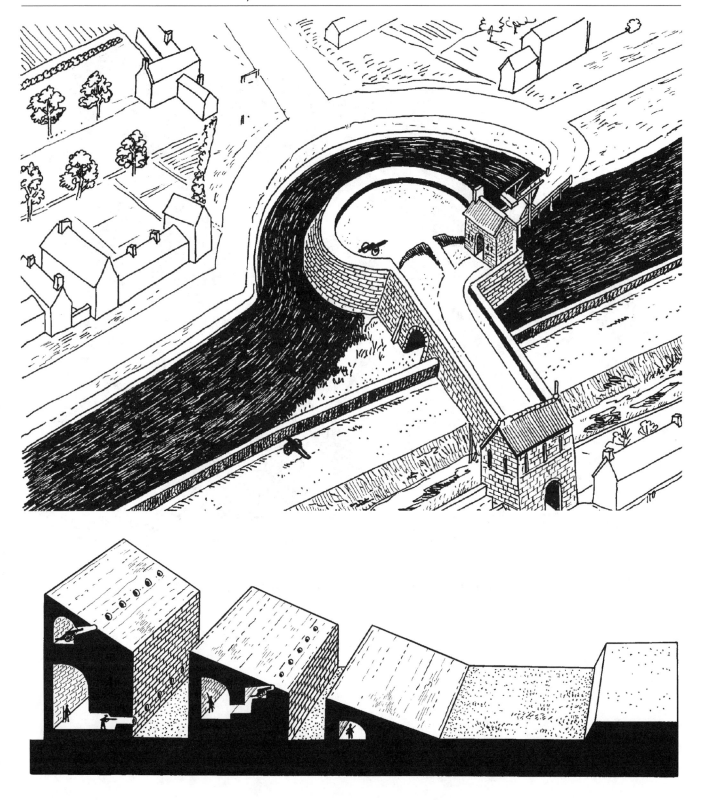

Top: *Groningen (Netherlands) Boteringerondeel. The artillery tower (rondeel in Dutch) was constructed in 1547 to protect the Boteringe gatehouse, in the north of the town.* Bottom: *Cross-section of a fort designed by Leonardo da Vinci*

Project of triangular fort designed by Francesco di Giorgio Martini

Opposite: *Project of towers and enceinte designed by Francesco di Giorgio Martini*

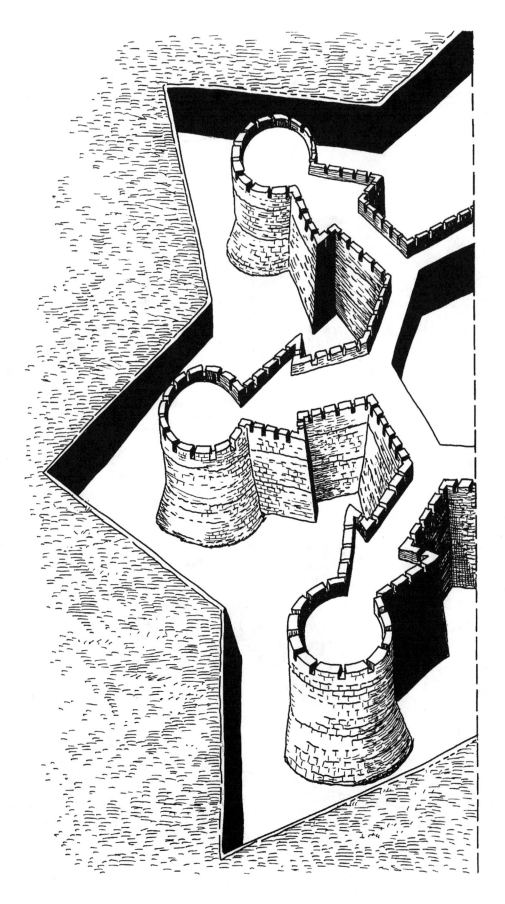

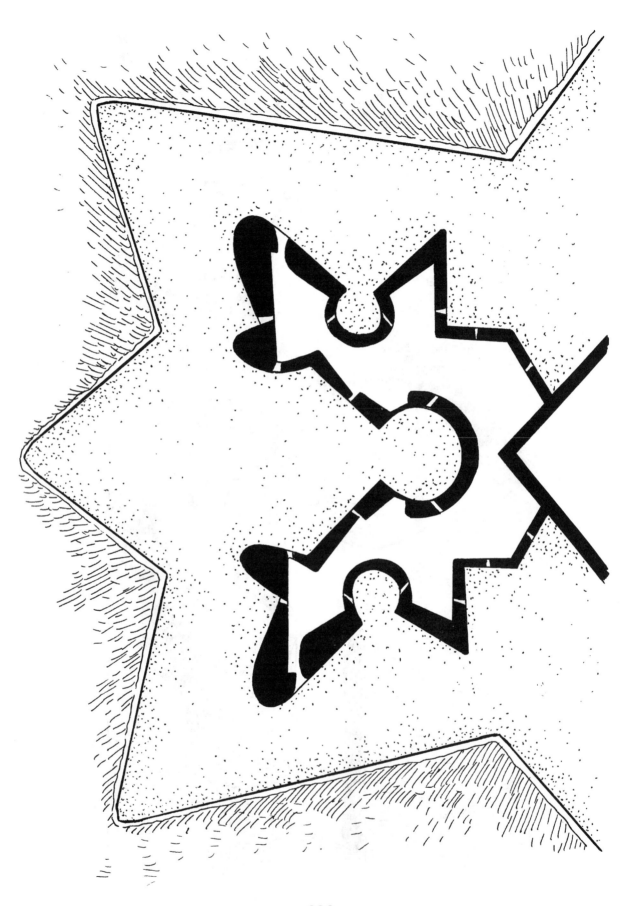

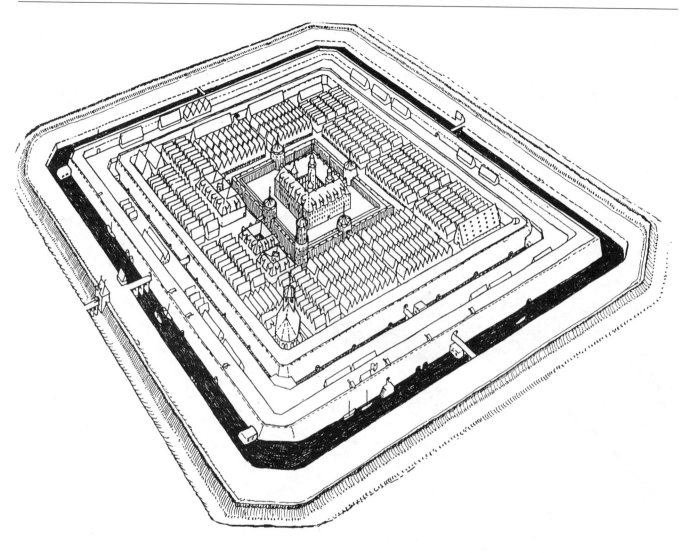

"Ideal city," Köningstadt, designed by Albrecht Dürer

Opposite: *Project of fortification in Prato d'Ognissanti in Florence by Michelangelo*

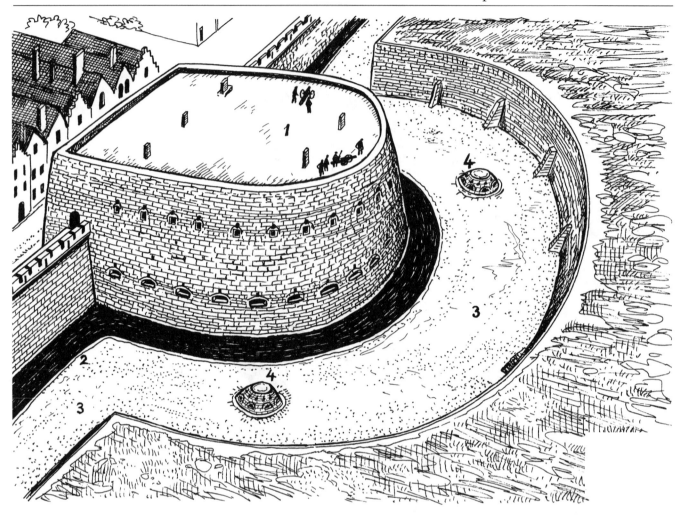

Project of a Bastei designed by Albrecht Dürer. Dürer's Bastei is a huge masonry artillery tower 40 m high and 130 m in diameter. The tower is fitted with a top platform (1) and casemated stories housing numerous pieces of artillery, giving it tremendous firepower. It has a scarp wet ditch (2) and a large dry moat (3) 40 m broad with a masonry counterscarp. Attention is paid to active close-range defense in the form of two rounded caponiers (4) housing musketry and probably accessible by underground galleries. Such towers would have been very expensive and therefore never built in Dürer's time. However, Dürer's theory was not without significance. Some works created later seem to bear his influence, such as the fortress Munot in Schaffhausen in Switzerland, built in 1585 by Heinrich Schwarz; the barbican of Warsaw, completed in 1656; or the barbican Florianska in Krakow, as well as urban artillery towers in Augsburg, Gotha, Kassel or Magdeburg. Huge masonry artillery towers were later revived by Marc René de Montalembert (1714–1800), whose theories dominated European fortification in the 19th century.

Opposite: *Castle Hochosterwitz (Austria). Castle Hochosterwitz is situated near Sankt-Veit an der Glan, northeast of Klagenfurt in province Carinthia near the border with Slovenia. The castle Hochosterwitz was created in 860 by King Ludwig the German. An important strategic place, it was enlarged and modernized by its successive occupiers, the archbishop of Salzburg, the lords of Osterwitz, the emperor Friedrich III and the lords*

Khevenhüller. The Hochosterwitz defensive system was remarkable: The castle lay on a 170 m high hill with steep slopes and included walls, towers and no less than fourteen gatehouses defending the 620 m long access road spiraling around the hill. At the end of the 15th century the pressure on Austria by the Turks was particularly strong, and the governor of Carinthia, Christoph Khevenhüller, and his cousin Georg made modifications, between 1570 and 1586, allowing the fortress to bear firearms.

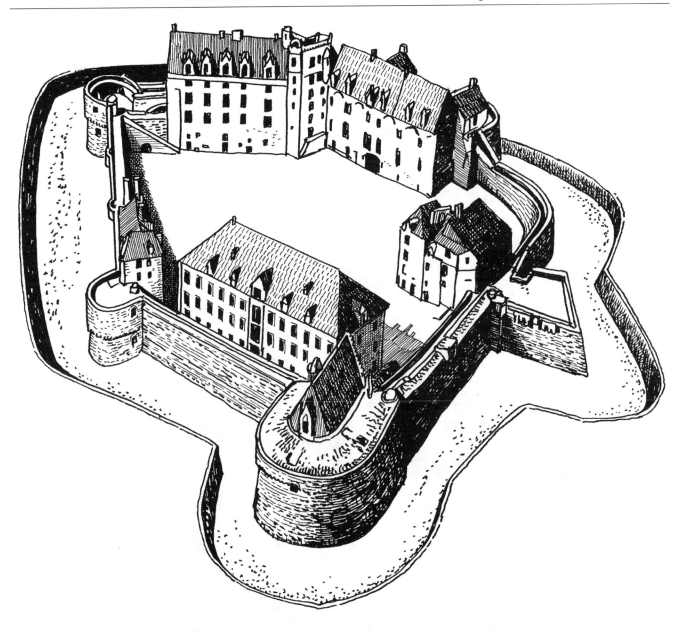

Castle Nantes (Loire-Atlantique, France). The castle of Nantes, overlooking river Loire, was originally a Roman tower, enlarged to a castle in 1205 by Guy de Thouars and completed in 1466 by the duke of Brittany, François II. Between 1582 and 1590, the castle was adapted to firearms by the duke of Mercœur, who added artillery towers. Nantes castle was also a luxurious royal residence with houses, palace and hall where many kings of France dwelled from Charles VIII to Louis XIV. The fortress was a prison and an arsenal during the French Revolution. Since 1915, the château has been municipal property; today it houses a museum.

Manzanares-el-Real (Spain). The castle Manzanares-el-Real is situated about thirty kilometers north of Madrid in the Sierra Guadarrama. Ordered by Iñigo Lopez de Mendoza and designed in 1475 by architect Juan Guas, the castle has a regular ground-plan with corner towers, a polygonal keep, a barbican and a low external enceinte adapted to firearms.

Evoramonte (Portugal). The fort Evoramonte is situated in the plain of Alentejo. Together with the fortified cities Estremoz and Evora, it was intended to defend the road to the Portuguese capital, Lisbon, from a Spanish invasion. Constructed on Roman and Moorish vestiges, the fort was reshaped in the 15th century to house artillery. The fort includes a square enceinte with four artillery corner-towers. Note the Manuelian-styled stone knots decorating the façade above the door.

Venetian fort in Heraklion (Crete). The island of Crete is situated southeast of the Peloponnese. Called Candia during the Middle Ages, the island was a possession of Venice from 1204 to 1669. The main city, Heraklion, was fortified by a bastioned enceinte and an artillery fort designed by the Venetian engineer Michel San Michele in 1538. Crete was taken by the Turks in 1669 after a very long siege.

Civita Castellana (Italy). Situated in the province Latium, the castle was ordered by the duke Caesar Borgia (1475–1507) and built between 1494 and 1497 by Antonio da San Gallo the Elder. The castle was a ducal residence but also a fortress fully adapted to firearms displaying a polygonal donjon, an enceinte flanked by five artillery towers, and a deep moat.

Rocca Ostia (Italy). The harbor Ostia, situated at the mouth of the river Tiber about twenty-four km from Rome, was founded in the 4th century BC when the Romans began to expand in the Mediterranean Sea. The port, called Ostia Antica, was defended by fortifications built in the time of Lucius Cornelius Sylla (138–78 BC). The rocca of Ostia was ordered by the pope and built between 1483 and 1486 by Guiliano da San Gallo and Baccio Pontelli. Probably influenced by the theoretical work of Francesco di Giorgio Martini, the rocca was a massive triangle with two circular corner-towers, a round donjon defended by a square artillery tower and a small forebuilding acting as a gatehouse in the deep moat.

227

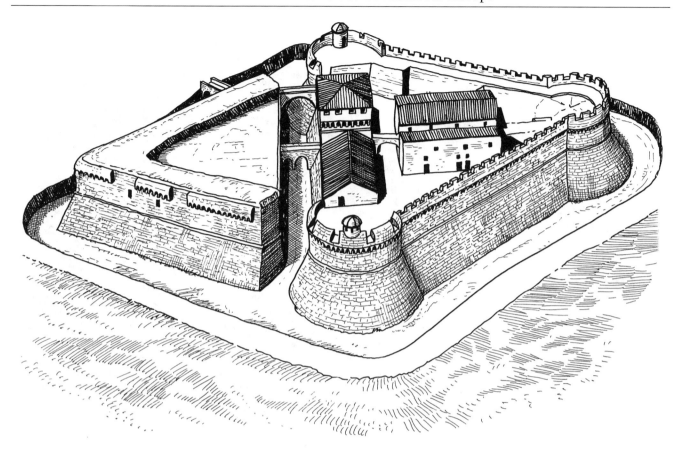

Fort Sarzanello (Italy). Fort Sarzanello dominates the city of Sarzana 16 km north of Carrare in Tuscany. The fort, built between 1493 and 1502 by engineer Francesco Giamberti, presented some similarities with Giorgio Martini's theoretical design: It was composed of two massive triangles, one with circular corner-towers, and the other in the shape of a ravelin, directly prefiguring the bastioned fortification.

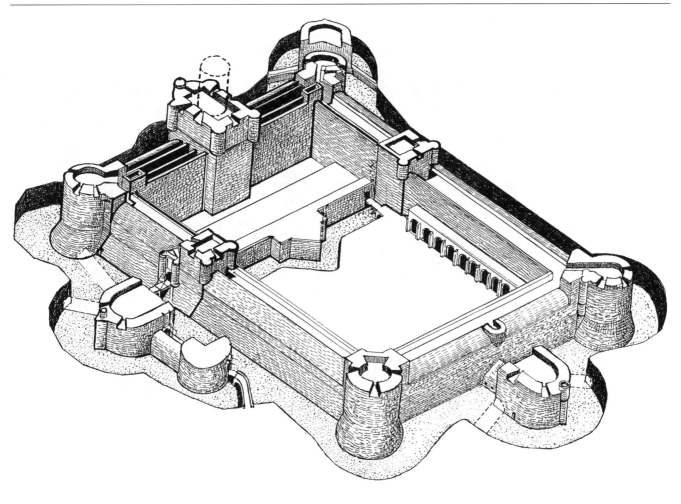

Fort Salses (France). The Spanish fort Salses is situated sixteen kilometers north of Perpignan in Pyrénées-Orientales. Ordered by King Fernando of Aragon to protect his territory in Roussillon against the French, the fort was designed by Francisco Ramirez and built between 1497 and 1504. Salses and the province Roussillon became French in 1642. Having thus lost its military border function, Salses was used as a prison and a powder supply place until 1889. Salses is a remarkable fort, especially designed both to support and to withstand artillery fire. It is an imposing rectangular fortress 110 m × 84 m, including four low cylindrical corner-towers, outworks placed in the moat 20 m wide and 7 m deep, a double barbican ahead of the main gatehouse, a reduit with a 20 m high donjon, a large central place of arms and various service buildings (supply-stores, barracks, stables, a chapel and others). Parapets are round to deflect enemy projectiles and fitted with embrasures. Walls and towers are casemated and particularly thick: 10 m to begin with, and after the siege of 1503, their base was enlarged to 14 m.

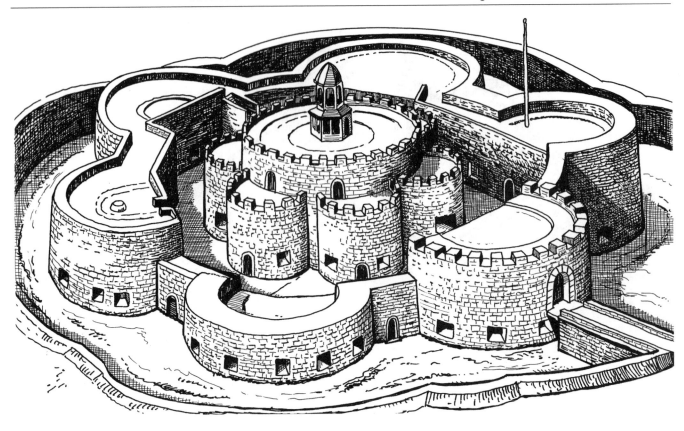

Deal Castle (Great Britain). Situated on the coast of Kent, Deal is a fort constructed on Henry VIII's order in 1540. Partly designed by the Italian engineer Girolamo Pennacchi, Fort Deal is composed of a round keep overlooking six half-circular towers, an internal moat, an outer enceinte with six semi-circular artillery towers, a single entrance with drawbridge in the west side and a wide external dry ditch. The fort housed numerous artillery placed on platforms and lighter hand-held guns concealed inside casemates. Deal was one of Henry VIII's coastal forts, intended to defend the south English shores.

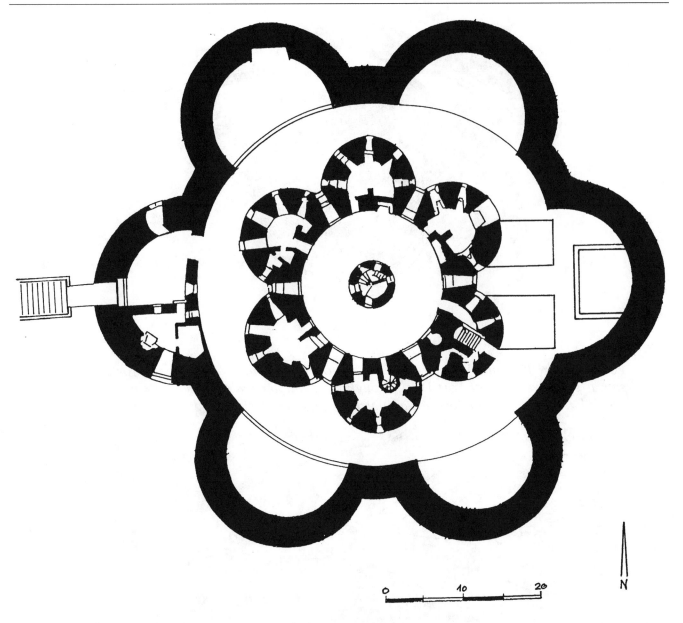

Ground-plan, castle Deal (Britain)

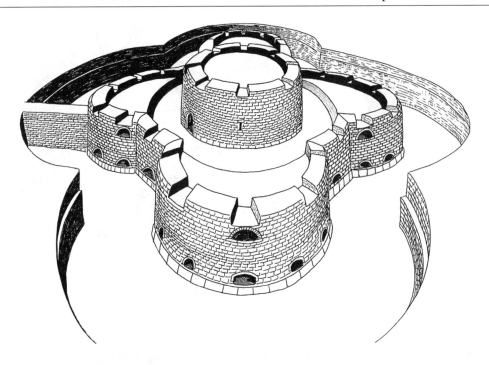

Fort Walmer (Britain). Walmer was another of King Henry VIII's coastal forts. Its design is similar to that of Fort Deal, though on a smaller scale. Instead of six main towers, it has only four. The fort has a quatrefoil plan and only two armed stages.

Fort Saint Mawes (Britain). Fort Saint Mawes, built in the period 1539–1543 by King Henry VIII, was intended to defend the mouth of the river Fal. The fort has a central circular tower and three half-circular artillery towers forming a generally triangular plan.

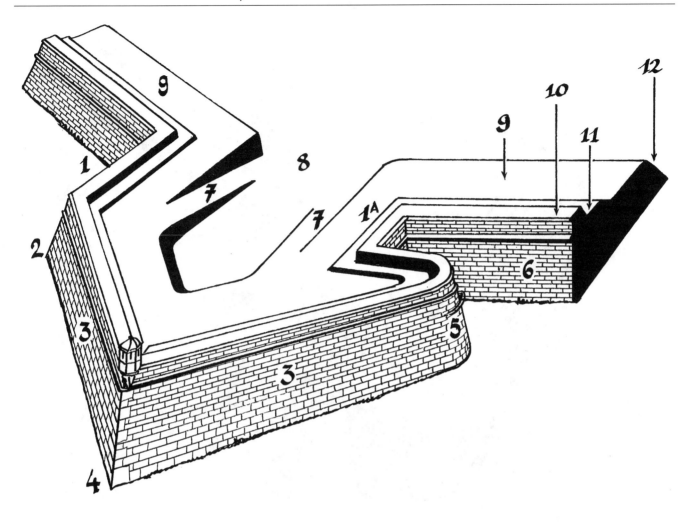

The main parts of a bastion: (1)The flank, which allowed the defenders to enfilade the moat. (2)The shoulder, the point of junction of the flank and the face. (3)The two faces met at the salient. (4) The sharp edge turned towards the enemy and therefore was reinforced with heavy clamping stones; note the échauguette or sentry-box for observation on top of it. (5) The ear or orillon, which protected the recessed flank (1A); the ear was either round or square. (6) The curtain was the wall between two bastions; this formed the scarp. (7) The gently sloping ramps allowed defenders to bring cannons and supply-carts on the wide wall-walk (9), which was both a communication and a place to install the artillery. (8) The open gorge, with a cross-section of the curtain showing the breast-work or parapet (10) fitted with a banquette (11), allowing infantry to fire en barbette over the breastwork. (12) The internal slope of the curtain, fitted with staircases for infantry. This bastion is "hollow" as its terre-plein is not filled with earth.

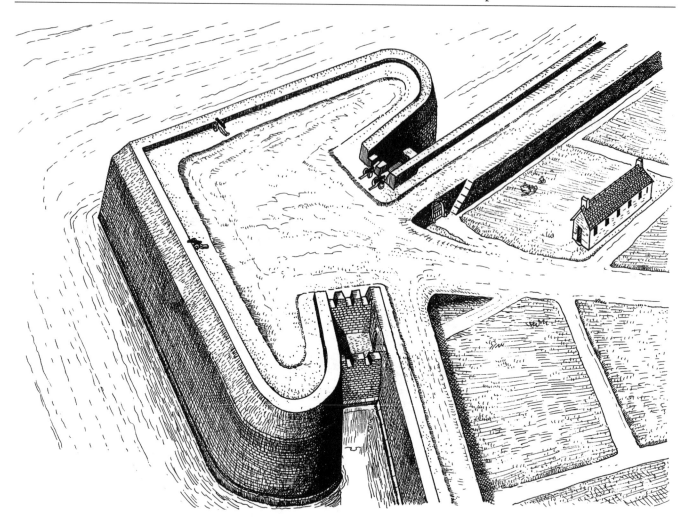

Italian bastion with orillon. Note the recessed flanks with two rows of guns. Access to the low story was via a postern and a gallery passing under the curtain. This bastion is "full," which means that its terre-plein is filled with earth, forming a vast terrace with an access ramp in the gorge. The moat could be either dry or filled with water.

Front view of a bastion. Note the overhanging sentry-box allowing observation on both faces and over the ditch. Note too that the flank casemates are perfectly concealed behind the orillons.

Flank of a bastion. On the left you see the protruding orillon protecting the recessed flank in the middle; this includes an upper open gun emplacement at wall-walk level and a lower casemated story with embrasures. On the right is the curtain.

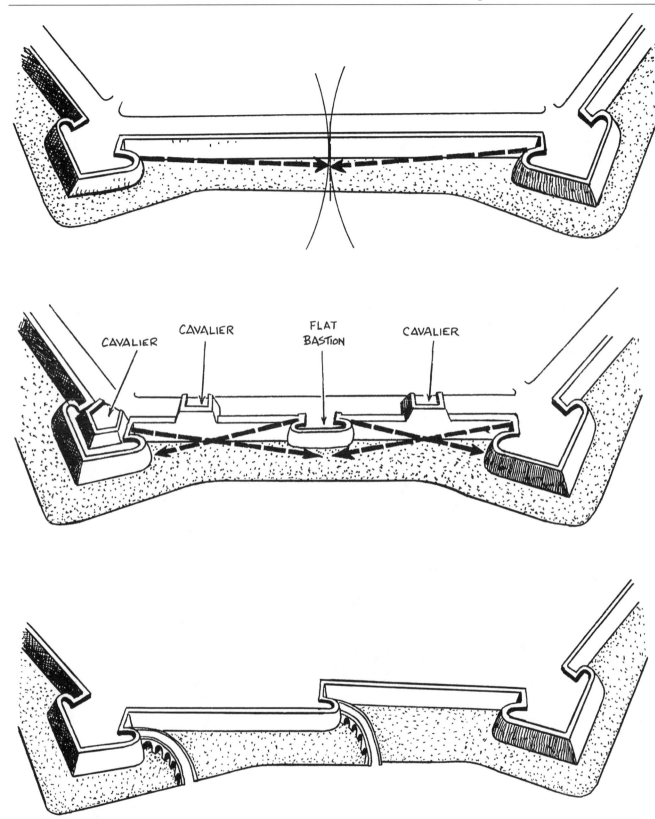

CAVALIER   CAVALIER   FLAT
BASTION   CAVALIER

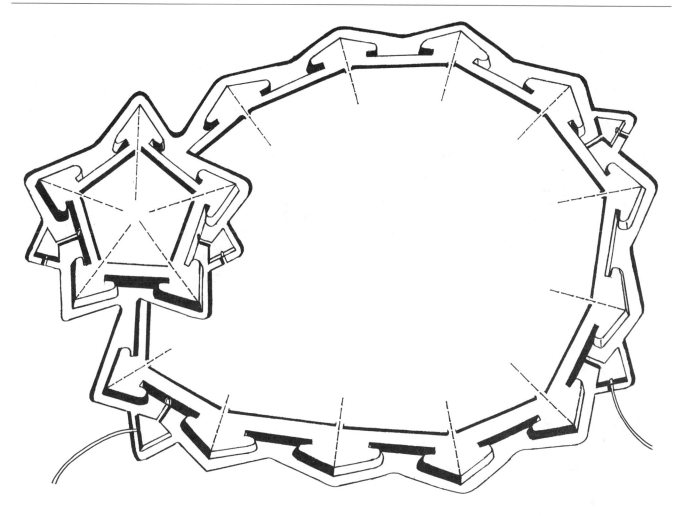

Bastioned fronts. Five fronts constituted a pentagonal citadel. The same front with a varying salient angle could be used to form an urban enceinte adapted to natural conditions.

Opposite: *Schematic views of the old Italian bastioned system. The sketch on top shows the basic style of flanking: the curtain length must not exceed the range of weapons placed in the flanks. The illustration in the middle shows the Venetian bastioned fortification with a flat bastion or piatta-forma in the middle of the curtain, increasing the flanking possibility, as well as the cavaliers, either placed on the bastion or on the curtain, increasing general firepower. The sketch at bottom shows the disposition of the access including a masonry bridge and a drawbridge in a gatehouse: This was generally placed in the flank of the bastion or in a recessed flank built in the middle of the curtain.*

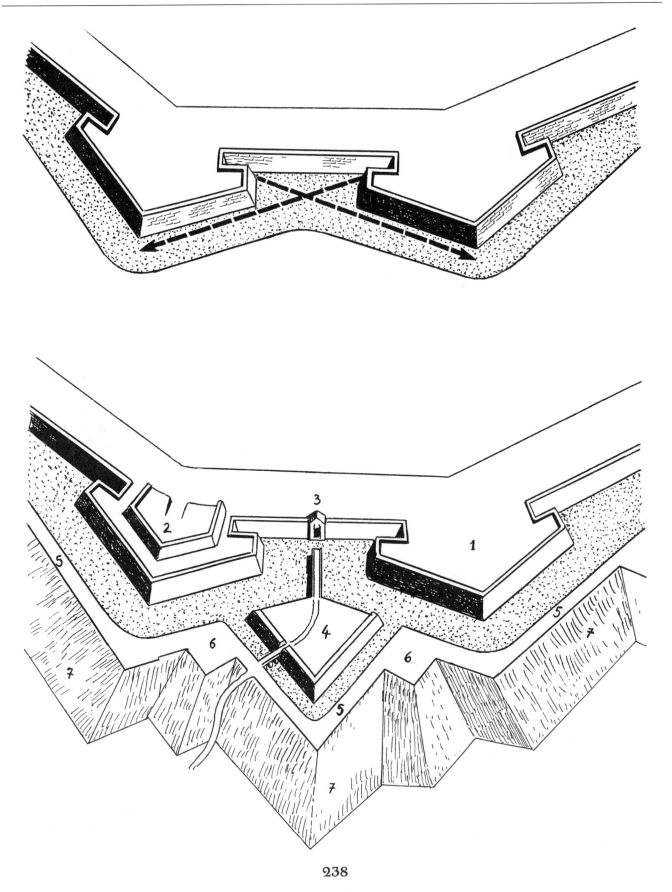

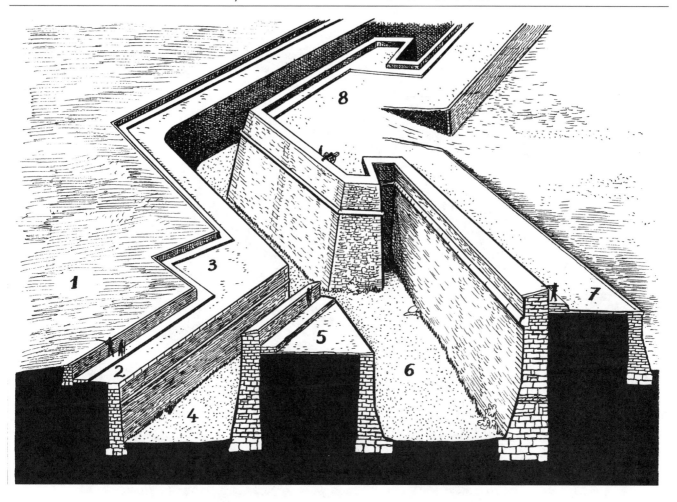

Cross-section, bastioned system. The cross-section shows the glacis (1), the covered way (2), and the place of arms (3), fitted with a breastwork and a banquette; the ravelin ditch (4), the ravelin (5), the main moat (6), the curtain (7) and the bastion (8).

Opposite: *Schematic views of the new Italian bastioned system. The sketch above shows the perfect flanking crossfire offered by the new Italian bastioned system, reducing or eliminating blind spots. The sketch below shows the main characteristics of the new system: the large bastion with orillons (1), often fitted with a cavalier (2), the gatehouse with a drawbridge (3) placed in the middle of the curtain, efficiently protected by a ravelin or demi-lune (4) in the wide moat, fitted with its own ditch and another drawbridge. On the counter-scarp, the covered way (5); the places of arms (6), which are fortlets placed in the reentering angles of the covered way; and the bare and flat glacis (7).*

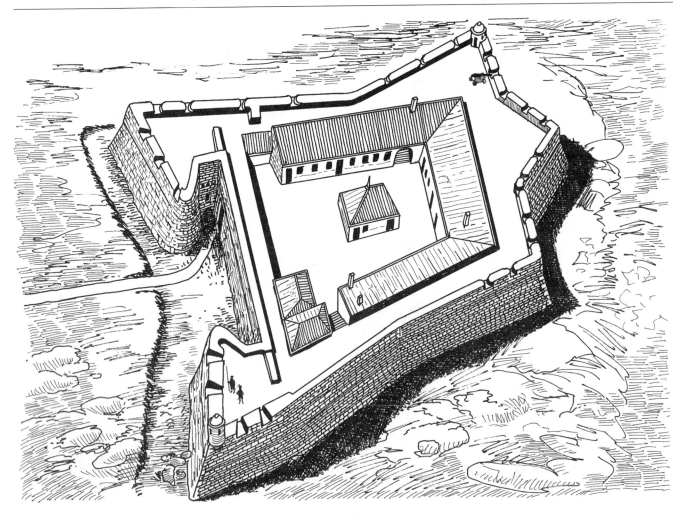

Fortaleza dos Reis Magos Natal (Brazil). Natal in Brazil was created in 1599 by the king of Spain and Portugal, Felipe II. To protect the mouth of river Potengy, a coastal fort called Fortaleza dos Reis Magos (fortress of the Wise Men) was built between 1599 and 1628. The fort was taken by the Dutch in 1633 and rechristened Fort Mathieu van Ceulen. The Dutch were driven out of Brazil in 1654, and the Portuguese used the Fortaleza as a prison until 1822, when Brazil became independent. Today the fort is a museum.

Fort Rammekens (Netherlands). Fort Rammekens, situated east of Vlissingen in Zeeland, was ordered by Maria of Hungary (emperor Charles V's sister and governor of the Low-Countries). Intended to control the mouth of river Scheldt and the approach to Antwerp, the fort was designed by engineer Donato de Boni and constructed by master-builder Peter Fransz in 1547. The coastal fort included a diamond-shaped enceinte, one casemated bastion turned towards the river, two flanking half-bastions and a portal with draw-bridge. The fort had a particularly long military career: Used by the Dutch after 1573, temporarily occupied by the British in 1809, reshaped by Napoleon in 1811, modernized as a Dutch coastal battery in the 19th century, Fort Rammekens was turned into an Atlantic Wall Stützpunkt (strong point) called StP Rommel in 1943. Abandoned since 1945, the fort is now a paradise for vegetation, birds and bats.

Fort Mont-Alban (France). The bastioned coastal fort Mont-Alban is situated on the steep promontory Boron dominating Nice in the French Riviera. It was ordered by the duke of Savoy to protect the entrance to the harbor Villefranche-sur-Mer, and designed by engineer Domenico Ponsello in 1557.

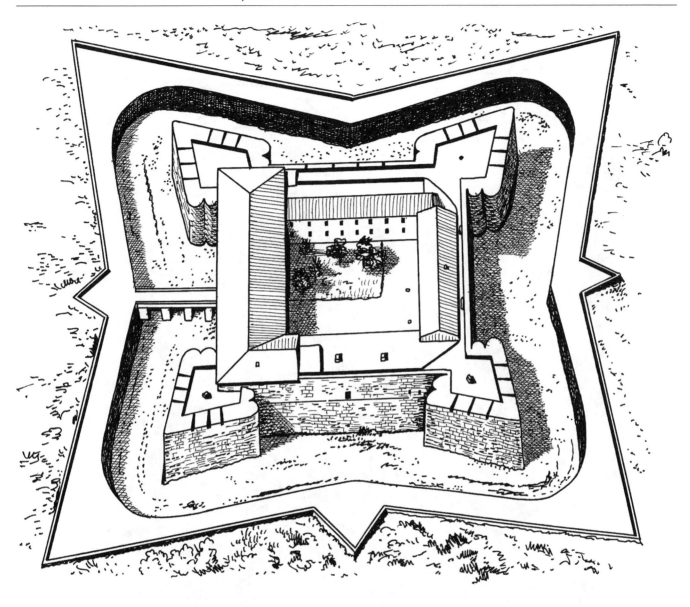

Castle Aquila (Italy). Aquila is situated on the mountain Gran Sasso in the Abruzzes. The town was founded in the 13th century by the German emperor Friedrich II von Hohenstaufen. After 1529, the town was under Spanish tutelage, and a citadel—called Castello Spagnolo—was built between 1535 and 1549 by the commandant Pedro Luis Escriva di Valenza.

Fort Filippo Porto Ercole (Italy). Situated on the promontory dominating Porto Ercole in Tuscany, the fort was constructed by the Spaniards in 1557.

Fort Jesus (Mombasa, Kenya). Fort Jesus was built in 1593 by the Portuguese engineer João Batista Cairato. The fort, intended to protect a Portuguese anchorage on the maritime route to India, was a square enceinte with four half-bastions with orillons.

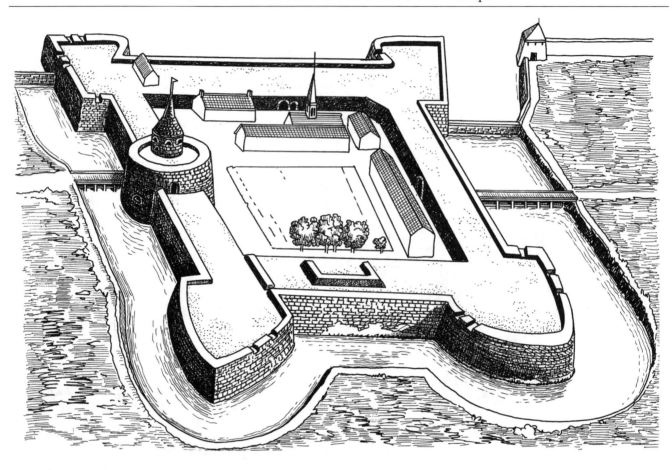

Citadel Vredeburg in Utrecht (Netherlands). Ordered by the German emperor Charles V in 1528, the citadel Vredeburg was intended to control the inhabitants of the town. Designed and built by the brothers Rombout and Marcellis Kelderman and Jean de Terremonde, the citadel was a square enceinte with four almond-shaped corner bastions. Utrecht was involved in the rebellion against the Spaniards in 1577, and the citadel Vredeburg was besieged, taken and later demolished by the population.

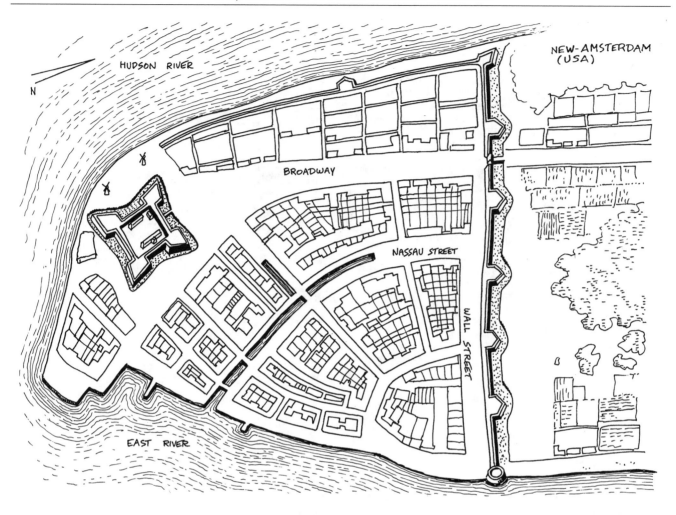

New Amsterdam (USA). The island of Manhattan is hemmed in by the Hudson, East and
Harlem rivers. In 1524, the Florentine explorer Giovanni da Verrazano, in French service, discovered the site and called it Angoulême after King François I of Angoulême.
Dutch merchants, headed by Peter Minuit, purchased the island in 1526 for sixty florins
($25).The Dutch colony was developed and fortified by a palisade and later (in 1653) a
bastioned earth wall; today that wall is remembered in the name of the street that runs
through the location, i.e., Wall Street. By the time the wall was constructed, a bastioned
square fort had been built at the place of the present Battery Park. In 1664, the Dutch
governor Pieter Stuyvesant was forced to yield the establishment to the English, and the
town of New Amsterdam was rechristened New York after the duke of York, who would
become King James II. New York's Dutch past is still reflected by some of the names of
today, including Nassau County, Harlem (named after the Dutch town Haarlem west of
Amsterdam), and Brooklyn (coming from the Dutch place Breukelen). In addition, the
term "yankee" originates from the Dutch Christian name Jan-Kees.

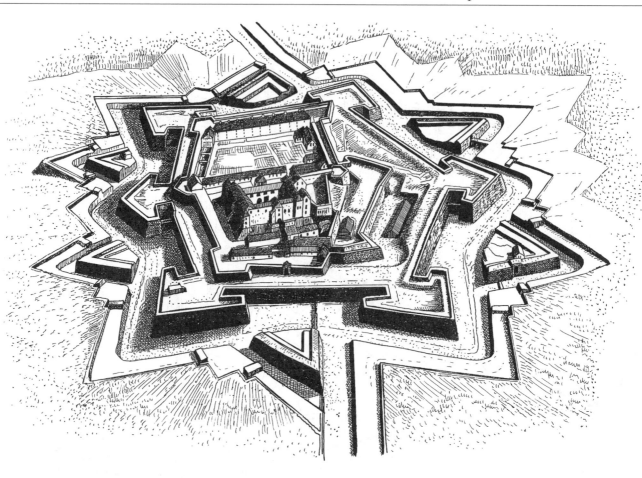

Citadel of Perpignan (France). The evolution of the citadel of Perpignan in Pyrénées-Orientales was directly connected to the troubled history of the town and the disputed province Roussillon. Its core was formed by the castle of the sovereigns of Majorca, built about 1277 by King Jaime I. At the end of the 15th century, Perpignan was temporarily annexed to France, and King Louis XI ordered the construction of an external enceinte, to which the king of Spain, Charles V, later brought additional defenses adapted to firearms. In 1560, Spanish king Felipe II ordered the construction of six Italian-style bastions and a moat. The fortifications of the citadel were further reinforced when Roussillon became definitively French: Vauban designed demi-lunes, a covered way and places of arms, which were completed in 1686 by royal engineer Christophe Rousselot.

Castel Sant'Angelo (Rome, Italy). The Castel Sant'Angelo is the Vatican stronghold on the right bank of river Tiber. Its core is formed by Hadrian's mausoleum, constructed between 135 and 138 AD. The mausoleum, formed of two cylindrical parts resting on a square base 60 m x 60 m, was used as sepulcher for the Roman emperors until Caracalla in 217. In the 6th century, Pope Gregory the Great built a chapel. In the 13th century, the mausoleum became a fortress where the popes might find refuge; that fortress was dubbed the Castel Sant'Angelo. During the pontificate of Nicolas V (1447–1455), the height of the tower's core was increased with a brick story, and round corner-towers were built. Between 1484 and 1493, during the pontificate of Alexander VI, the castle was em-

bodied in the Vatican fortifications and enclosed by five bastions designed by Antonio da San Gallo the Older. Later popes, notably Clement VII and Paul III, embellished the fortress between 1492 and 1569. Today the Castel Sant'Angelo, linked to the left Tiber bank by a beautiful bridge, is one of the great glories of Rome.

5

EUROPEAN TOWNS FROM THE 12TH TO THE 16TH CENTURIES

THE REBIRTH AND GROWTH OF CITIES

From the 5th to the 10th centuries, towns were reduced in size, limited in importance and greatly depopulated. Some vanished altogether. Most of those remaining were merely big villages, though others were modest commercial or episcopal centers.

After the year 1000, the decrease in invasions and the reestablishment of relative security favored demographic growth, trade and commercial activities. The instauration of money exchange and the installation of markets and fairs made possible the rebirth of towns. Consequently, urban population increased, while transport means were more rapid and less expensive owing to significant inventions and technical improvements such as collars for horses and stern-rudders for boats.

During the Crusades, large parts of the Mediterranean Sea were purged of Arabian pirates, permitting Italian ports to control commercial sea routes with the East. In this favorable context, many towns grew and got rich. In the 13th century, feudalism was slowly dying out, but the social changes made some of the nobility richer and many peasants poorer. Many among the lower classes found themselves unable to pay their rent. As a result, some lost or sold their lands and moved to the towns, which often offered a better hope for the future.

The origins of European cities are extremely various. Many cities were ancient settlements founded by the Romans (villa, castra and castella) that were developed owing to the effort of a bishop or because they were near the protection of a feudal lord and his castle. Some towns grew around monasteries or places of pilgrimage. Certain cities owed their growth to the installation of a royal, imperial, princely or episcopal court and became national, regional or provincial capitals. Many others were rebuilt or created because of a favorable geographical situation (for example, a passage in a marsh or between mountains, a ford on a river, a junction of important crossroads, or a protected anchorage) because accessibility favored the installation of trading-places and markets. In the 12th and 13th centuries, many new hamlets, villages and towns were founded in vast areas conquered on wastelands all over Europe, and their names acknowledged them as brand new creations (Villeneuve, Bourgneuf, Neustadt, Newtown, and Villanova, for example). In southern France, some newly created cities were gaven famous or exotic names such as Cologne, Grenade or Valence. Others were named after their creators: the bastide of Libournes was founded in 1270 by Sir Roger Leyburn, seneschal to English king Edward I. Many new cities were created as military strong points or as supply bases on the borders of disputed lands. Others were colonies and economical centers in new lands. Their inhabitants came from ancient overpopulated villages and towns; to attract them, kings and lords granted privileges, rights, freedom and various fiscal advantages, sometimes reflected in the names of those cities (Villefranche, Freistadt, Freiburg, Villafranca, Freetown).

Bastides were fortified villages founded mainly in the 13th century. In southern France there were about 350. Created by the kings of France and England, who were fighting over the rich province of Aquitaine, bastides had

250

a square or rectangular plan inspired by ancient Roman urbanism. Inside, the city space was divided into regular living parcels with a church and a market square. Bastides were fortified with a masonry enceinte composed of curtains, flanking towers, moats and gatehouses. In southern France, the best preserved are Libournes, Cadillac, Sauveterre-de-Guyenne, Monpazier and Saint-Macaire. Bastides were also created in Britain, notably during the conquest of Wales by King Edward I (Caernarvon, Beaumaris, Flint, Conwy and Winchelsea, for example).

Bastides were also founded by the Teutonic knights to conquer and evangelize eastern Europe. In Pomerania, the knights created about forty new settlements, including the town of Rostock, which was built between 1190 and 1252. Many other colonies and towns were founded in Bohemia to fight the Turks, and the same thing happened in Spain and Portugal during the Reconquista against the Moors.

Colonial bastides were also created in the Netherlands in lands and polders conquered on marshes and low seashores. Elburg was founded in 1230, Naarden and Arnemuiden in 1288, and Brouwershaven in 1285 by the count of Holland, Floris V. The Dutch cities of Culemborg, Montfoort, Heusden, Bredevoort and Helmond developed around existing castles, which related them to *castelnaux*.

Castelnaux (also called new-castle, châteauneuf or castet) were newly created fortified villages in the vicinity of previous castles. The development of the castelnau was either spontaneous or encouraged by the local lord, who granted economic and juridical advantages to settlers coming to work and live on his domain. Created between 1000 and 1300, they were particularly numerous in southern France.

Sauvetés (also called salvetat or sauveterre) were new villages created by the Church. Their development was generally connected to pilgrimages and Crusades. Sauvetés were stopping-places along the routes leading to sanctuaries and places of pilgrimages such as Santiago-de-Compostella in Spain, and along the roads going to the main Mediterranean ports of embarkation to Palestine.

In the 14th century the creation of towns and the conquest of new lands was slowed down by epidemics, disorder and war.

URBAN EMANCIPATION

Peasants, whose lives were strictly framed by the system of feudal domains, did not move about a lot. But in spite of danger, in spite of the ill-controlled forces of nature, and in spite of rudimentary means of transportation, medieval society saw many travelers. Juxtaposed with the immobility of the peasant societies coiled in upon themselves were the continuous travels of merchants, royal officers, militaries, clergymen, Crusaders and pilgrims. Cities offered accommodations and safe resting places on their journeys, as well as local markets where country folk came to sell their products.

On the whole, peasants were rather poor, isolated in their villages, and more or less resigned to their fate; to use a modern word, they tended to be somewhat "conservative." On the other hand, citizens—called burghers, later bourgeois—were generally more "progressive," being active, dynamic, enterprising, open to novelties and accustomed to bargaining with strangers and coexisting with foreigners. Making common cause with each other within their towns, citizens, craftsmen and merchants were realistic people who transformed raw materials into goods, sold those goods, and got acquainted with bargaining and negotiation. They believed in experience, progress, reason, and above all, profit.

Traders were initially ill thought of because by introducing import and export, they disturbed a rural world living more or less in autarky. The Crusades gave a strong impulse to travel and trade, however, and from the 12th century onwards, burghers and merchants formed the driving force of economic development. Now wealthy and aware of themselves and their position, they determined to abolish or at least limit the local lords' despotism. Just like peasants, the citizens were obliged to pay taxes and dependent on the justice of the lord, earl or bishop. In an essentially rural society, the citizens began to claim a certain autonomy, to demand administrative and juridical institutions adapted to their way of life. No longer would they tolerate the slowness and the archaic nature of medieval justice. They suffered under uncontrolled authority, excessive tolls, abuse from boisterous warriors, and the mistrust of the Church, which condemned profit and lucrative activities. They wanted to free themselves from feudal ties and interference.

In spite of the authorities' resistance, the burghers were gradually admitted into society and obtained their freedom. As early as 1032 the burghers of Venice proclaimed their freedom and bound themselves by oath to defend it. The same happened in Milan in 1067 and Lucca in 1068. In 1070, the city of Le Mans in France was in rebellion, followed by Cambrai in 1077 and then by the northern Italian cities of Lombardy and Genoa. In the 12th century large-scale city emancipation began in all the areas between the Seine and Meuse rivers, as well as in Thuringia, Saxony and Bavaria.

The process of urban liberation was extremely complex, long and multiform. Many tactics were used to achieve the goal. Urban merchants needed peace because business could flourish only in order and calm. Citizens

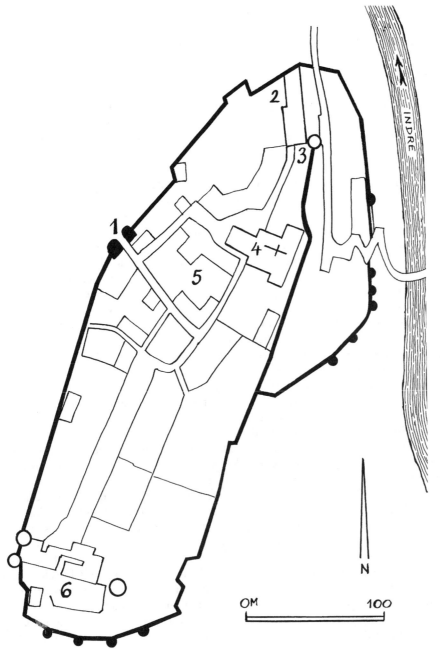

were therefore opposed to boisterous and warlike lords and tried to obtain the king's protection. For their part, kings were quick to understand the growing potential of citizens. They realized that cities could become effective centers of royal authority, to balance the power of the local nobility. Cunningly, kings gave their support to the new class and discouraged local lords from taking the wealth from nearby towns. The alliance of monarchy and bourgeoisie weakened the local power and, in the long run, was one of the ways by which royal authority was restored, particularly in France.

In other European lands the growth of the bourgeoisie had other effects. In Germany and Italy, because of the weakness of the central authority, the emancipation of towns was adverse to the cause of unity, and these lands would not be nationally united until the second half of the 19th century. Since the fall of the Hohenstaufens in 1250, Germany had ceased to be a great power; it was merely a collection of countries, principalities and smaller fiefs of inextricable complexity. The emperor was elected, and the title became honorary with little authority behind it. The fragmentation of Italy was less pronounced than that of Germany; instead of numerous tiny units, Italy had half a dozen regional city-states, perpetually at war with one another, living in a tangle of shifting diplomatic combinations and torn by in-

Ground-plan, Loches (France). Situated near Tours in the Indre-et-Loire, Loches was enclosed by a 2 km long wall erected by the king of England, Henry II, about 1154. Loches was retaken by the French king Philippe Auguste in 1204. In the centuries that followed, Loches was a royal residence. Fortifications were improved and enlarged with many buildings, notably the Logis du Roi (king's house) for Charles VII and his mistress Agnès Sorel. In the 15th century the dungeon of Loches became a state prison where, according to legend, King Louis XI (1461–1483) imprisoned his enemies in iron cages. The ground-plan shows the Royal Gate (1), the Royal House (2), the Agnès Sorel Tower (3), the Saint-Ours church (4), the medieval village (5) and the donjon (6) built by Fulk the Black in the 11th century.

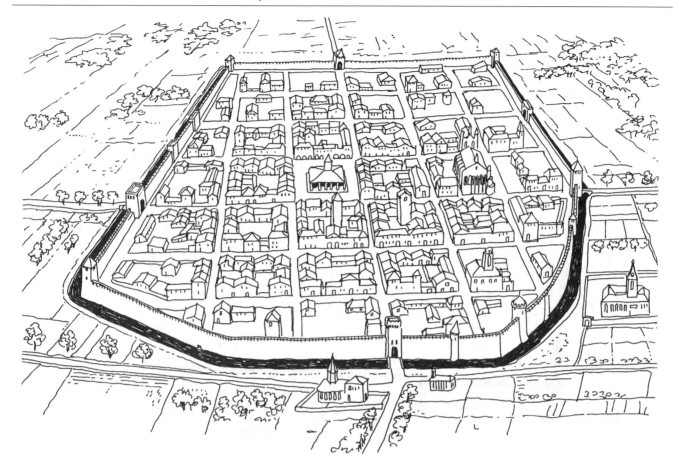

Bastide Mirande (France). Situated on the left bank of river Grande Baïse in the Gers, Mirande was a bastide created in 1281 by the seneschal Eustache de Beaumarchais by order of the French king Philippe III. The bastide counted one large market square, two main streets with four gatehouses, walls, towers and moat.

ternal rivalry between the Gibelins (partisans of the German emperor) and the Guelf party (partisans of the pope).

As for Spain and Portugal, their cities were still on the fringe of medieval Europe. Until the 14th century both countries were engaged against the Moors and divided by internal struggles, dynastic squabbles and conflicts between sovereigns and nobles. The end of the 15th century, however, marks the starting point for the great maritime adventures of these two countries, decisive for the history of the world.

In England, the cooperation of the nobles and the urban merchants forced King John, in 1215, to accept the Magna Carta, reducing the authority of the sovereign.

Another way for an urban community to obtain freedom was to bargain. When the lord departed for the Crusades, he needed funds, and when he came back from Palestine he might be ruined. The urban citizens might lend money and negotiate with him to buy back some feudal rights and duties to redeem debts. Freedom thus had to be paid for—sometimes a high price, but it was worth the money.

Another way, much more dangerous, was violence. Some urban communities entered into armed rebellion against the lord and attempted to impose freedom by force.

Emancipation, whether obtained by royal grant, negotiation or violence, was noted, authenticated and sealed in an official document called a charter. The content of the charter was extremely variable according to many factors such as local customs, circumstances, and the strength and position of the concerned parties. Generally, however, the charter officially recognized the freedom of the city (i.e., recognized the city as an autonomous political body) and stipulated immunities, concessions, exemptions, the annual tax paid to the king, and the rights and duties of each side as well as the privileges, fundamental freedoms and institutions of the city.

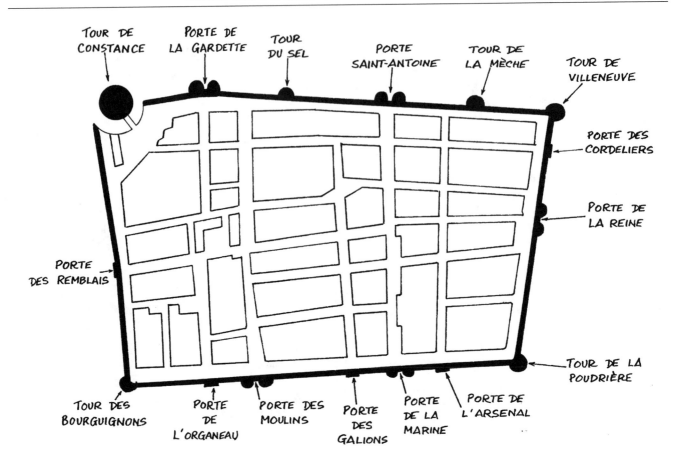

Ground-plan, Aigues-Mortes (France). Aigues-Mortes was a bastide created by the king of France, Louis IX (called Saint-Louis), who reigned from 1226 to 1270. The purpose of this creation was to provide the French realm with a port on the Mediterranean Sea to communicate with Palestine during the Crusades. In 1241, a road was built through the marsh, a colony was established, and a huge tower was erected. The construction proceeded during the reign of Philippe III le Hardi from 1270 to 1285. Built between 1272 and 1300, the enceinte was designed by the Genovese architect Guilhelmo Boccanegra. It was composed of a rectangle approximately 1.7 km in perimeter enclosing a surface of 16 hectares. The curtains were 11 m high and 2.5 m thick with corner- and wall-towers, five main gatehouses and five posterns. The decline of Aigues-Mortes as a port was due to the silting up of the site and to the fact that Provence—-with the harbors Marseille and Toulon—became French in 1481. Today Aigues-Mortes is situated a few kilometers inland, and the remarkable 13th century walls and the powerful Tour de Constance are perfectly preserved.

The town was governed by a college of elected aldermen and municipal magistrates headed by a mayor or a burgomaster. However, the urban government was never democratic. By the middle of the 14th century, the power was monopolized by the richest merchants. This upper class oligarchy created the capitalist economy driven by a bourgeoisie who drew their living from properties and investments.

Towns also generated a new middle class of society including educated men, managers, bankers, financiers, and lawyers. This class provided state officials, civil servants, jurists, councilors, administrators, and ministers as well as intellectuals and teachers as the Church gradually lost its monopoly over science and education.

Merchants were able to develop social and economic organizations free from feudal rule. Foreign traders and bankers were always welcomed in the main cities, especially those from Venice, Florence and northern Germany; they helped to organize international exchange and developed fairs held in the big market towns. The rich bourgeois dominated the urban people, the lower classes composed of craftsmen, workers, companions and apprentices; this subordinate population formed a lumpen proletariat, ill-paid, living in miserable conditions with uncertain resources and exposed to economic crises, famines and epidemics. Social struggles and political conflicts between the common man and the patrician sometimes resulted in riots and armed rebellions.

Though they had limited juridical rights, urban craftsmen and workers were strictly controlled by a guild, similar in some ways to our modern trade unions. The guild was a brotherhood, a hierarchical organization of skilled workers, a society of men who practiced the same trade. The term guild comes from the Saxon word *gildan*, to pay, because members paid towards the costs of the association. Guilds controlled the standards of products, prices, wages and training of craftsmen. They gave board and lodging to young apprentices and made rules requiring sick pay and

Cross-section, Tour de Constance in Aigues-Mortes (France). The huge Constance tower, completed in 1248, was a 32 m high cylinder, 22 m in diameter with walls 6 m thick. Built in a swampy site, the tower rests on solid foundations composed of pillars. The tower includes two vast vaulted chambers and a crenellated top platform with a watch-tower used as a lighthouse.

forbidding night work. Their leaders formed the borough council headed by a guild-master or chairman.

Some cities obtained only privileges but remained under the direct tutelage of the local lord, prelate, bishop or archbishop. Other cities were submitted to the authority of a prince, king or emperor. Still other urban communities became totally independent. Called communes in northern Europe and municipalities in the South, free-towns became collective powers, autonomous laic republics or independent principalities. According to the charter, free cities had the right to maintain a permanent army, build fortifications, make war, and conclude alliances and peace treaties. Many towns had their own justice system, their own minted money, their own weights and measures and their own collective heraldic emblems such as seals, flags, banners, devices, and coats-of-arms.

Certain free cities established strong economic connections with one another. Created in the 12th century, the Hansa—officially called Stete van der Dudeschen Hense—was a group of about 150 merchant cities in northern Germany and the Baltic Sea. The main Hansa towns were Lübeck, Hamburg, Minden, Cologne, Dortmund, Bremen, Rostock, Brunswick, Stralsund, Danzig, Vwasby and Riga. The Hansa worked closely with the Teutonic knights in eastern Europe and included commercial establishments in western Europe, in England (London), in Belgium (Bruges), in Netherlands (Amsterdam, Groningen, Kampen), in Scandinavia (Bergen in Norway) and in Russia (Novgorod).

Others cities and towns made military unions, such as the Cinque Ports, a group including Dover, Sandwich, Romney, Hythe and Hastings that secured the defense of the southern English coasts. Some concluded temporary political and military alliances, such as the league of Lombardian towns grouped together to resist the German emperor's pretensions in northern Italy. But towns did not always work together; in fact, rivalry between them sometimes resulted in conflict and even war.

Hence in addition to their economic significance, towns played a more and more important political role from the 13th century onwards. A slow displacement of forces took place, with the coastal areas taking on primary importance as the revival of commerce, the rise of the towns, and the creation of wider areas of agriculture (which could feed a larger population) came at the expense of the older, inland regions.

The amount of urban rebirth was not, however, the same in all areas, nor did it take place with the same speed everywhere. The implantation of a network of cities varied a great deal. The most significant urban development happened principally along the major European communication roads, coasts and rivers. Urban development and commercial activities were particularly strong in northern Italy (in Tuscany and principally in Lombardy between the Alps and the Mediterranean maritime ways), in Flanders and northern Germany (trading with England, Scandinavia and Baltic regions) and in northeast France (on rivers Seine, Meuse, Scheldt and Rhine, at the junction of north German and Italian commercial roads).

URBAN FORTIFICATIONS

Unlike our modern, wide-open cities, medieval towns were completely closed. The first concern of a free city was to build a wall protecting the city's inhabitants and wealth. The role of the enceinte was to define the urban surface and to indicate the space to be populated. The wall was an object of pride and prestige, a sign of independence and of union, a source of confidence and self-awareness. It was the expression of physical and moral solidarity, the reflection of the citizens' spirit. The city wall was the legitimate conclusion of the process of emancipation that made the inhabitants no longer villeins but a recognized social group.

The urban wall also constituted a juridical border. The town had tutelage over the surrounding countryside, which furnished raw materials, food and manpower. The town's authority (ban) generally spread about one lieue (about 4 km), whence the French term *banlieue*, meaning suburb. A very important city might dominate a whole region, even a whole province. In such cases the defensive system was composed of a network of strongholds and might even include allied or submitted cities. Venice, for example, dominated a wide empire including a part of northern Italy, towns and ports on the shores of the Adriatic sea, trading posts in Corfu, and parts of Greece up to the islands Cyclades, Crete and Cyprus.

Urban defenses, when they existed, were in many cases vestiges of ancient Roman enceintes or improvised fortifications dating from the time of Viking invasions. Fortifications were built or reconstructed according to the richness and importance of the city. Because a city wall was a heavy financial burden, the strength of such walls varied greatly. Certain towns could not afford strong defenses and had to be satisfied with rudimentary and symbolic fortifications consisting of moats, earth entrenchments, wooden towers, palisades and simple gateways. Many cities retained earthwork defenses until quite late in the medieval period; at both Coventry and Sandwich (Great Britain) such fortifications were replaced by stone walls only in the 15th century. Though stone walls were by no means universal, some towns with regional and even international influence had huge budgets and were able to build defenses as strong as those of the most impressive castles.

The construction of the urban enceinte was a long process, lasting for years. The periphery was generally marked out by a moat, an earth wall and a palisade. Then the high-priority works such as towers and gatehouses were built in stone. The masonry walls were constructed last, when funds permitted. The construction depended on budget but also on the population growth, the threat of danger, and the probability of war. Certain enceintes were never completed.

Construction and maintenance were financed by the municipality and the citizens themselves. While the building of a castle was due to a lord's private initiative, construction of a city wall was a collective undertaking. The urban wall, therefore, was possible only with the resumption of the ancient concept of public interest, a concept that had disappeared with the collapse of the Roman empire. To finance the design, construction and maintenance of a wall, the municipality set up a fiscal system managed by civil servants. A town under the authority of a king, emperor, prince, lord or religious prelate usually asked the ruler for subventions, fiscal exonerations, privileges or the right to levy taxes and tolls. Because maintenance was so costly, urban fortifications were usually neglected during peacetime or when the immediate danger had passed. In wartime they were hastily refurbished and put in a state of readiness, but restorations, adaptations and consolidations were generally improvised and rather poorly done. In all circumstances, urban medieval walls were subject to an immutable law regarding their dimensions: they invariably followed the smallest perimeter. Every extension of the town diameter, every foot of masonry, implied greater building costs, greater maintenance expenses, and a larger garrison for adequate defense.

While a private castle housed a tiny group of combatants in a small space, a town embraced a rather large number of non-combatant inhabitants whose lives and work were spread over a relatively large surface. The urban enceinte was an ensemble of comprehensive military constructions established around a place of life and work and intended to provide security. Its configuration was the result of difficult compromises between the requirements of defense, which demanded inaccessibility (possibly equal to that of a castle), and living and trading conditions, which tended on the contrary to establish the city near a commercial road, to develop the surface, and to provide multiple access points. Obviously, efficient fortification of a large city was a difficult and expensive task.

The evolution of urban military architecture was directly connected to castle fortification, and most elements used to protect castles were applied in the protection of towns. Cities were enclosed by curtains of various thickness (usually about 2 m) and height (usually 7 to 10 m, but in some cases up to 20 m). Walls were insurmountable obstacles to normal transit and furnished with wall-walks and crenellated breastworks. Within range of bow and crossbow, curtains were flanked by brattices, échauguettes, pepper-pot turrets and towers of varied height, strength and shape. These elements were fitted with combat emplacements such as crenels and merlons, loopholes and crosslets, hoarding, and later machicolation. Walls and towers were sometimes surrounded by a ditch or a wet moat.

While one tends to think of the city walls in terms of siege, with defenders behind the crenellation casting down projectiles on ascending invaders, the everyday and even more important purpose of walls was control and entry in peacetime. The defining characteristic of urban fortification was, therefore, the importance given to the access, by definition the most vulnerable place in a fortified unit.

The main streets of the city were always anterior to the construction of the wall; at the junction of the new wall and older roads, gatehouses were built. Urban gatehouses had the same structure as those of castles. They included a wide, arched portal deeply recessed between two strong flanking towers, heavy doors, a drawbridge, and a portcullis with a chamber for windlass on the first floor. Active combat emplacements on the gatehouse included shooting chambers, a guard-house, loopholes, crosslets, murder-holes and a brattice. Beside military defensive elements, the city gatehouse also included a custom-office where taxes and tolls were levied on all persons and goods coming in or out the city. The gate taxes were the major form of income for medieval cities. Obviously a heavily guarded point, the gatehouse might also include an arsenal for weapons and ammunition, apartments for civil servants or a prison. The city gatehouse also played a prestigious and symbolic role: Its imposing defenses displayed the city's strength, and its many ornaments made an ostentatious show to visitors and travelers, bespeaking the city's wealth and importance.

For security reasons, access to the town was as limited as possible, and the result was often annoying traffic jams, particularly on market days. To alleviate the problem, secondary accesses, called posterns, were arranged and opened in peacetime. But from dusk to dawn, all drawbridges, gates and posterns were closed.

Road transport was dangerous, difficult and slow in the Middle Ages, especially for heavy loads. River transportation was the favored alternative. Despite the dangers and problems rivers sometimes presented—including sandbars, currents, eddies, floods, tolls, bridges and water-mills—they were used to convey communications, cargo and passengers. Rivers were also valuable as sources of energy for mills and water to supply defensive wet moats. Cities situated on waterways were generally prosperous, with much commercial activity, and inland navigation guilds were very powerful.

Cities situated on waterways were generally walled off against the riverbanks, with special gates leading to landings and bridges. But if the waterway bisected the town it formed a very dangerous breach in the defensive system. In this case the river access was defended by strong towers and chains if the waterway was broad. If the river was rather narrow, it was fortified by a water-gate. Water-gates were usually similar to gatehouses, but the portal was replaced by one or more arches allowing navigation. Like gatehouses, water-gates were fitted with defensive elements (towers with shooting chambers, loopholes and so on) and with the customary check-points for cash tolls, dues and taxes. The arches were closed at night and in case of danger by a portcullis and heavy chains.

SUBURBS

Towns were growing bodies, attracting more and more people. The story of medieval cities is the story of people trying to get into town, not out of it. Only towns, with their special legal status, offered freedom, as well as the conditions and facilities for an existence based on the production and exchange of goods and services as opposed to the rural life on the land outside. That is primarily what medieval cities were for, as is illustrated by a common German saying: "Stadtluft macht frei" (city air makes free).

Outside the town, in front of the gatehouse, there was generally an inn or two for travelers who arrived after the gates were closed at night. A few artisans and shopkeepers might move alongside, and after a while, economic activities just outside of the main gates would begin to mushroom. A new settlement was created, called a faubourg or suburb. The suburb might also be built by new settlers and growing populations who found no place left inside the town and built houses outside, where the ground was available and cheaper. A faubourg might also come to existence because of the installation of a convent outside the walls; this sometimes happened as Franciscan, Dominican and other mendicant orders sought to fulfill their twofold mission of helping the poor and purging the heretics. In other cases suburbs grew between two inhabited centers which developed and fused.

Suburbs of course were a bit risky; lying outside the protection of the walls, they were exposed to theft in peacetime and destruction and looting in wartime. They were also sometimes seen as undesirable; municipalities tried to regulate and sometimes to forbid the illegal and spontaneous occupations. After a while, however, the temporary settlement became a part of the town. The faubourg might even turn into a major satellite of economic life in competition with the older and usually smaller markets within the walls.

In a typical situation, a town was constructed on one bank of a river, and the opposite bank was occupied by a suburb called a bridge-head. The bridge connecting both parts of the city was fortified like a gatehouse. This very common disposition can be seen in Besalú (Spain), Frankfurt (Germany), Scaliger bridge in Verona (Italy), and Valentré bridge in Cahors (France), just to mention a few.

In most cases, there came a point at which the economic pressure of the suburbs and of the growing population could not be denied and the risks and fiscal burden of a new wall could not be resisted. At that point, a faubourg was integrated within the town and fortified with new walls, towers, a moat and a gatehouse. If growth continued, a second, third or even fourth enceinte had to be built. Previous walls were swallowed up in the urban landscape, or they were demolished and their materials used to make the new one. In some cases the poorest inhabitants would squat in the ruins; in others, rich bourgeois would buy towers and turn them into habitations. Old wet moats might be filled in, or they might be converted to an internal network of concentric canals, as can be seen in Amsterdam (Netherlands).

By the end of the Middle Ages, many European towns had developed the physiognomy they would generally keep until the Industrial Revolution in the second half of the 19th century. The oldest part of a settlement was the administrative and religious city (cité in French, Altstadt in German, castrum in Italian, ciudad vieja in Spanish), while the economic suburbs formed the town (ville, Neustadt or civitas).

Most town fortifications have been swept away since the Middle Ages. Most of them were either torn down during the Industrial Revolution, when more space was needed, or lost in the large scale destruction of World War II. Even today, however, there are a great number of places where a tower, a section of wall or an original gateway can still be seen. These surviving structures represent only a fraction of the thousands of towns in Europe that are known to have had enclosing walls.

At any rate, despite later construction, the ravages of fire or war, and modern renovations and enlargements, many European cities have preserved charming and delightful sights from the Middle Ages such as cathedrals, churches, narrow streets, old houses, squares, canals, bridges and many other historical, architectural and cultural places of interest.

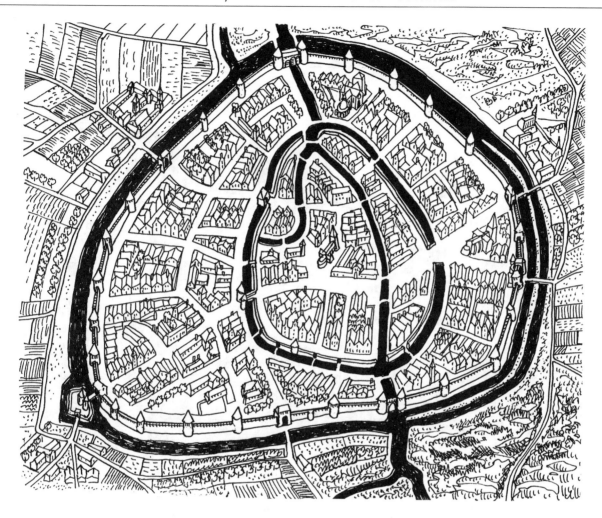

Ground-plan, Amersfoort (Netherlands). Amersfoort, situated near Utrecht, developed in the 12th century. The bishop of Utrecht, Hendrik van Vianden, granted the inhabitants city-right in 1259, and the first enceinte was raised about 1269. The town, enriched by the trade of cloth and the production of beer, was enlarged, resulting in new walls built between 1380 and 1450. Measuring 2,850 m in perimeter, this enclosure was reinforced between 1560 and 1570 by an earth bulwark. During the war against the Spaniards (1568–1648), the fortifications were modernized by five Italian-style bastions designed by engineer Adriaan Anthonisz between 1591 and 1594.

PRIVATE URBAN FORTIFICATIONS

The collective character of the city walls did not exclude private fortification inside the town. Relationships between rich and poor were not always peaceful, and for this reason wealthy merchants, rich bourgeois, patrician families and noblemen dwelled in fortified stone houses. Such houses reflected the urban aristocracy's preoccupations: to protect persons and property and to show off the power of the ruling class, which intended to keep economic, military and juridical control over the town and its inhabitants.

The characteristics of fortified stone houses varied quite a bit according to place, period and, of course, the wealth of the owner. A fortified house could be a tower or a large masonry house, featuring elements of the previously described rural 12th century donjon. It generally included several stories divided into rooms, a hall, store-places, apartments and other accommodations. The ground-floor might be arranged as a blind store-room, and the entrance to the house was often placed on the first

Amersfoort (Netherlands). View of the Koppelpoort water-gate

floor with a defensive staircase. The top of the house might include military elements such as a wall-walk with crenellation, a watch-tower, a brattice, or a turret in order to deter or repulse a rebellious, rioting mob. The richest and the highest placed in the hierarchy dwelled in luxurious residences, some of them so large and so magnificent that they could be called palaces, composed of several buildings, fitted with many facilities, opening up to a yard or a garden enclosed by walls.

Palaces, residences and stone houses were numerous in all European cities. A good preserved example of urban patrician strongholds is San Gimignano in Tuscany (Italy).

Urban private fortified houses were not the monopoly of the rich laic oligarchy. Bishops and archbishops dwelled in a tower, a residence or a palace generally built near the cathedral. Prelates' houses were on the whole similar to those of the richest men in town; they were both prestige buildings and military strongholds protecting clergymen and their property. The monks of the

neighborhood often had an urban establishment (called a refugium) which they occupied in troubled time. Rich abbots generally made use of an urban pied-à-terre, either living there permanently or occupying it only during their visits in town; an example was the Hôtel de Cluny in Paris.

In the regions exposed to pirates and raiders, and in Spain and Portugal during the Reconquista against the Moors, cathedrals and churches were frequently fortified. The same was true for abbeys and convents. When Benedictine and Cistercian abbeys were isolated in the countryside, Dominican and Franciscan convents were established in towns or in the suburbs. Nevertheless urban convents and rural abbeys had many architectural similarities combining material and spiritual life. They included an abbatial church, chapels, cloisters, a chapter-hall, and various conventual buildings such as a scriptorium, a library, and sleeping and eating accommodations for the brothers; service facilities such as store-places, a kitchen, an infirmary, and washing facilities; a

260

Gatehouse in Nancy, Lorraine (France)

The Grand Châtelet gatehouse in Paris (France). The Grand Châtelet, built in 1130, was intended to defend the access to the island of the Cité. Used as a prison in the Middle Ages, it was demolished in 1800.

garden, a cemetery and a guest-house. Rural or urban, monasteries were always enclosed by a wall, which isolated the community and marked the border between a sacred sanctuary and the profane world outside. Some monasteries were genuine fortresses; others were just enclosed behind a poor wall.

URBAN MILITIA

Among the urban privileges stipulated by the charter of freedom was the right for a free city to raise troops. The urban militia was an armed force composed of physically able volunteers recruited from among the inhabitants. Militiamen were not paid, and therefore they were recruited from the richest men of the town—the only ones who had spare time to train and enough money to pay for weapons and military equipment. Militiamen were usually well motivated, for they defended their family and property. They fought for a simple cause and concrete interests: customs, privileges and liberty.

The municipal militia's main purpose was to defend the town. The city walls were divided into sectors manned by neighboring militiamen who were grouped in companies under command of a captain. In time of trouble, the militia was on a war footing; gatehouse control was reinforced, and persons, boats and vehicles were searched. The municipality might also raise the entire male population in case of siege or for an expedition into enemy territory. In wartime, the militia might be reinforced by a royal contingent or allied units, but the municipality was often reluctant to introduce foreign troops within its walls, partly for financial reasons and partly for fear of losing a part of its independence.

In peacetime, the militia served as a police force for keeping public order. Its members arrested criminals and thieves, guarded the accesses and walked night-watch. The militia also played a significant political role by securing the established order and, possibly, repressing rebellion against the ruling class.

Medieval municipal armed forces obtained several resounding military victories. In 1176, Italian militias de-

Bargate in Southampton (Britain)

263

Westgate in Canterbury, Kent (Britain)

feated the German emperor Friedrich Barbarossa in Legnano, a disaster that stupefied the entire feudal world. In Kortrijk in 1302, the Flemish militiamen crushed the élite of French chivalry in the so-called Golden Spurs battle. In 1315, the Swiss won the battle of Morgarten over the German emperor Leopold of Austria, marking the freedom of the Helvetic confederation.

Overall, however, the military value of urban mili-

tias was dubious. They were largely composed of dilettante civilians, men more at ease in their shops, behind their desks or in their workshops than on the battlefield. Moreover, many rich bourgeois found the condition of soldier unworthy of their rank, considered fighting too dangerous for themselves and their sons, and felt they had better things to do than training, patrolling at night and guarding the windy city walls. Instead, rich citizens ob-

Porte Saint Michel in Guérande, Brittany (France)

tained exemptions and gladly agreed to pay taxes that would allow the municipality to recruit professional soldiers and mercenaries.

In the late Middle Ages and during the Renaissance, urban militias proper were usually deprived of active military service. They were relegated to auxiliary police forces or fire-brigades, or became mundane associations or shooting clubs, marching with colorful uniforms, drums and flags on parade and feast days.

THE CITADEL

Until now we have discussed the medieval town in its ideal form: the free and independent city-republic, run by and for the bourgeois and dominating a wide area of the surrounding agriculture land. But this ideal was achieved by only a few cities, and in many cases the secular barons, dukes, and kings, the ecclesiastical princes, and their fortified residences remained a significant and characteristic part of medieval towns. The interests of the nobility and the bourgeoisie were often in fundamental contradiction, and both parties tried to settle down to a more or less mutually beneficial coexistence. As a voracious parasite, the feudal urban magnate took wealth from the citizens in return for "protection" from a very particular kind of fortification: the citadel.

The term citadel comes from the Italian word *cittadella*, meaning small city. The citadel was a fortress built within a fortified city. It was placed in a dominant position inside the town and often overlapped the urban

Groningen (Netherlands). Oosterpoort

266

Hainburg (Austria). Vienna gatehouse, 1260

Templin (Germany). Preslau gatehouse

Marvejols (France)

269

La Rochelle (France). Tour Saint-Nicolas. Together with the Tour de la Chaîne and the Tour de la Lanterne, the huge Saint-Nicolas tower was intended to defend the harbor of La Rochelle.

Maastricht (Netherlands). Helpoort gatehouse, 13th century

271

Verdun (France). La Porte Chaussée gatehouse

fortifications, which allowed its access to be independent from the city gates. The citadel was accessible by a main gate turned toward the city and a secondary access leading directly to the countryside.

In certain cases, the citadel was an ancient preexisting castle or an enlarged and fortified residence around which the city developed. It might also be a newly created fortress fulfilling three distinctive roles.

The first role was logistical: The citadel contained everything needed in order to resist a long siege, such as living accommodations; stores of food, water and forage; and arsenals and workshops. It was also a supply point and winter quarters for armies in a campaign, as well as a military, fiscal and administrative center.

Secondly, the citadel was a powerful military bulwark. Just like the keep in the medieval castle, it acted as a final fall-back position, a retreat from which to continue the defense even when the town was conquered.

The citadel was therefore strongly fortified with powerful towers, high walls, and a fortified gatehouse with drawbridge and deep ditches. This display of strength was also intended to deter enemies from laying siege.

The third and most important role was political. The fortress on its rocky height dominated the city and its approach; the town nestled below in its shadow, perpetually reminded of its dependence.

Citadels were often built in the most important cities of realms, duchies, counties or ecclesiastical principalities as residences for kings, dukes, earls or high prelates. These powerful rulers—living on the resources of the nation as a whole—dwelled within splendid palaces with gardens and dependencies. In less important cities where the rulers did not live permanently, the citadel was occupied by royal, ducal or episcopal representatives and governors. In some cases the citadel was intended to subjugate, control and overawe conquered populations of questionable loyalty or municipalities with rebellious propensity.

The citadel had its own garrison, loyal to the ruler and ready to repress insurrections, as well as its own civil servants collecting taxes. The garrison might also discourage the inhabitants from surrendering at a premature stage in a siege. Very often the construction and maintenance of the expensive citadel as well as the occupying garrison's pay were financed by citizens' money.

For all these reasons, the citadel represented a threat. It was an unpopular, even hated place, an object of terror and dictatorship as well as a financial burden. Consequently, as soon as relationships between the occupiers and the conquered population improved, urban authorities usually asked for the dismantling of the citadel, or at least military takeover of its expenditures.

In Britain the castles built by King Edward I in Wales in the second half of the 13th century were citadels intended to secure his communication lines, to house English garrisons and to submit the rebellious Welsh. In France the citadels were directly linked with the consolidation of the royal power and the territorial expansion which principally begin under Louis XI's reign (Beaune, Dijon and Auxonne citadels, for example, were built after the annexation of Burgundy in 1577). In the Netherlands, Germany, Spain and Italy, the citadel, respectively called dwangburcht, Festung, alcazaba and rocca, was often both a dwelling place and a fortress occupied by the local ruler.

Citadels played an important role in the 16th and 17th centuries. In the 18th century, however, citadels lost their political role because of the population's loyalty, and in the 19th century they lost their military function because of the creation of outer rings of detached forts. Today many citadels remain military or civil administrative centers, and some are still palaces occupied by nobility, while others have been turned into prisons or museums.

Zwolle (Netherlands). Sassenpoort

Top: *Verona (Italy). Ponte Scaligero and Castel Vecchio, 1354.* Bottom: *Schematic view of a bridge-head: (1) city enceinte; (2) city gatehouse; (3) fortified bridge; (4) fortified bridge-head with walls and gatehouse*

San Gimignano (Italy). San Gimignano, situated near Sienna in Tuscany, in the 12th century was a prosperous free city. However, like many other Italian towns, San Gimignano was divided by internal rivalry, the Gibelins (partisans of the German emperor) opposing the Guelf party (faithful to the pope). During those troubled times, rich families built square fortified living towers called torri gentilizie. The highest tower (Torre della Rognosa) was 51 m high. The city had seventy-two towers in the Middle Ages; today, thirteen are left.

MEDIEVAL URBANISM

From the 12th century onwards, towns and ports became again what they were in ancient Roman times: places of life, tools for the production and exchange of goods and service, as well as religious, cultural, industrial, political and administrative centers. However, in spite of their growth, medieval towns maintained rather small populations; a population exceeding 30,000 was large for the time.

Though it is very difficult to know the exact number of citizens before the 15th century, the most populated European towns were found in Italy. Milan and Venice, with probably 200,000 inhabitants each, and Paris with probably 100,000 were exceptionally large. Ghent and Bruges, the richest towns in Belgium, each counted about 50,000. London had 40,000, as many as Cologne, one of the most important German cities. Barcelona, capital of the kingdom of Catalonia in Spain, had about 35,000 inhabitants; Narbonne and Toulouse, important towns in southern France, each had about 30,000; Vienna, the capital of Austria, had only 20,000. Many towns counted only a few thousand inhabitants, many others even fewer.

Enclosed within their walls, cities developed without an urban plan. Unlike Roman settlements, which were

Dutch patrician stone house

Cross-section of a patrician stone house

Hôtel de Clisson, Paris. The Hôtel de Clisson, located at 58 rue des Archives (3rd arrondissement), was built in 1371 by constable Olivier de Clisson. Today only two pepper-pot turrets are preserved. The rest of the hôtel is incorporated in the Hôtel de Rohan and the National French Archives buildings.

Hôtel de Sens, Paris. The archepiscopal residence, located in the rue de l'Hôtel-de-Ville, was constructed from 1475 to 1507 by the archbishop of Sens. The bishopric of Paris depended on the archdiocese of Sens until 1622.

more or less regularly planned and carefully organized, medieval towns were labyrinths of streets, lanes, alleys and back-streets. Such irregular layouts developed as a result of landowners (including noblemen, the rich bourgeois, and religious communities) jealously preserving their possessions. Insistence on private property rights defeated any attempts at regulation or the application of measures aimed at improving municipal facilities for the common good.

Today we tend to picture medieval towns as squalid and chaotic, with their accumulated houses, overcrowding, absence of urban services, congested circulation, traffic-jams in narrow streets, noise and swarming citizens. Beyond their aspect of confusion, however, towns usually did have a measure of organization, being made up of small cells of sorts with their own particularities. Artisans of the same craft were grouped in special streets or neighborhoods. Clergymen clustered around the cathedral; convents, canons-chapters, the bishop's house, chapels and other religious buildings formed a distinct ecclesiastical establishment within the city. Intellectuals, teachers and

Palais des Papes in Avignon (Vaucluse, France). Situated at the junction of rivers Rhône and Durance, the site of Avignon was occupied from the neolithic period onward. The place was successively dominated by the Celts, the Greeks from Marseille, the Romans, the Visigoths, the Moors, the Franks, the realm of Aquitaine, the duchy of Provence and the German empire. In 1129, Avignon became a free city, then passed under the tutelage of the duke of Anjou in 1290.

At the beginning of the 14th century, Christiandom entered a serious crisis, resulting in two rival papal powers, one in Rome and the second established by the French king in Avignon. From 1309 to 1377, seven popes (Clement V, John XXII, Benedict XII, Clement VI, Innocent VI, Urban V and Gregory XI) ruled the Church from Avignon. This division came to an end after the council of Constance in 1418, when the pope was restored and reestablished in Rome.

The papal palace of Avignon, the fortified residence of the popes, was created by Benedict XII between 1334 and 1342, enlarged by Clement VI between 1342 and 1352, modified by Innocent VI from 1352 to 1362 and completed by Urban V from 1362 to 1370. Officially Avignon and its region, the Comtat-Venaissin, belonged to the papacy until May 1791. During the French Revolution, the Palais des Papes was used as a prison, and after that as barracks until 1906. Since that time the palace has been a historical monument.

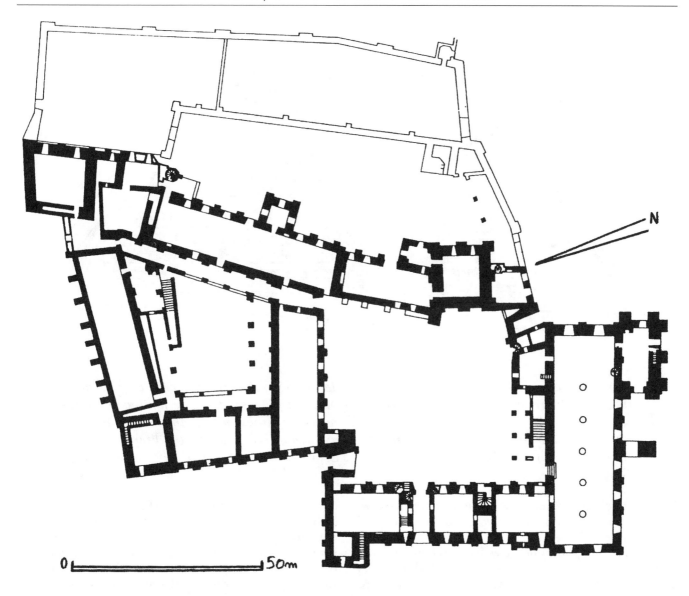

Ground-plan, Palais des Papes, Avignon

students (later printers, publishers and booksellers) were gathered in a part of the city called the university (the Latin Quarter in Paris, for example). Merchants and traders established their offices, shops and warehouses near the market, along the main roads and near the harbor. Foreign bankers, traders, money-changers, and financiers had their own street or ward.

In some cases, urban space was so limited and the parcels of ground so expensive that houses were even built on both sides of the bridges (Ponte Vecchio in Florence or Pont au Change in Paris, for example). In other cases, densely populated areas were concentrated around the main square and main streets, leaving a kind of countryside near the walls within the city where scattered houses, huts and barns stood here and there amid fields, meadows, vegetable gardens and waste-grounds.

Public squares were not numerous, and those that existed were rather limited in area. They were formed by the junction of two or more alleys, and in the center there was a pillory, a cross, a statue or a fountain. Towns did often have a main central square where the largest streets converged. The central square, whose dimensions varied from town to town, played an essential role in daily economic and social life. Similar to the Greek agora and the Roman forum, it was the heart of the town, on the sides of which were built the houses of the rich citizens and the main public buildings.

Streets are the basic units of public space in a city.

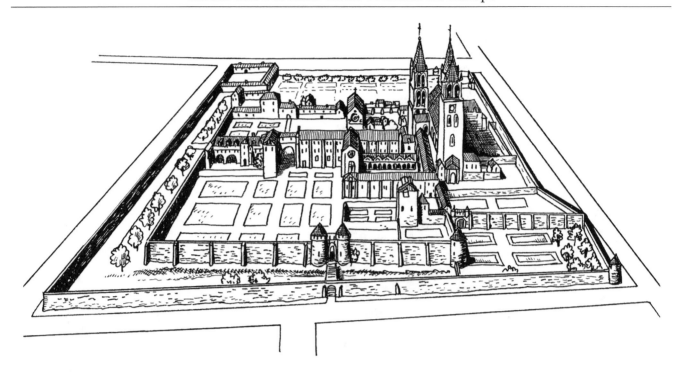

Saint-Germain-des-Prés abbey, Paris. Completed in 558, the site was created as a sanctuary for the relic of Saint Vincent's tunic. A place of pilgrimage made famous by miracles and wonders, the sanctuary became a benedictine abbey in the 8th century and was renamed Saint-Germain-des-Prés. The abbey was demolished during the French Revolution in 1794, and today only the Romanesque church is preserved on the boulevard Saint-Germain.

In the Middle Ages they were tortuous, dark, narrow, muddy, filthy and bad-smelling because of the absence of public services. Some cities did at least order garbage to be carted to dumps outside the walls. Street dirt and manure were generally washed away by rain, and the rivers were even more important as open sewers than they were as traffic arteries. Streets were in most cases unpaved with a central draining gutter. They were bumpy and broken by the coming and going of carts; encumbered with domestic animals; and spoiled by garbage, dirty water, and filth. Most of them were so narrow that they were actually mere footways and lanes exclusively suitable for pedestrians. In southern Europe (Spain, Portugal, southern France and Italy) the width of the streets was influenced by considerations of climate: a narrow street enjoyed maximum shade.

Streets had names, but no signs on which the names were indicated, and houses did not carry numbers. The houses were packed together and were usually three to four stories high, sometimes even higher. Cellars and attics were generally storing-places, and the upper stories were arranged as apartments; ground-floors were the domain of professional activity, housing both manufacture

and sale. The combined workshop and storefront encroached upon the street. Consequently, the street was not only a public circulation way but also a private working and trading space as well as a collective social place of daily life where people met each other, hung around, shopped, were entertained, played, ate, quarreled, and so on. In spite of regulations issued by some municipalities regarding the width of streets, the frontage lines that could not be exceeded, and the minimum height at which a building projection was permissible, encroachment sometimes went to such extremes that a house might extend all the way across a street, leaving only an underpass of minimum viable height.

Stone was an expensive material reserved for the rich and used mainly for public buildings. Houses for the common urban people were generally covered with tiles or thatched roofs, and walls were made of bricks or timber frameworks filled with cob and dried mud. Walls might also be made of wattle-and-daub: wattle was a frame of wooden stakes with long twigs woven between them, and daub was a kind of plaster that was smeared on top of the wattle to make a smooth, thick cement.

Houses' internal arrangements and creature comforts

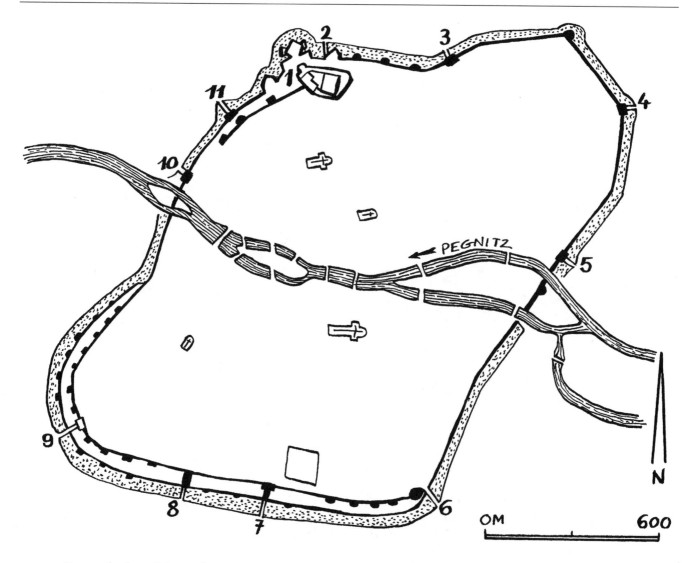

Ground-plan, Nuremberg (Bavaria, Germany). Nuremberg (Nürnberg in German) was heavily fortified, with walls 5 km in perimeter, 128 towers, and ditches 12 m deep and 20 m wide. The medieval fortifications (Stadtbefestigung), completed about 1452, are preserved today. The ground-plan shows the imperial palace Keiserburgau (1) and the main city-gates: Vestnertor (2), Maxtor (3), Laufertor (4), Hubnerstor (5), Königstor (6), Karthausertor (7), Frauentor and Färbertor (8), Ludwigstor (9), Hallertor (10) and Neutor (11).

varied according to region, period and the wealth of the dwellers, but on the whole, living conditions were rather primitive and home facilities were poor. Citizens had to fetch water from the nearest public fountain and attend public baths.

Life in town was hard, but the population was regularly entertained. Local feasts, numerous religious ceremonies (notably the days of saints), harvests, the coming of the king, the birth of a prince, the marriage of an important personality or a military victory—all were celebrated with church bells ringing, decorated façades, colorful parades, receptions, tournaments, jousts, popular feasts, and banquets with music and dance. The church organized imposing free shows before the cathedral; these so-called mystery plays are ancestors of secular theater. Inns and taverns, too, were places of meeting, discussion, music, dance and fun. Public baths and taverns might also be places of prostitution.

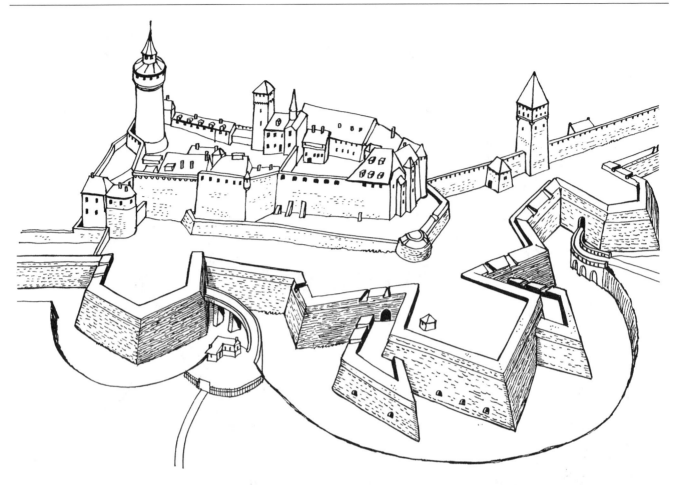

Kaiserburg, Nuremberg (Germany). The imperial palace (Kaiserburg) is situated north of the city. It was the residence for the burgraves and emperors from the 11th to the 15th century. The Kaiserburg is composed of a circular donjon (Sinwellturm) erected about 1200 by the Hohenstaufen emperors. Construction continued throughout the Middle Ages, with various accommodations and buildings. Between 1538 and 1545, the fortress was reinforced by Italian-style bastions designed by the engineer Antonio Fazzuni Maltese. Note the typical old Italian-style entrances placed in the bastion flanks and the curious angular artillery bulwarks added to the flanks of the middle bastion.

Opposite: *Ground-plan, Nantes (Loire-Atlantique, France). Nantes is situated at the junction of rivers Erdre and Loire. The city, created by the Romans, was one of the residences of the dukes of Brittany in the Middle Ages. The ground-plan shows the Roman enceinte (1), the 13th century walls (2), the Saint-Pierre gate (3), the Sauvetout gate (4), the Saint-Nicolas gate (5), the Poissonière gate (6), the city extension in the 16th century with its bastioned enceinte (7) and the castle of the dukes of Brittany (8) built and reshaped between 1205 and 1466.*

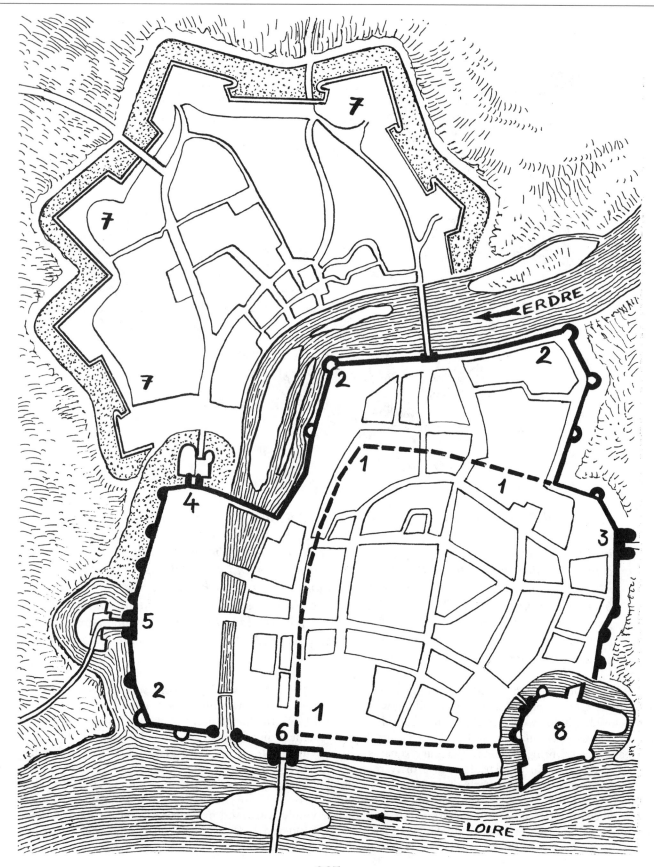

ERDRE

LOIRE

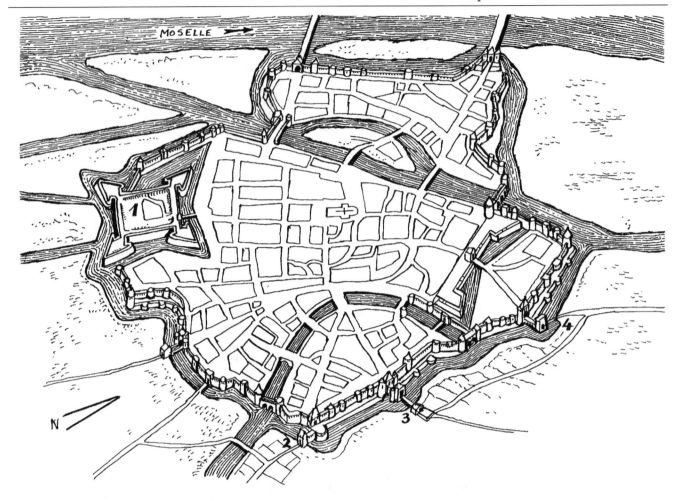

Ground-plan, Metz (France). As early as 561 Metz was the capital of the Merovingian realm of Austrasia and an important bishopric. In the 12th century it became a free city within the German empire, and in the following centuries the municipality constructed a wall 6 km in perimeter with 38 towers, wet ditches and 18 gatehouses. In 1552, the king of France, Henri II, took Toul, Verdun and Metz from Charles V, emperor of Germany and king of Spain. The duke François de Guise reshaped the fortifications in 1552 and erected a bastioned citadel in 1560. The ground-plan shows the fortifications, the ducal citadel (1) and the main gates: the Mazelle gate (2), the Allemands gate (3) and the Sainte-Barbe gate (4).

At twilight, the town lost all animation; curfew time had come. City gatehouses, posterns and drawbridges were closed. Chains were stretched out across the main streets to forbid circulation, and each and every home was barricaded. During the night, streets and squares were dark and deserted. In the darkness, insecurity reigned, thanks to the misery of large parts of the population, the absence of public lighting, the shortage and inadequacy of the police force (the night-watch recruited from among the municipal militia). From dusk till dawn, streets were the exclusive domain of thieves and brigands who would likely rob or even kill anyone so imprudent as to walk in the darkness without armed escort.

With their closely packed houses, in a time when light required flame, medieval towns were particularly vulnerable to fire. Fire brigades, if they existed, were poorly organized, the streets were narrow, and most houses were made of flammable material. For all these reasons, a fire could spread rapidly from one house to a whole ward and even destroy the entire city. Between 1200 and 1225, Rouen (Normandy) was devastated six times by fire.

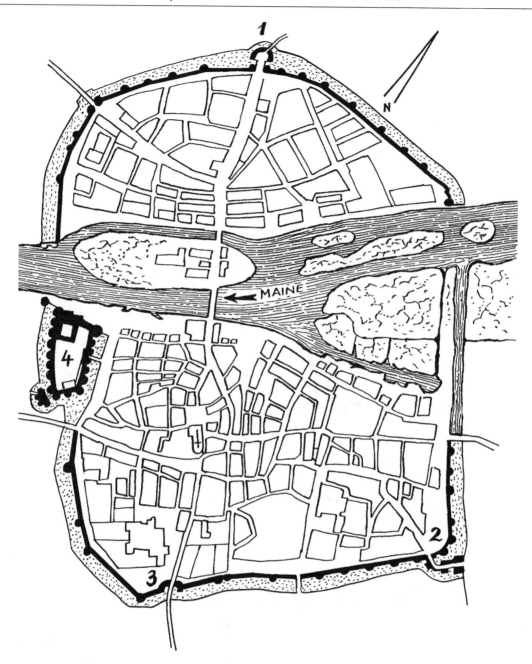

Ground-plan, Angers (France). Angers, situated on the river Maine in the department of Maine-et-Loire, was the oppidum and the ancient capital of the Andicave Celtic tribe and then a Roman town called Juliomagnus. In the 10th century Angers was the capital of the county of Anjou, cradle of the Plantagenet family that would rule England. Angers was reattached to the realm of France in the beginning of the 13th century. The fortifications were then extended and a huge castle-citadel was built between 1228 and 1238. The ground-plan shows the suburb Doutre on the right bank of river Maine with the Lionnoise gate (1), the old city on the left bank with the Saint-Michel gate (2), the Saint-Aubin gate (3) and the castle (4). The urban fortifications were demolished in the 19th century, but the castle is perfectly preserved today.

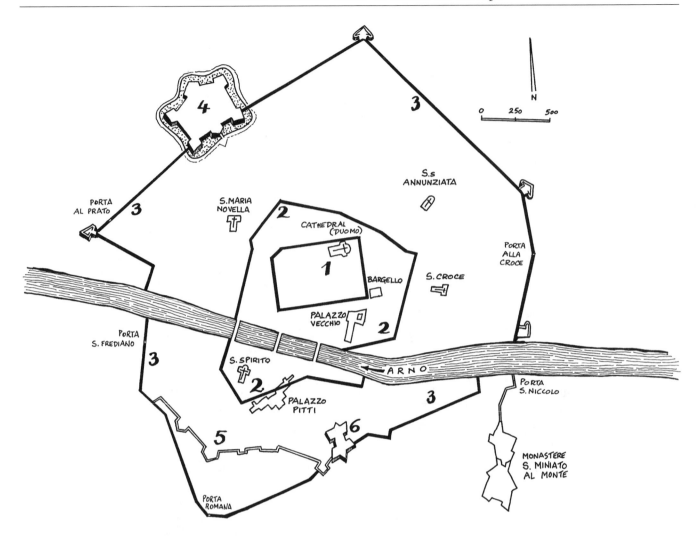

Florence (Italy). Florence (Firenze in Italian) is the capital of Tuscany. The town was founded about 59 BC by the Romans on the right bank of river Arno. In the 12th century Florence was a prosperous city with fortifications erected from 1173 to 1175. In the 13th century, the city grew significantly, resulting in another wall 8.5 km in perimeter with 73 towers and 15 gates. Florence, ruled by the banker family Medici, played a major role in the Renaissance. After the siege of October 1529, the emperor of Germany and king of Spain, Charles V, ordered the construction in 1532 of a bastioned citadel (Fortezza Da Basso) designed by the military engineer Antonio da San Gallo the Younger. In 1569, Florence became the capital of the great duchy of Tuscany. Between 1590 and 1595, the great duke Ferdinand I ordered the construction of a bastioned wall and another fortress (Fortezza Di Belvedere) in the southern part of the town. The capital of Italy from 1865 to 1870, Florence is a cultural and architectural wonder.

The ground-plan shows the principal buildings, the city-gates, the ancient Roman castrum (1), the first enceinte from 1173 (2), the second wall from 1284 (3), the Fortezza Da Basso from 1532 (4), the southern wall (5) and the Fortezza Di Belvedere (6) from 1590.

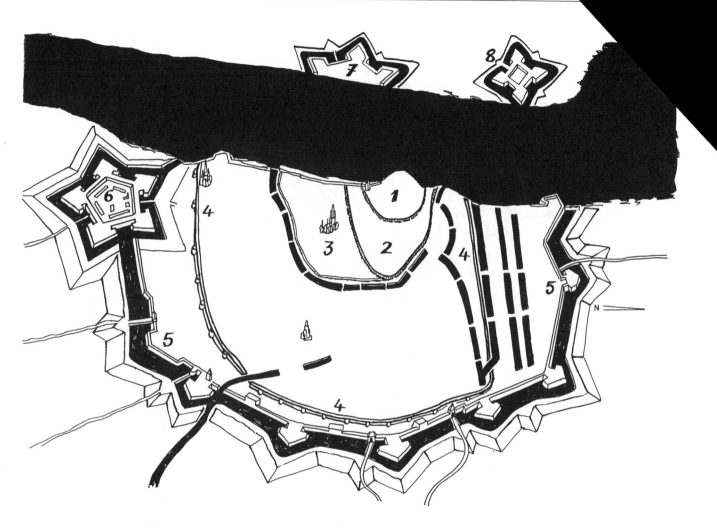

Ground-plan, Antwerp (Belgium) in 1610. Antwerp was the second main Belgian city after Brussels. The town appeared in the 3rd century near a Benedictine abbey. The fortifications developed in several phases. The first core (1), called Burcht, dating from about 980, included the Steen castle and the Saint-Walburg church. In the 11th century the town was enlarged with a suburb called Ruienstad (2). The city was then a member of the German Hansa, and because of growth and wealth a third wall (3) was built between 1240 and 1291. In the following centuries Antwerp was such a rich port and prosperous city that a fourth wall (4) was erected in 1415. This fourth wall was 5.50 km in perimeter and included masonry walls, 52 towers, wet ditches and seven gates. In the 16th century, the city and the harbor continued to be enlarged. Emperor Charles V ordered the modernization of the fortifications by adding new curtains with Italian-style bastions (5) designed in 1540 by the engineer Donato Boni di Pellezuolo. A bastioned citadel (6) was built in 1567 by the engineers Francesco Pacciotto and Bartholomeo Scampi. Completed in 1569, the citadel made manifest the ideal of the pentagonal bastioned citadel. The defenses also included two bastioned strongholds on the opposite bank of river Schelde: fort Flander Headbridge (7) and fort Isabella (8). Enceinte and citadel were demolished in the 19th century when the fortifications of Antwerp were completly renewed to form the Belgian National Réduit.

289

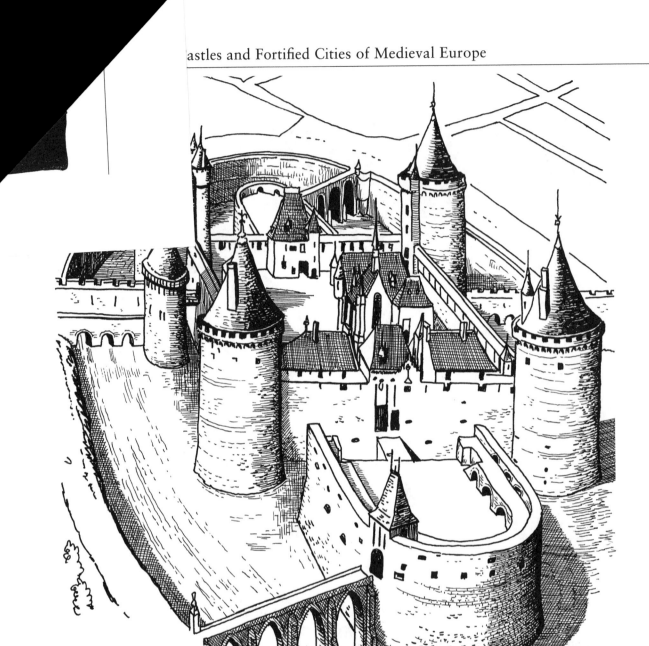

Citadel of Dijon, Burgundy (France). After the death of the duke of Burgundy, Charles le Téméraire, in 1477, the province of Burgundy was annexed to the French realm, and King Louis XI decided to build a strong citadel to control the inhabitants. Continued by King Charles VIII, the construction of the castle was completed in 1512 during King Louis XII's reign. The Dijon citadel was a huge square with four high circular corner-towers with traditional crenels and machicolation. The citadel was adapted to firearms with casemates, embrasures and two huge artillery towers defending both gatehouses, the Boulevard de la Ville towards the town and the Boulevard Louis XII turned towards the countryside. Dijon citadel was dismantled in 1890.

Another danger for the urban population was epidemics. The spread of disease was facilitated by domestic animals, promiscuity and lack of hygiene.

Does this mean that medieval cities, badly lit, deprived of trees and parks, overcrowed and unsanitary, were not good places to live? Perhaps not; for in spite of social inequality, hardship, insecurity, fire and sickness, towns grew, became more populated, increased the range of their activities, and reached prosperity at least until the end of 13th century. The fact that cities were crowded only proves that they were successful. There is only one criterion of failures for cities: depopulation. In the 14th century, however, epidemics, disorder and war resulted in urban regression, depopulation, paralysis of transport, decline of economic productivity, business breakdown, social troubles and moral crisis.

RELIGIOUS AND PUBLIC BUILDINGS

Seen from the countryside, the medieval city displayed a severe barrier of moats, walls, towers and gatehouses marking a strict frontier between the urban area and the rural space. Behind this façade, one saw the roofs with chimneys, turrets, pinnacles, gables, échauguettes, pignons, church bell-towers and convent chapels as well as several huge religious and public buildings. Because the growing urban populations required larger churches, generally the most impressive of the buildings was an enormous and vertiginous cathedral.

Romanesque religious art dominated the period from 1050 to 1150. Its main characteristics were a Latin cross–shaped plan, a rectangular nave (preceded by a narthex and a portal), a transept, aisles continuing around the apse forming a choir with ambulatory, an underground crypt, a chevet with radiating apsidioles and chapels, thick walls, small windows and a round vaulted ceiling. The interior decoration included sculptures and polychrome frescos.

In the 12th and 13th centuries, the ideology of the Church was fully developed, and the intense desire for salvation in the next world, coupled with an awful fear of damnation, gave rise to a preoccupation with life after death—probably the most intense preoccupation since the days of Ancient Egypt. All actions were colored by their imagined effects on chances of salvation, and Heaven and Hell were no longer figures of speech but very real places for which mankind was inevitably bound. Outside the body of the Church there were few intellectuals, and practically no one could read, so medieval builders symbolized their religious beliefs in stone, making churches and cathedrals into dramatized and educational representations of their ideals. Meanwhile, engineering skills greatly increased, stone cutting improved beyond all recognition, and builders came to a proper understanding of thrusts.

Gothic or ogival architecture, created about 1140 in Ile-de-France (the very heart of the French kingdom around Paris), fully deserves the name *opus modernum* or *francigenum* (modern or French work) given by contemporary commentators. Spreading on beyond northern France, the Gothic style became the art of the entire West until the Renaissance. The elegant, weightless and luminous Gothic art is closely linked with the primacy of French civilization and the authority of the French sovereigns, but its tremendous development is also explained by its intrinsic value: Its three basic features—ogave ribs, the broken arch, and the flying buttress—concentrate thrusts at a few critical points and thus eliminate the solid Romanesque walls. Gothic cathedrals reach out for universality; they reflect a harmonious balance and express the cultural upsurge of the golden age of the 13th century.

If the cathedral was the pride of the city, churches were a daily necessity everywhere. Each district of a town, called a parish, had its own place of worship, and even in towns, the parish church was often hemmed by a cemetery.

City growth, overpopulation and emancipation necessitated new public buildings, which were witnesses of the prosperous, proud and dynamic medieval urban civilization. The town hall was frequently built on the main square. This official functional building was intended as meeting place for the municipal council. It included a vast hall for deliberations, meetings, feasts and receptions; offices for civil servants; and a room for the city archives. The town hall was also the expression of the city's wealth, authority and freedom, and for this reason it was richly decorated with high-pitched roofs, pinnacles, statues, sumptuous staircases, high windows, and carvings. The town hall was frequently crowned by a high tower used as an observatory to watch over the vicinity of the town. The tower was fitted with a bell to use as an alarm for fire. The town-hall tower was both a donjon with crenellation, machicolation, watch-tower and échauguettes and a cathedral bell-tower with rich Gothic architectural decorations.

Some towns had a semi-fortified building for the administration of justice, such as the Bargello in Florence, built about 1250. The guilds formed political and economic organizations with their own houses or halls. A guild hall was generally composed of a large room for meetings and feasts, administrative offices and a room for archives.

Cities were economic centers, places of production and consumption. The increasing importance of trade

Sainte-Chapelle, Paris (France). The Sainte-Chapelle was completed in 1248. It was built inside the royal palace in the Ile de la Cité by the king of France, Louis IX, to house the relic of Christ's thorn-crown. The chapel is a jewel of Gothic art with a few buttresses, wide windows and a 75 m high clock-tower.

292

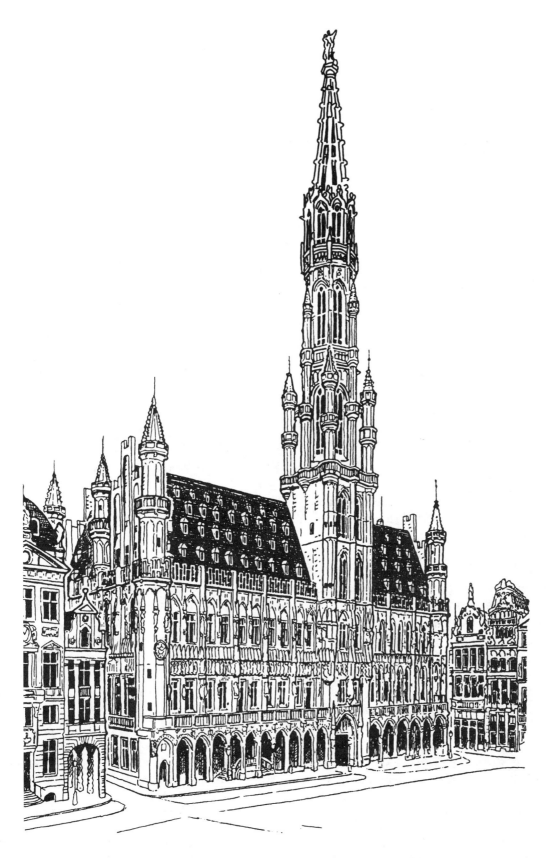

Town hall and tower in Brussels (Belgium). The town hall of Brussels was built between 1402 and 1454. The tower is 96 m high.

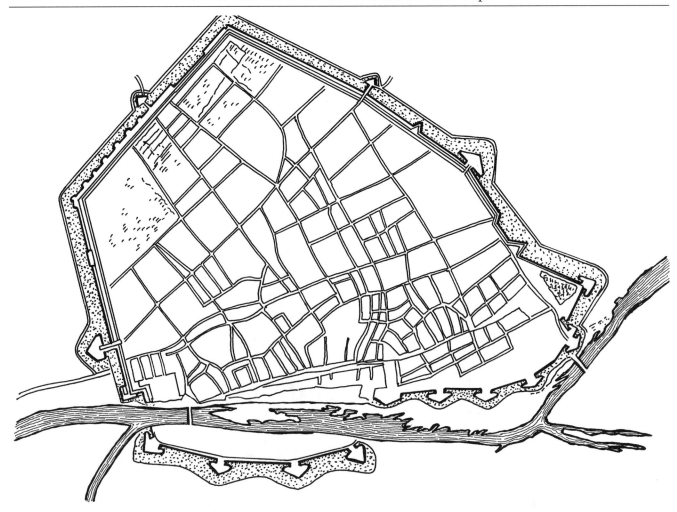

Ground-plan, Ferrare (Italy). Ferrare, on the river Po in the province of Emilia-Romagna, was ruled by the family Este from 1208 to 1598. The medieval town was defended by walls and towers designed in the 13th century by master-builder Bertolino Ploti de Novare. Ferrare was enlarged in 1451 by Borso d'Este and completed in 1492 by Ercole I with wide avenues, walls, towers and Italian-style bastions. The castle (Castello Estense) situated in the middle of the town was built in 1385 by Bartolino Ploti de Novare. The castle was both the residence to the family Este and a powerful fortress with a high donjon (Torre dei Leoni). After 1598, Ferrare was taken and placed under the tutelage of the pope. The family Este then established itself in Modena. The fortifications of Ferrare are partly preserved.

necessitated the creation of adapted commercial public spaces open to all. In great towns, markets were specialized according to the goods exchanged (fish market, hay market, flower market, horse market, herb market and so on). Spots of colorful activity, of shouting, hawking and movement, markets were installed in open squares, in covered spaces fitted with timber roofs (such as in Dives-sur-Mer in Normandy, for example), or in splendid Gothic-decorated houses such as the Lakenhalle (drapery market) in Ghent, Belgium. The existence of these specialized spaces of trade should not, however, blind us to a basic fact: The entire medieval city was a market, and most streets were places of production and business.

Each kingdom, duchy, and region—and many a town as well—had its own measure system and its own money. Changers, traders, bankers, financiers and merchants met in a special place that became a public house, called a

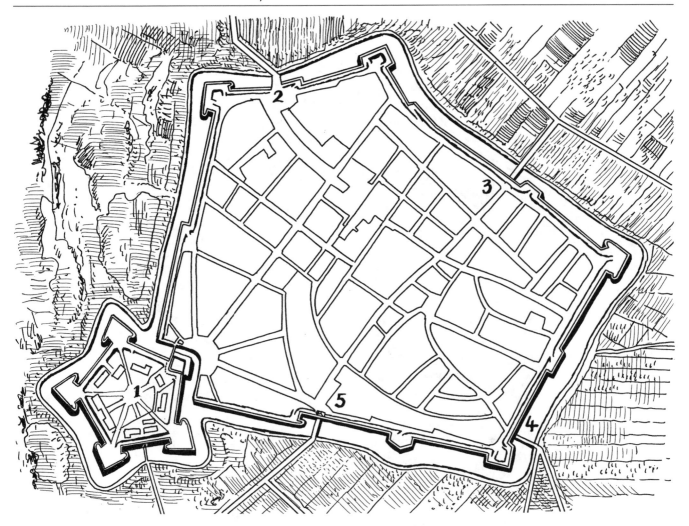

Modena (Italy). Modena, in Emilia-Romagna, was founded by the Etruscans and became the Roman town Mutina in 183 BC. From 1336 until 1796, Modena belonged to the family Este from Ferrare. After 1598, the family Este was driven off Ferrare by the pope, and the Estes established their capital in Modena. The ground-plan shows the bastioned castle-citadel (1), the Venetian-style fortifications and the main gates: the Castle gate (2), the Bologne gate (3), the Saint-Francis gate (4) and the Saint-Augustine gate (5).

stock exchange or money market, for commercial transactions and banking operations.

Cities had sanitary problems: Growing populations, poor sanitation, impure water and vermin led to recurrent epidemics. Fleas, lice, mice and rats were an unwelcome but common sight. In the 14th century the problem of vermin-spread disease reached disastrous proportions, culminating in the Black Death in the years 1348–50. Traditionally it was the Church who provided accommodations for the sick, as well as for pilgrims and beggars. Beginning in the 13th century, municipal authorities took over part of this task, and many towns had their own orphanages, old people's homes, hospices and hos-

pitals. Financed by the municipality, the king or a charitable rich citizen, a hospital generally included latrines, a chapel, various service buildings, separate dormitories for men and women and several specialized wards for the sick, the newly delivered mothers, the dying and the recovering. Volunteer nurses organized in semi-religious orders took care of the sick and dying. Service was free, the costs covered by the income from gifts and legacies.

Because private commerce and public administration required a much greater supply of trained jurists, scholars, notaries and scribes, cities began to develop universities. At first students lived in public inns, where their lives were ruled more by drink, women, and songs

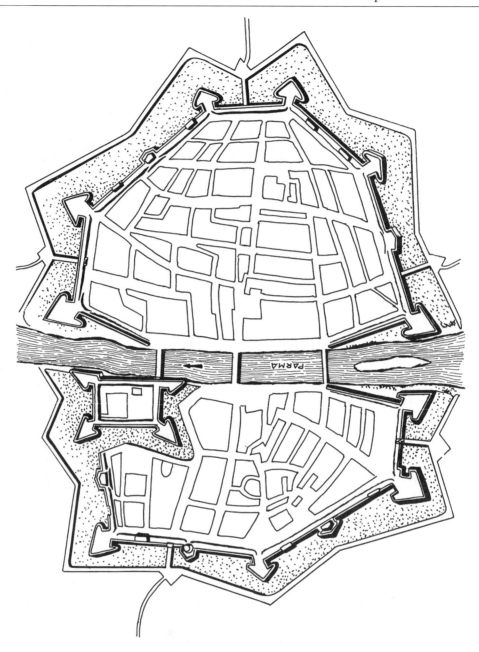

Ground-plan, Parma (Italy). Parma is situated on the river Parma in the province of Emilia-Romagna. An important crossroads between Piacenzia, Modena, Mantova and La Spezzia, the town was created by the Etruscans about 525 BC and became a Roman colony called Julia Augusta in 183 BC. The real development of Parma began with the Ostrogoth king Theodorik (489–526) and was continued during the Byzantine domination from 553 to 568. Conquered by the Lombards in 579, Parma became a free city in the 11th century. From 1341 until 1513, Parma was ruled by the family Visconti from Milan. It then became a part of the pope's territory. In 1445, Pope Paul III Farnese made Parma a duchy for his son Pietro-Ludovico. The dukes of the Farnese family ruled until 1731. The ground-plan shows the situation in the 16th century, when Parma was defended by bastioned fortifications.

than by study. Gradually, however, the college system produced order and discipline, which resulted in a high standard of learning. Usually situated on donated lands and financed by gifts, colleges offered education in Latin, along with board and lodging. Their architecture followed the pattern of the mendicant convents and the urban Gothic hospitals. The most highly reputed medieval university was the Sorbonne in Paris, attracting students and teachers from all parts of Europe.

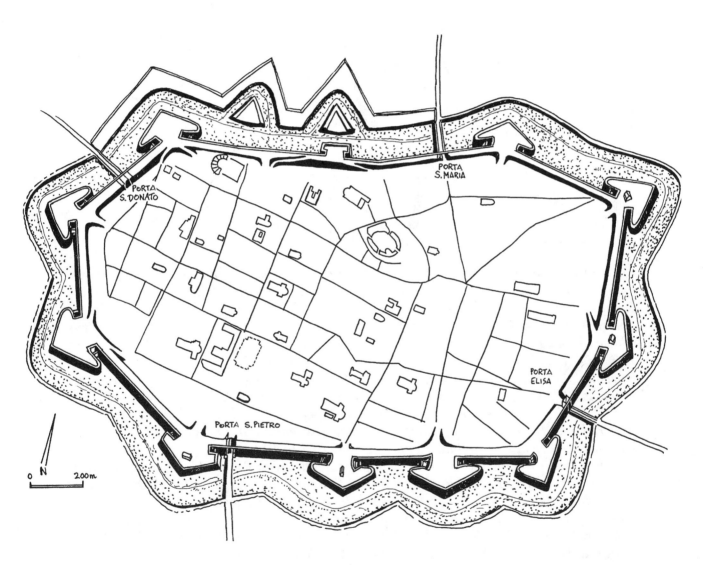

Ground-plan, Lucca (Italy). Lucca is situated north of Pisa in Tuscany. It was founded by the Etruscans and became a Roman camp and a colony in the 2nd century BC. In the 12th century, Lucca was a free city, and during the Renaissance it was ruled by the condottiere Castruccio Castracani. Between 1554 and 1568, the engineer Francesco Paciotto built new fortifications in the Italian style, composed of 12 m high curtains, arrow-headed bastions and four gates. Reshaped and completed in 1645, the fortifications of Lucca are 4 km in perimeter, and are today perfectly preserved.

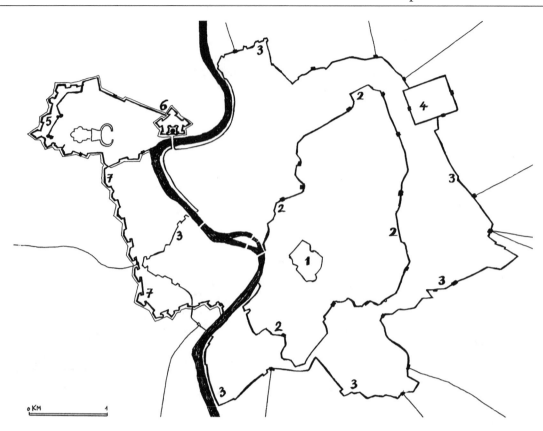

Ground-plan, fortifications of Rome (Italy). Fortifications around Rome date from the creation of the town: According to legend, the first wall (1) was built in April 753 BC by Remus and Romulus. After the disastrous Gallic raid in 387 BC, the Roman republic undertook the construction of a larger enceinte (2) enclosing the seven hills of the Urbs. Those fortifications, called Servius Tullius's wall, were built about 390 BC. The walls were 10 m high and 4 m thick with a 9 m wide moat. Between 270 and 275 AD the emperor Aurelian had new enlarged fortifications built. The resulting wall, called Aurelian's wall (3), was 19 km in perimeter, 6 to 8 m high and 3 to 4 m thick; it included 380 towers and 12 gatehouses. The emperor Tiberius (42 BC–37 AD) built a castle-barracks for the imperial guard, the Praetorian camp (4). In the 5th century, because of the Barbarian invasions, the height of Aurelian's wall was increased to 10 to 16 m.

The state of Vatican was the ancient papal territory in Rome. The first fortifications were constructed by Pope Leon IV from 847 to 855 after a devastating raid launched by Moorish pirates in 846. In 1527, Rome was looted by mercenaries in service of the German emperor Charles V, and Alexander Farnese, who became Pope Paul III, undertook new fortifications (5). These included bastions and moats built between 1537 and 1548, designed by engineers Antonio da San Gallo the Younger and Castriotto.

Hadrian's mausoleum was built between 135 and 138 AD and used as an imperial cemetery. In the 13th century the mausoleum became a fortress for the popes. Between 1484 and 1493, it became the castle Sant'Angelo (6), defended by bastions designed by Antonio da San Gallo the Elder. The popes that followed continued the defensive works until 1569, enclosing the Saint-Peter church, completed in 1614. The last Vatican fortifications were bastions and walls (7) built on Mount Gianicolo during Urban VIII's pontificate between 1623 and 1644.

298

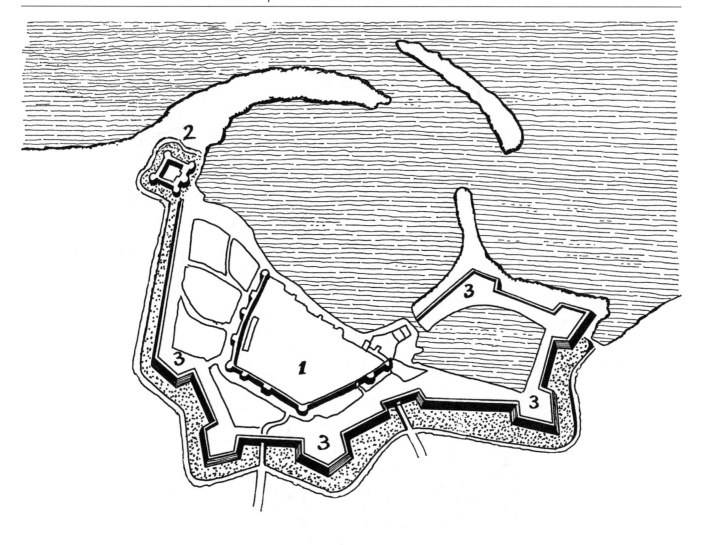

Ground-plan, Civitavecchia (Italy). Civitavecchia is situated northwest of Rome on the coast of Latium. In ancient times called Centum Cellæ, this harbor and the town were created by the Romans and became the advanced port of Rome during the reign of emperor Trajan. The castle dominating the harbor was constructed by Bramante in 1508 and completed by Michelangelo in 1557, whence its name, Forte Michelangelo. It was a massive rectangular fortress with four heavy artillery corner-towers. Civitavecchia was one of the first Italian cities to be defended with modern bastioned fortifications, designed and constructed by engineer Antonio da San Gallo the Younger in 1515. The ground-plan shows the medieval city (1), the castle Michelangelo (2) and the bastioned enceinte (3).

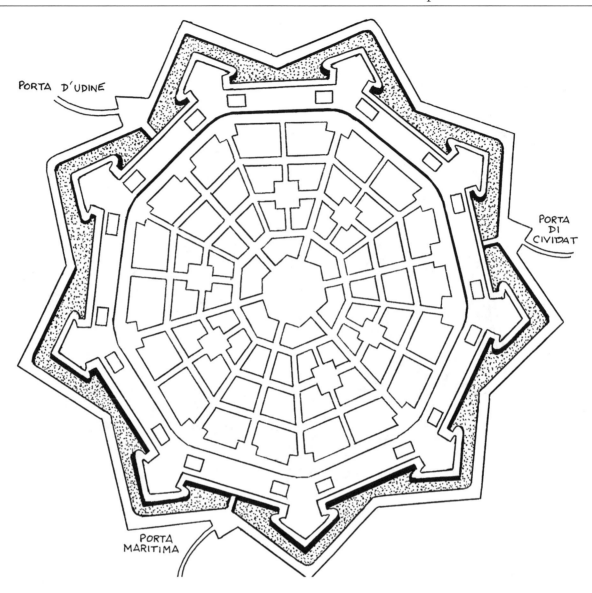

PORTA D'UDINE

PORTA DI CIVIDAT

PORTA MARITIMA

Ground-plan, Palma Nova (Italy). In the Renaissance, Italian urbanists and military engineers designed what they thought to be the ideal city. Combining urban life and defense, it was composed of streets regularly radiating out from a central square to circular bastioned fortifications. The ideal radio-concentric city was, however, a mixed blessing in practice. The living districts were too narrow at the center of the circle and too wide on its periphery, and the fortifications transformed the city into a militarized zone in which all public facilities were submitted to defensive purposes. The fortifications imprisoned the inhabitants in a strict frame, excluding any possibility of further urban development. Palma Nova, situated near Udine in the valley of the river Po, was an "ideal" city created ex nihilo *by Venice. Intended to be a part of the Venetian defense network, Palma Nova was designed in 1593 by Vicenzo Scamozzi and Guilio Savorgnano. Perfectly preserved today, Palma Nova is one of the few realizations of the Italian theoretical ideal city. Divided in a radial organization, it includes nine bastions, a moat, a covered way and three gates.*

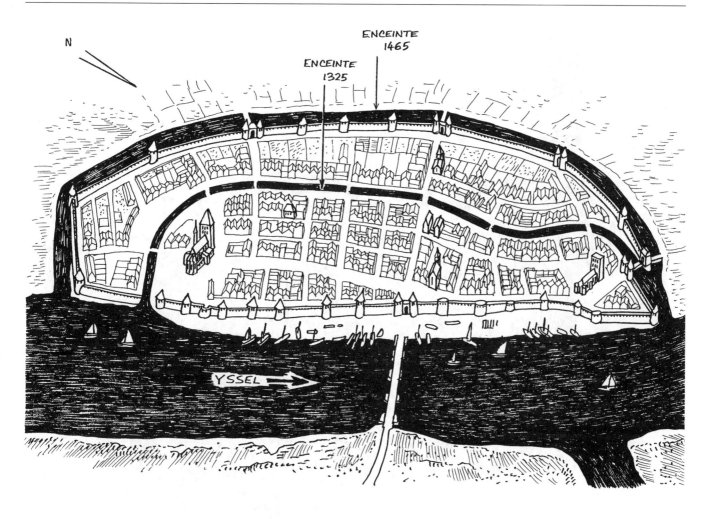

Kampen (Netherlands). Kampen in the province of Overyssel was a prosperous medieval city associated with the German Hansa. A first wall with wet ditch was constructed in 1325, but because of growth another wall with wet moat was constructed between 1465 and 1493. In 1580 these defenses were reinforced by an earth bulwark on which five bastions were erected in 1598. The fortifications of Kampen were demolished in 1809 and turned into public gardens in 1830.

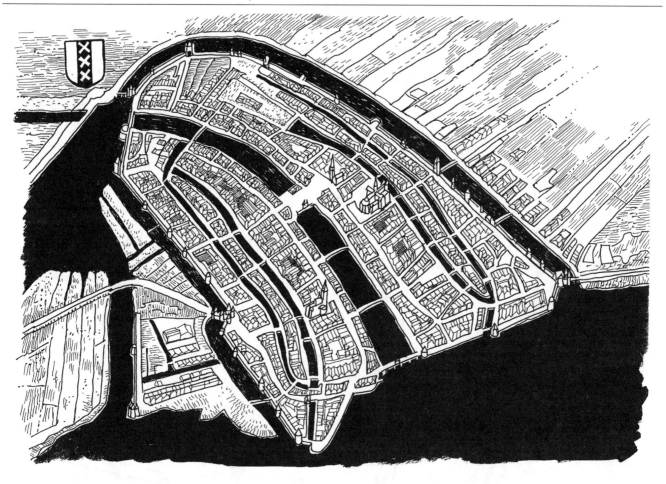

Amsterdam (Netherlands). The capital of the Low Countries, Amsterdam—whose name means "dike on the Amstel"—appeared about 1200 as a modest fishermen's village. In 1275, the village obtained its city-right from the count of Holland, but not until 1425 did the town have the financial means to construct real defenses. Composed of a stone wall with towers and wet moat, these defenses were completed by 1481. In the 16th century, the defenses were adapted to firearms by the dukes of Burgundy. Amsterdam had tremendous growth in the 17th century; the marshy lands around were dried and turned to polders, while bastions, walls and moats were built in 1612. This enceinte rapidly became too small, and another bastioned wall was constructed between 1658 and 1665. Amsterdam's fortifications were demolished between 1839 and 1848, and only a few medieval towers are preserved (Montelbaan and Munttoren). All moats, however, have been turned into canals, giving the city its particular concentric appeal. The ground-plan displays the situation at the beginning of the 16th century.

Opposite: Ground-plan, Zwolle (Netherlands). Zwolle in the province of Overyssel obtained its city-right from the bishop of Utrecht in 1230. A stone wall was built between 1326 and 1329. The town became a rich merchant place associated with the German Hansa, resulting in growth and another wall, erected between 1396 and 1408. The defenses were adapted to firearms between 1488 and 1524, and reinforced by eleven bastions between 1629 and 1631.

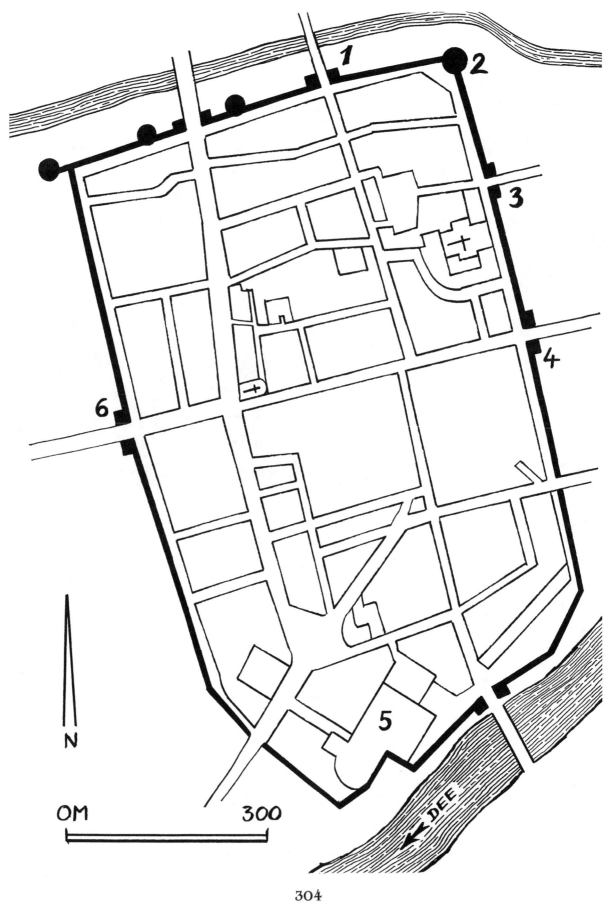

OM   300

N

DEE

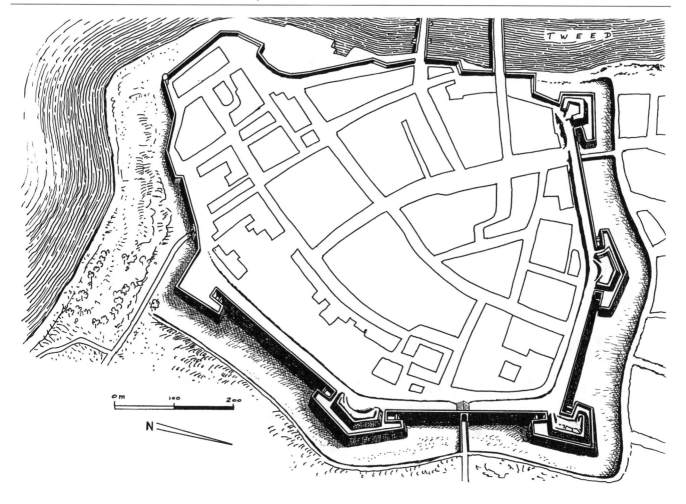

Ground-plan, Berwick-upon-Tweed (Great Britain). Berwick-upon-Tweed is situated at the border between England and Scotland. From the time of its founding about 870, Berwick was disputed until its annexation by the English in 1482. The medieval walls were reshaped between 1522 and 1588 by the architects Richard Cavendish, John Rogers and Sir Richard Lee. Giovanni Portinari from Florence and Jacopo Aconcio from Milan completed the fortifications in 1564 by adding Italian-style arrow-headed bastions. The fortifications of Berwick-upon-Tweed, today well preserved, give a unique and excellent illustration of the influence of the Italian engineers in 16th century Britain.

Opposite: *Chester (Britain). Situated in Cheshire south of Liverpool, Chester was a castrum created by the Romans in a bend of the river Dee. For about 200 years, Chester was garrisoned by Roman legion XX (Valeria Victrix). The Roman fortifications were reshaped in the beginning of the 10th century by Aethelflaed, King Alfred's daughter. The ground-plan shows the fortifications—which today are well preserved—with (1) Northgate, (2) King Charles tower, (3) Kalevards gate, (4) Eastgate, (5) the castle and (6) Watergate.*

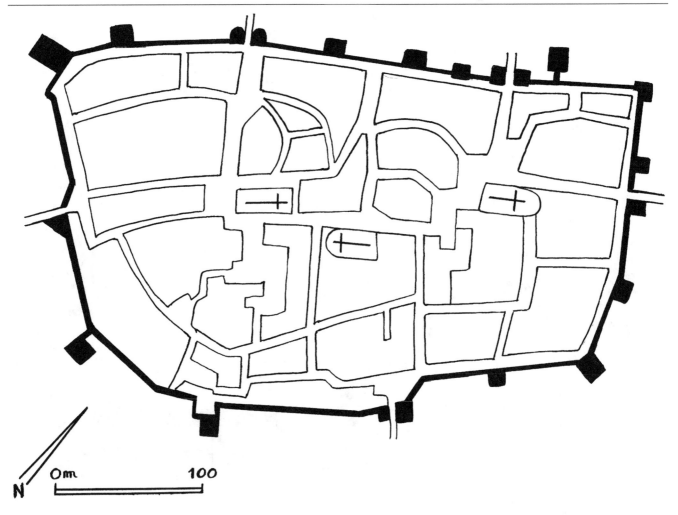

Ground-plan, Caceres (Spain). Caceres is situated in the western province of Estremadura. The city has kept a remarkable center with the central market (Plaza Santa Maria), a palace (Palacio de Los Golfines de Abajo), churches, and unique houses dating from the Middle Ages and Renaissance, with walls and towers from the Moorish occupation.

Opposite: *Ground-plan, Avila (Spain). Avila is situated on the 1,131 m high plateau of Meseta, dominating the Río Adaja northwest of Madrid in Castilla. An ancient Celtic oppidum, Roman castrum and Moorish stronghold, Avila has preserved all of its fortifications (las Murallas), built in 1090 by Raymond de Bourgogne during the Reconquista. Designed by master-builders Cassendro and Florian de Ponthieu, the defenses of Avila form a rectangle 900 m x 450 m. The enceinte includes crenellated walls 12 m high and 3 m thick, flanked by 86 high half-cylindrical towers and eight main gatehouses.*

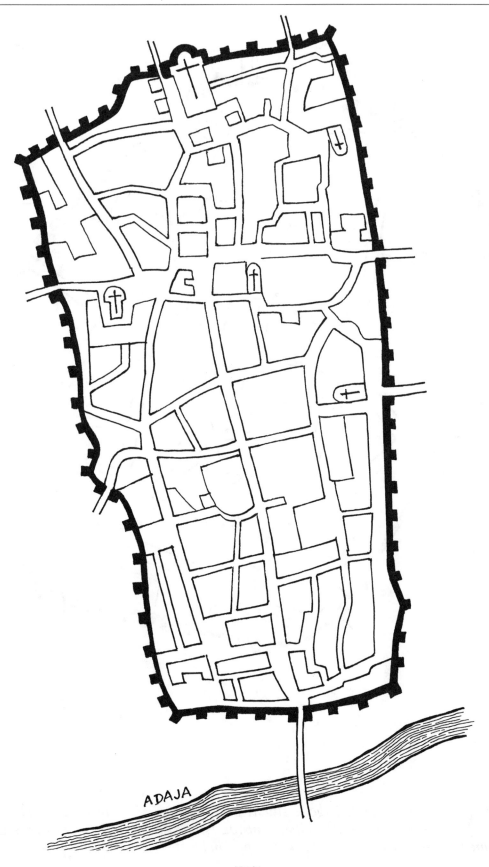

ADAJA

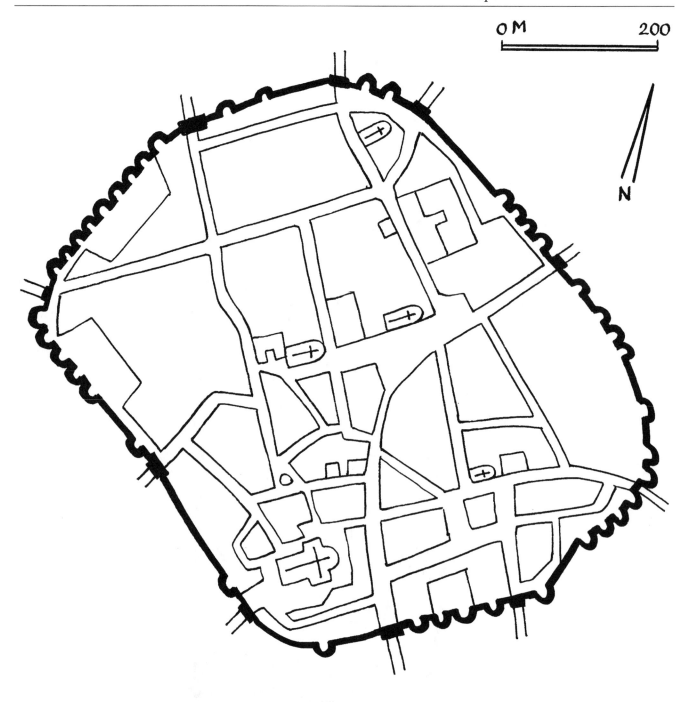

Ground-plan, Lugo (Spain). Lugo is situated on the river Miño in Galicia. The ancient capital of the Roman province Gallæcia in the 1st century AD, Lugo has preserved its entire medieval-era wall, which is 2 km in perimeter.

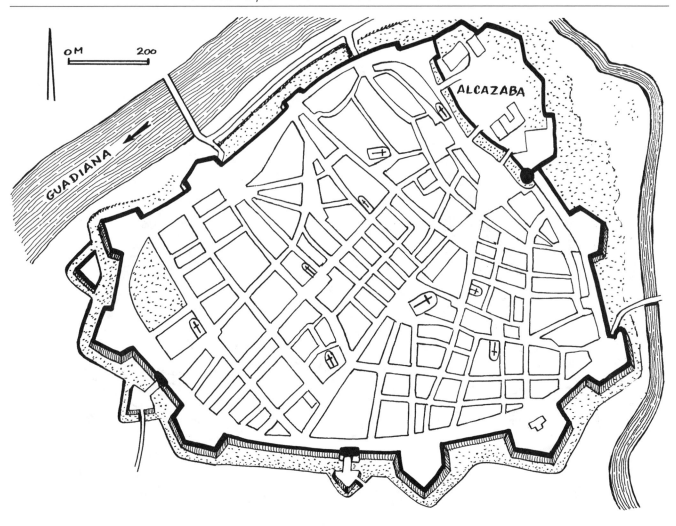

Ground-plan, Badajoz (Spain). Badajoz lies on the river Guadiana in Estremadura, near the border with Portugal. Created by the Romans, the town was the capital of the small Moorish realm in the 11th century, which was fortified with walls and an alcazaba. The king of León reconquered Badajoz in 1228, and from then on, the city was an important fortress facing Portugal. The medieval fortifications were adapted to firearms, and in the 16th century Badajoz was enclosed by a bastioned enceinte, which today is well preserved.

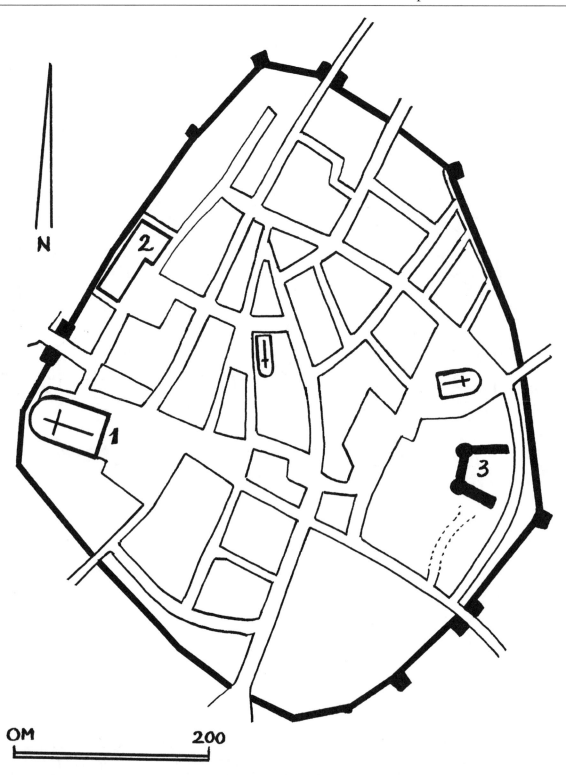

N

OM   200

Ground-plan, Portalegre (Portugal). Portalegre is situated in the north of the province Alto Alentejo. Strategically placed at the border with Spain, the town was fortified by order of King Dinis I in 1290. The ground-plan shows the enceinte with square towers, the cathedral (1), the Palacio Amarelo (2) and the ruins of Dinis's castle (3).

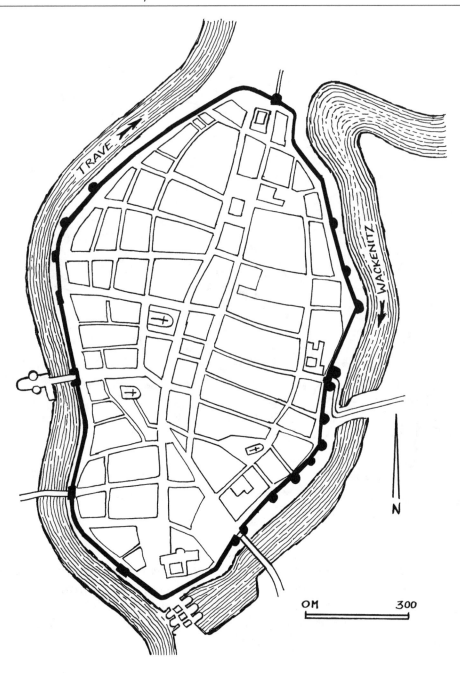

Ground-plan, Lübeck (Germany). Lübeck is situated at the junction of rivers Trave and Wackenitz near the Baltic Sea in the northern province of Schlewig-Holstein. The town was created in 1143 by the count of Holstein, Adolf II von Schauenburg. Beginning about 1159, through the influence of the duke of Saxony, Heinrich the Lion, Lübeck became an important town trading with Baltic and Slav merchants. The fortifications, including walls, towers, gatehouses and wet moats formed by both the Trave and the Wackenitz, were built about 1230. Populated, active and prosperous, Lübeck was one of the most important cities associated with the German Hansa. Between 1595 and 1604, the town was fortified with Italian-style bastions designed by the military engineer Giovanni Pasqualini. The fortifications were demolished between 1783 and 1803.

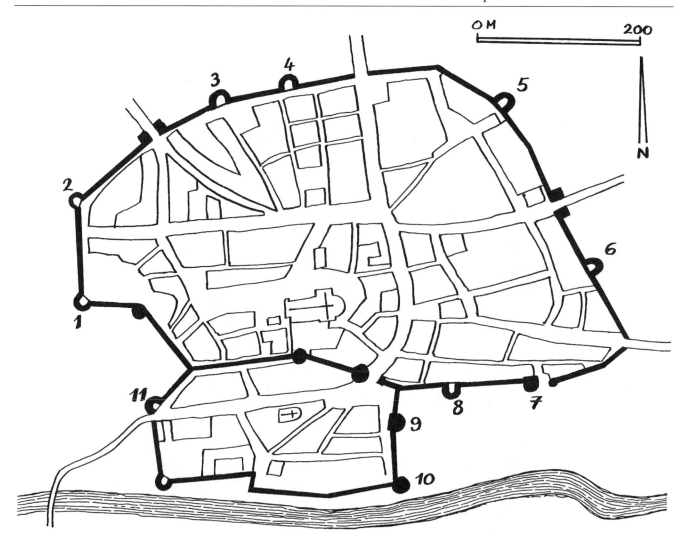

Ground-plan, Fritzlar (Germany). Situated on the river Eder, south of Kassel in the province of Hesse, Fritzlar has retained all of its 13th century fortifications. The ground-plan shows the main towers: (1) Frauenturm, (2) Grauerturm, (3) Grebenturm, (4) Rosenturm, (5) Jordansturm, (6) Rundturm, (7) Regilturm, (8) Steingossenturm, (9) Turm am Bad, (10) Bleichenturm and (11) Winterturm.

Opposite: *Ground-plan, Rothenburg-ob-der-Tauben (Germany). Rothenburg is situated on a steep hill overlooking the river Tauber west of Nuremberg in Bavaria. Though the town was probably fortified as early as Frankish times, the fortifications were probably rebuilt around 1200, reshaped and enlarged in the 14th century and adapted to firearms in the 16th century. The latest additions to the fortifications are preserved today. This plan shows the walls, the towers and the gates: (1) Klingentor, (2) Wurzburger Tor, (3) Rödertor, (4) Spitaltor, (5) Koboldzellertor and (6) Burgtor.*

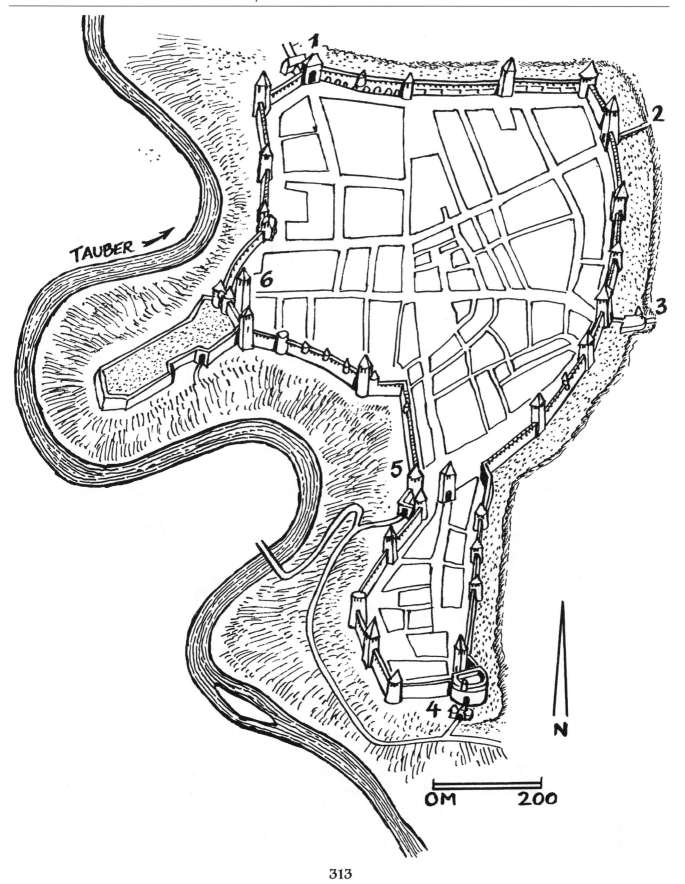

TAUBER

1

2

3

6

5

4

N

0M   200

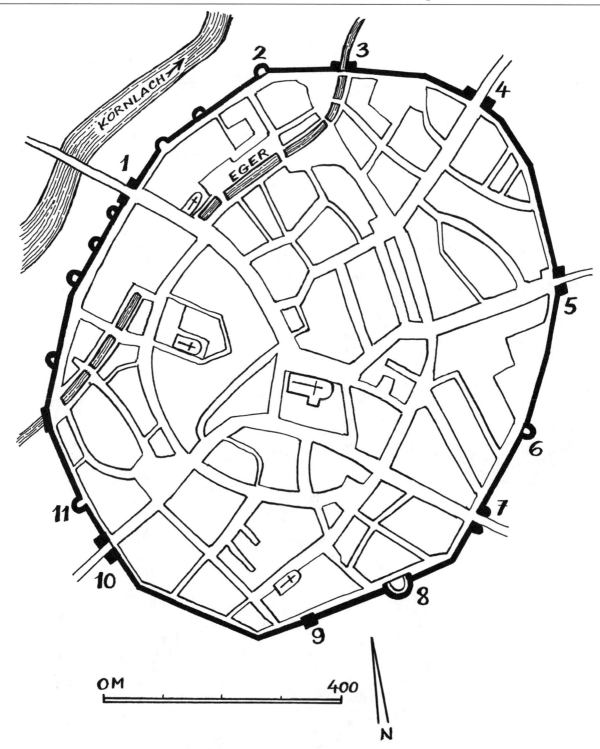

Ground-plan, Nördlingen (Germany). Nördlingen is situated south of Rothenburg in Bavaria. The medieval fortifications (Stadmauer) are perfectly preserved. The ground-plan shows the towers and the gates: (1) Baldingertor, (2) Spizturm, (3) Unter Wasser Turm, (4) Lupsingertor, (5) Deinigertor, (6) Reisturm, (7) Reimlingertor, (8) Alte Bastei, (9) Feilturm, (10) Bergertor and (11) Lowenturm.

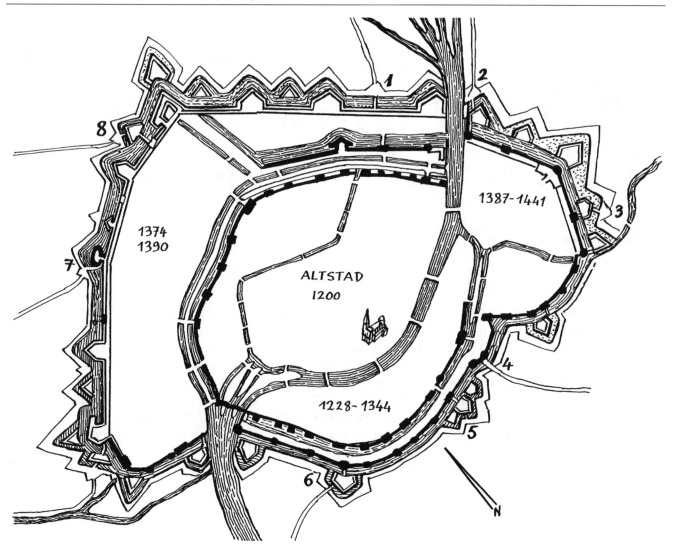

Ground-plan, fortifications of Strasburg in 1643 (France). Strasburg is situated on several arms of river Ill near the Rhine in the department of Bas-Rhin in Alsace. The city was founded by the Romans about 15 BC and called Argentoratum. Devastated during the invasions in the 4th and 5th centuries, the town reappeared during the Carolingian era. Strateburgum, as it was then called, belonged to the realm of Lotharingia, then to the German empire from 870 until it became a free city in 1201. The medieval town was composed of the ancient core, called Altstadt, and three main suburbs, which were incorporated within the town and fortified. Between 1577 and 1589 the city was reinforced with bastioned fortifications designed by the military engineer Daniel Specklin. Strasburg became French in 1681 during the reign of Louis XIV and was further fortified by Vauban. The ground-plan shows the situation in 1643 before the French annexation, with the Altstadt, the three suburbs created in the periods 1228–1344, 1374–1390 and 1387–1441, and the main city-gates: (1) Judentor, (2) Fischerstor, (3) Neutor, (4) Metzgertor, (5) Spitaltor, (6) Elisabethator, (7) Cronenburgertor and (8) Steinstraßertor.

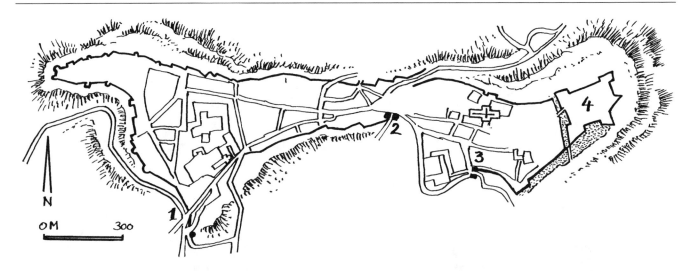

Ground-plan, Laon (France). Laon is the ancient Gallic-Roman town of Laudanum, situated on a 181 m high chalky hill northwest of Reims in the department of Aisne. In the 5th century Laon was an important bishopric, and during the Carolingian time (8th to 10th century), Laon was one of the capitals of the Frankish kings. The town lost its political importance when the Capetian kings transferred the capital to Paris, but Laon remained a significant religious and intellectual center. The ground-plan shows both parts of the town: The western part is the Bourg with the Soissons gate (1); the eastern part is the Cité with the Chenizelles gate (2), the Notre-Dame cathedral, the Ardon gate (3) and the bastioned citadel (4) built by engineer Jean Errard during the reign of the french king Henri IV at the end of the 16th century.

Opposite: Ground-plan of the enceinte of Philippe Auguste in Paris (France). The site of the actual capital of France was occupied as early as 300 BC by the Celtic tribe Parisii, who established an oppidum on the small island in the middle of river Seine. In 52 BC the oppidum was conquered by Julius Caesar and became a Gallo-Roman town called Lutecia. During the Barbarian invasions about 253 AD, the town was reduced in size and fortified. Paris became the capital of the Frankish realm, but it was in full decline during the Carolingian era when the emperors established the capital in Achen in Germany. Paris was attacked by Norsemen in 845, 856 and 861. In the 10th century Paris was the capital of the Capetian dynasty and grew to be one of the largest European medieval cities. King Philippe Auguste, who reigned from 1180 to 1223, undertook the construction of stone fortifications in 1190. Philippe Auguste's enceinte was composed of curtains flanked by 39 towers, a ditch and 18 gatehouses. In 1204 began the construction of the Louvre fortress. The French king Charles V, who reigned from 1364 to 1380, had a second wall built in 1370 to protect new suburbs developing on the right bank of the Seine.

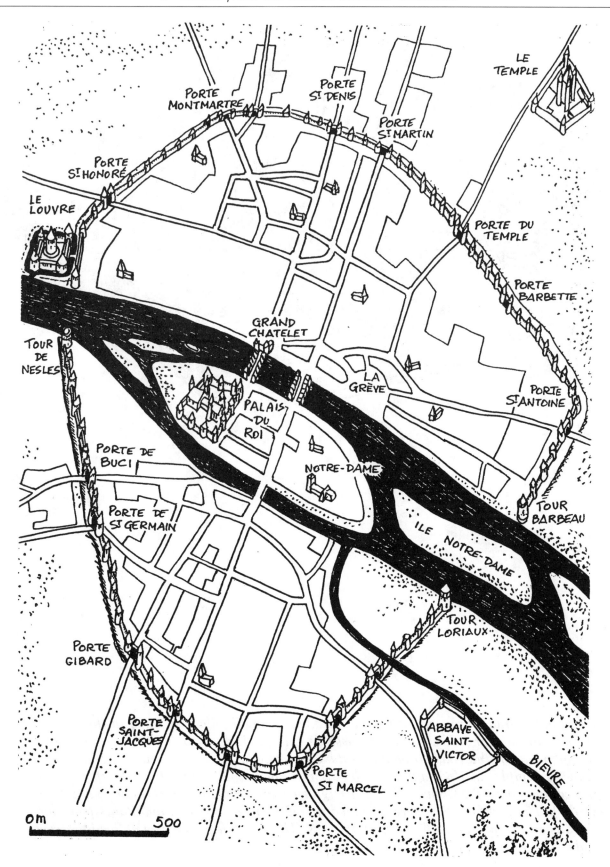

LE TEMPLE

PORTE MONTMARTRE

PORTE St DENIS

PORTE St MARTIN

PORTE St HONORÉ

LE LOUVRE

PORTE DU TEMPLE

PORTE BARBETTE

TOUR DE NESLES

GRAND CHATELET

LA GRÈVE

PORTE St ANTOINE

PALAIS DU ROI

NOTRE-DAME

PORTE DE BUCI

PORTE DE St GERMAIN

TOUR BARBEAU

ILE NOTRE-DAME

PORTE GIBARD

TOUR LORIAUX

PORTE SAINT-JACQUES

PORTE SAINT-JACQUES

ABBAYE SAINT-VICTOR

BIÈVRE

PORTE St MARCEL

0m 500

317

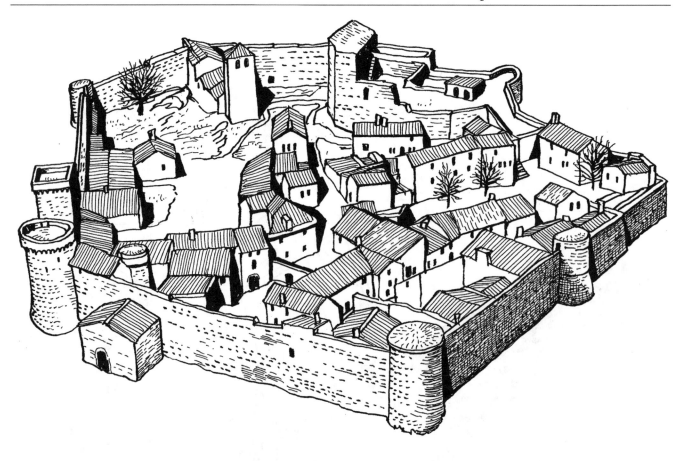

La Couvertoirade (France). La Couvertoirade is a small village situated in the valley of river Dourbie near Lodève in the Causse de Larzac. It was originally a stopping place for pilgrims on the road to Santiago da Compostella. The village was yielded to the Knights Templar in 1182, and after the dissolution of the Order of the Temple in 1312, the commandery La Couvertoirade was given to the Knights Hospitaler (Saint John's Order). The fortifications were reshaped in 1439 to protect the inhabitants from local bandits established in the Causses mountains. Those fortifications remain well preserved today.

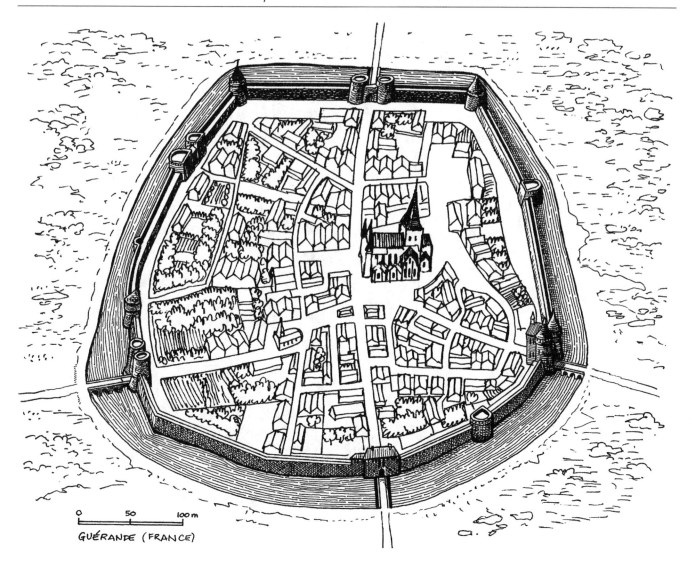

0   50   100 m

GUÉRANDE (FRANCE)

Guérande (France). Guérande in Loire-Atlantique was a border town between the realm of France and the duchy of Brittany. The 14th century fortifications, including walls, towers and four gatehouses, are perfectly preserved.

319

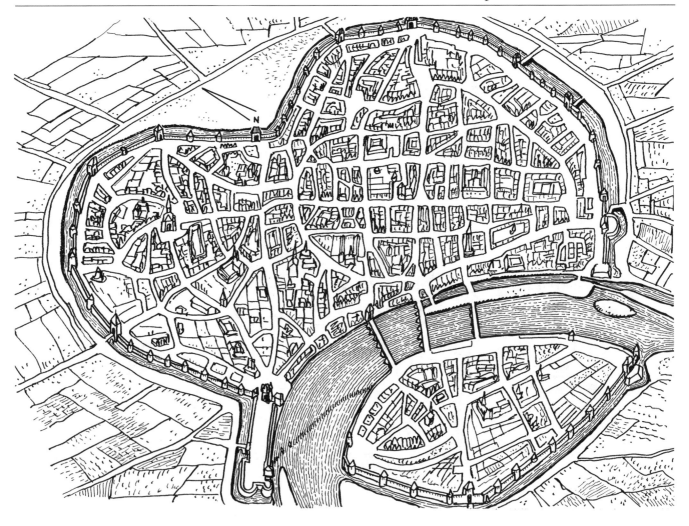

Toulouse (France). Toulouse (Tolosa in the Occitan language), situated on the banks of river Garonne, was the ancient capital of the Celtic tribe Volsque. A bishopric and an important trading center, Tolosa became the capital of the Visigoth realm in 419. Conquered by the Franks in 507, it then became the capital of the rich province of Aquitaine, then that of the county of Toulouse. In the 12th century Tolosa was an independent free city, and the ancient Roman enceinte was reshaped and enlarged in the period 1140–1152. In the beginning of the 13th century the suburb Saint-Cyprien on the opposite side of the Garonne was incorporated and linked to the town by three bridges. Toulouse was severely damaged during the Albigenese Crusade. It was besieged and taken and its fortifications demolished by order of Crusade leader Simon de Montfort. The town and the county of Toulouse were then annexed to the French crown in 1271.

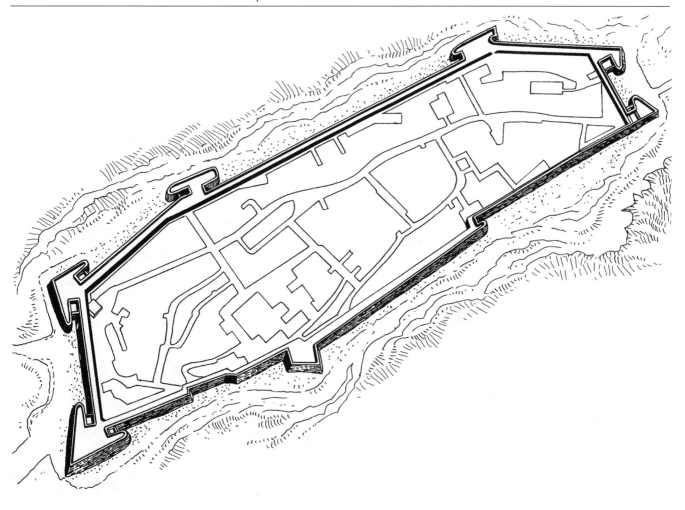

Ground-plan, fortifications of Saint-Paul-de-Vence (Alpes-Maritimes in France). The small village of Saint-Paul, situated north of Nice, is typical of the fortified strongholds that once guarded the border river Var. The ramparts and the bastions in early Italian style have scarcely been touched since King François I had them built in the years 1537 to 1547 in answer to a challenge from the citadel of Nice.

321

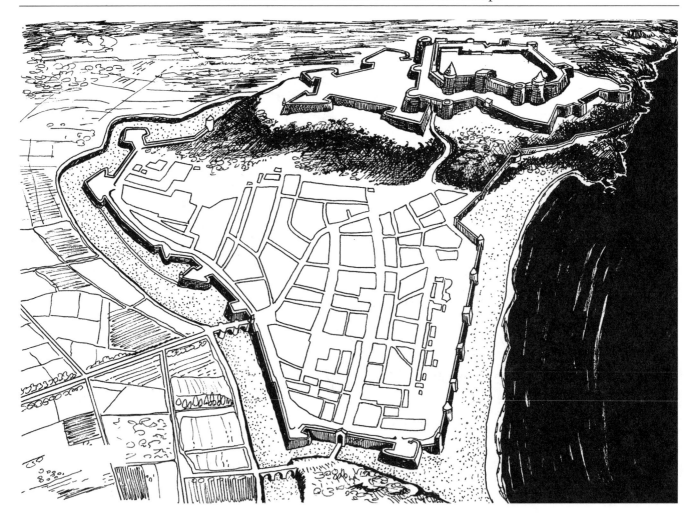

Nice (France). Nice in the Alpes-Maritime is the queen of the French Riviera. The city was founded by the Greeks of Marseille in 350 BC as a modest trading post. The Romans concentrated their colonization efforts on nearby Cimiez, whose splendor overshadowed that of Nice. Barbarian and Saracen invasions, however, reduced Cimiez to nothing, so it was Nice that began to develop under the counts of Provence in the 10th century. At the beginning of the 14th century Nice was ruled by the dynasty of Anjou and was annexed by the dukes of Savoy in 1388. Except for a few short interruptions, Nice belonged to Savoy until 1860. But before Nice was reattached to France, it was a strategic border town and therefore had many fortifications, including medieval walls and a castle built on the dominating hill. In the 16th century, the defenses of Nice also included bastioned citadels and coastal forts built by the dukes of Savoy around the city in Villefranche-sur-Mer (a harbor created in 1295 by Charles II of Anjou): Citadel Saint-Elmo, Fort Mont-Alban and Fort Saint Hospice.

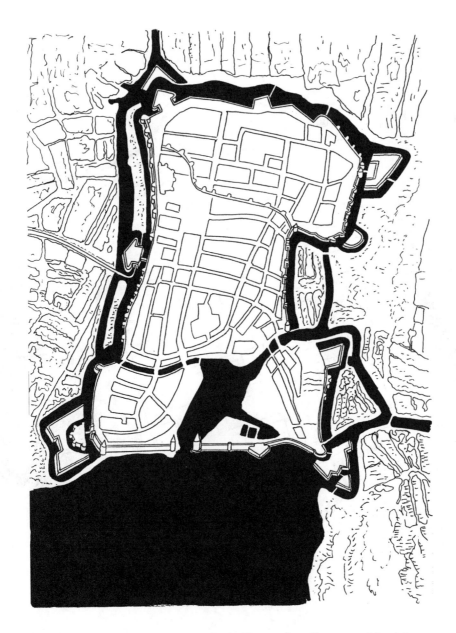

Ground-plan, La Rochelle (France). La Rochelle in the Charente-Maritime was the capital of the medieval province Aunis. Founded in 1130 by the duke of Aquitaine, Guillaume II, La Rochelle belonged to the Plantagenet English empire and became French in 1372. Fortifications were built in the 14th and 15th centuries to defend the city and the harbor (remains are the Saint-Nicolas tower, la Chaîne tower and la Lanterne tower). About 1500, the fortifications were enlarged and modernized, and the gatehouses were fitted with artillery bulwarks. La Rochelle became a Protestant place and was fortified during the wars of religion between 1558 and 1568 under the direction of François "Iron-arm" de La Noue and engineer Scipione Vergano. The fortifications of La Rochelle were again modernized between 1596 and 1602. A port open to the English, nicknamed "synagogue of Satan" by the Catholics of the area, La Rochelle and its rebellious Protestant population were finally brought into submission by Cardinal Richelieu and King Louis XIII after a long and tragic siege that began in September 1627. In spite of help provided by the duke of Buckingham, the city was forced to surrender in October 1628. The ground-plan shows the situation in the period 1558–1568.

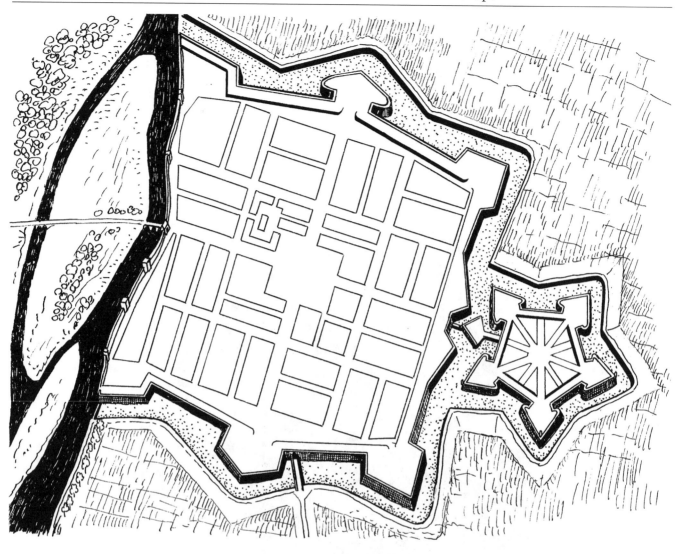

Vitry-le-François (France). The village Vitry-en-Perthois in the department of Marne having been destroyed by the German emperor Charles V in 1544, King François I decided to create ex nihilo *a town named after him. Vitry-le-François was designed according to Renaissance Italian principles. It was a square 612 m x 612 m with a regular urban organization. The Italian-style fortifications, designed by Girolamo Marini and Aurelio Pasini, included an enceinte with six large bastions and a pentagonal citadel (dismantled in 1598). Vitry was 90 percent destroyed in May 1940 and rebuilt in its original plan after World War II.*

CONCLUSION

The monuments of yesterday are documents worthy of study. In a rapidly changing world, with different values, this is more true than ever. And if such documents are worthy of study, then they are surely worthy of preservation for what they are and what they represent. Any civilization that neglects its future will certainly come to regret it someday. But a civilization that neglects its past will find its regrets much more profound and long-lasting. In Europe, although much has been lost, much of this priceless heritage is still preserved—and it is priceless, for no amount of money can ever replace it. There is still time to ensure that it continues to be preserved for the pleasure and instruction of generations to come.

Castle Pierrefonds (France). Situated near Compiègne department Oise north of Paris, Pierrefonds was originally an 11th century motte-and-bailey castle built by Lord Nivelon. Enlarged in the 12th century, then abandoned and ruined, the site was rebuilt between 1390 and 1407 by the royal architect Jean le Noir to serve as residence to Louis d'Orléans, king Charles VI's brother. Dismantled in 1617 by Cardinal Richelieu, Pierrefonds lay in ruins until 1857, when the architect Eugene Viollet-le-Duc rebuilt it to serve as a residence to the French emperor Napoléon III. Viollet-le-Duc's reconstruction was historically rather reliable but also showed the architect's enthusiasm for neo–Gothic architecture. Pierrefonds is less a medieval castle than an expression of the 19th century romantic attitude regarding the Middle Ages, and teaches us to be careful about architectural reconstruction.

BIBLIOGRAPHY

Books about the Middle Ages, medieval castles and towns are numerous. Even more numerous are the books, brochures, leaflets and articles concerning local fortifications. Because it is impossible to enumerate all publications, I shall list below only a subjective selection of a few works particularly relevant, useful and interesting, in the hope that they may provide sources of further reading.

Benevolo, L. *La Citta Europea*. Rome, 1993.

Boussart, J. *Atlas Historique et Culturel de la France*. Paris, 1957.

Braun, G., and Hogenberg, F. *Civitates Orbis Terrarum*. Cologne, 1572.

Brice, M.H. *Stronghold*. London, 1984.

Brochart, P. *Chevaliers et Châteaux-forts*. Paris, 1985.

Chatelain, A. *Châteaux-forts*. Paris, 1987.

Douglas-Simpson, W. *Castles in Britain*. London, 1966.

Duchet-Suchaux, G. *Les Châteaux-forts*. Paris, 1994.

Forde-Johnson, J. *Castles and Fortifications in Britain and Ireland*. London, 1977.

Gistel, G. *Burgen und Schlösser in Osterreich*. Vienna.

Harouel, J-L. *Histoire de l'Urbanisme*. Paris, 1995.

Haucourt, G. *La Vie au Moyen Age*. Paris, 1987.

Herrera-Casado, A. *Castillos y Fortalezas*. Madrid, 1989.

Huizinga, S. *Vestingsteden*. Amsterdam, 1990.

Hugues, Q. *Military Architecture*. Hants, 1974.

Janneau, G. *Cités et Places Fortes*. Paris, 1979.

Janse, H. *Stadswallen en Stadspoorten*. Zaltbommel, 1974.

Le Halle, G. *Précis de Fortification*. Paris, 1983.

Lepage, J-D. *Vestingbouw*. Zutphen, 1995.

Libal, D. *Châteaux-forts et Fortifications en Europe*. Paris, 1993.

Marchand, P., and Jusserand, N. *La France Médiévale*. Paris, 1997.

Martin, P. *Armes et Armures*. Fribourg, 1967.

Merian, M. *Theatrum Europaeum*. 1635.

Mesqui, J. *Châteaux-forts et Fortifications en France*. Paris, 1997.

Moerman, I. W. *Kastelen*. Bussum, 1970.

Monnier, G. *Histoire de l'Architecture*. Paris, 1994.

Neumann, H. *Festungsbaukunst*. Bonn, 1988.

Paluzie de Lescazes, C. *Castles of Europe*. Barcelona, 1981.

Reyen, P. *Middeleeuwse Kastelen*. Bussum, 1965.

Rocolle, P. *2000 Ans de Fortification Française*. Paris, 1989.

Saalman, H. *Medieval Cities*. London.

Sailhan, P. *La Fortification*. Paris, 1991.

Salch, C. L. *Dictionnaire des Châteaux et des Fortifications du Moyen-Age en France*. Strasbourg, 1979.

Salch, C. L. *Les Plus Beaux Châteaux-forts en France*. Strasbourg, 1987.

Schellart, A. *Burchten en Kastelen*. The Hague.

Treu, H., and Sneep, J. *Vesting*. The Hague, 1982.

Vercauteren, F. *L'Europe Histoire et Culture*. Brussels, 1972.

Viollet-le-Duc, E. *Histoire d'une Forteresse*. Paris, 1874.

INDEX

DATE DUE